TABLE ◇ OF ◇ CONTENTS

DOWNLOAD YOUR FILES

Tiger Head	01-02
Tiger	03-04
Tengu	05-06
Tsuchigumo	07-08
Snake | Hebi	09-10
Frog | Kaeru	11-12
Koi Fish | Nishikigoi	13-14
Phoenix | Hou-ou	15-16
Dragon | Ryu	17-18
Dragon Head | Ryu	19-20
Demon | Oni	21-22
Kirin	23-24
Three-Legged Crow | Yatagarasu	25-26
Cherry Blossom | Sakura	27-28
Peonies | Botan	29-30
Chrysanthemums | Kiku	31-32
Maple Leaves | Momiji	33-34
Lotus Flower | Hasu	35-36
Bamboo | Take	37-38
Plum Blossoms | Ume	39-40
Waves | Nami	41-42
Clouds | Kumo	43-44
Fire | Hi	45-46
Samurai	47-48
Geisha	49-50
Traditional Fan | Uchiwa	51-52
Japanese Lantern | Chochin	53-54
Sword | Katana	55-56
Severed Head | Namakubi	57-58
Woman-Spider | Jorogumo	59-60
Fox Spirit | Kitsune Kabuki Mask	61-62
Fox | Kitsune	63-64
Daruma Doll	65-66
Beckoning Cat | Maneki-Neko	67-68
Crane | Tsuru	69-70
Rooster | Ondori	71-72
Samurai Crab | Heikegan	73-74
Octopus Monster | Akkorokamui	75-76
Kappa	77-78
Shisa	79-80

Downloading your files is simple. To access your digital files, please go to the last page of this book and follow the instructions.

For technical assistance, please email: info@vaulteditions.com

Copyright

Copyright © Vault Editions Ltd 2025.

Bibliographical Note

This book is a new work created by Vault Editions Ltd.

ISBN: 978-1-922966-63-6

VAULT EDITIONS

TIGER HEAD

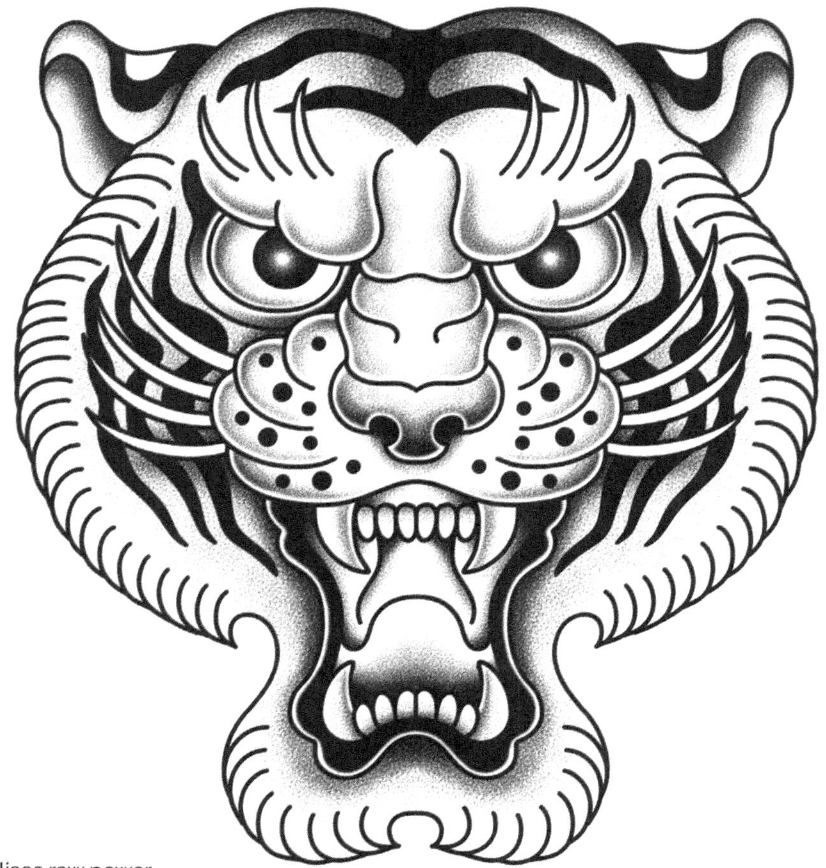

The tiger's head symbolises raw power, courage, and fierce protection in Japanese tattooing, often used to ward off evil and embody inner strength.

01

02

03

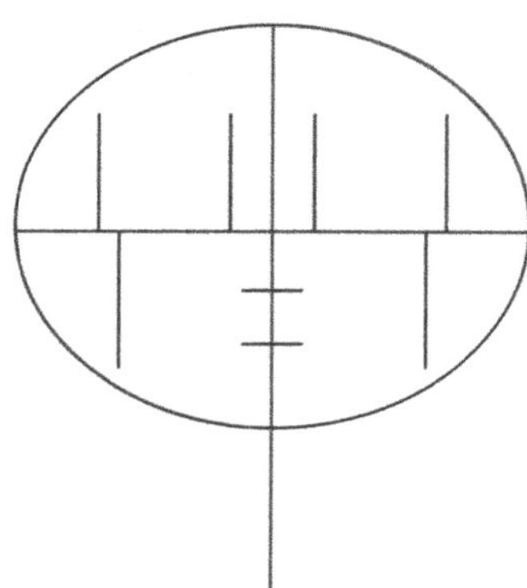

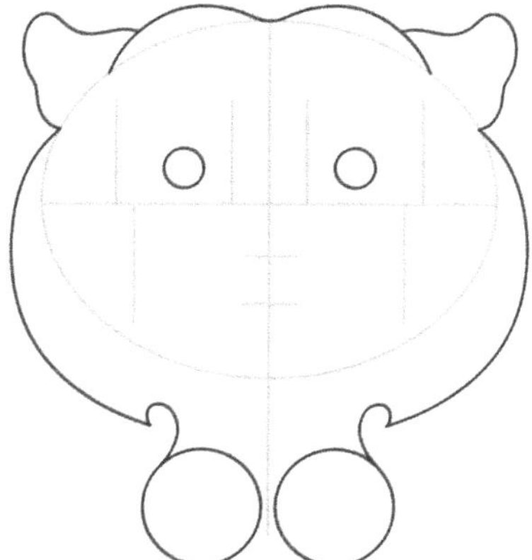

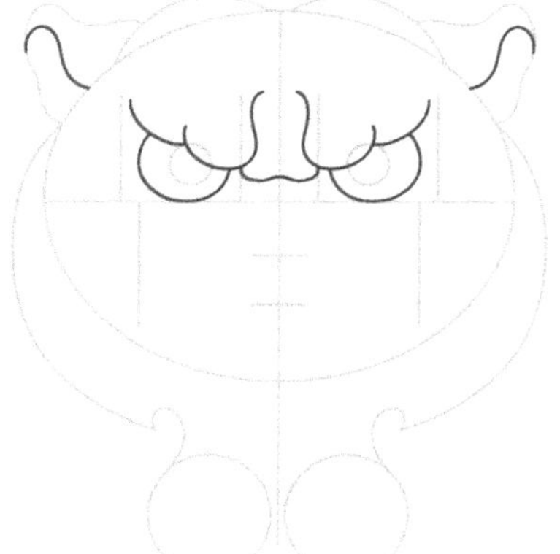

HOW TO DRAW
JAPANESE TATTOOS

A HELPFUL MANUAL FOR ARTISTS AND DESIGNERS

STEP BY STEP

HAND DRAWN

UNIQUE **40** DESIGNS

BEST QUALITY

EDITIONS
Vault

INTRODUCTION

Japanese tattooing, known as irezumi, is a centuries-old art form rooted in mythology, folklore, and deep cultural symbolism. With its bold lines, flowing compositions, and powerful imagery, this style has become one of tattoo culture's most recognisable and respected traditions worldwide. Each motif carries layered meanings, representing values such as courage, protection, transformation, and spiritual power, and is often used to tell personal stories, reflect inner character, or express a connection to cultural heritage.

How to Draw Japanese Tattoos is a step-by-step drawing guide that introduces artists to the timeless visual language of traditional Japanese tattooing. Using the Vault Editions 12-step drawing process, this book breaks down complex motifs into clear, easy-to-follow stages designed to build confidence and technical skill.

This guide features 40 iconic designs and explores the rich symbolism found in Japanese tattoo art, from legendary creatures and deities to animals, plants, and folkloric figures. Each motif has been carefully selected for its cultural significance and visual impact. The artwork was created by Abrom Rose, an accomplished and highly skilled artist whose exceptional ability for visual instruction makes each step clear, engaging, and accessible.

Whether you're a tattoo apprentice, illustrator, or creative looking to expand your drawing repertoire, this book provides a structured, easy-to-follow way to engage with a powerful artistic tradition.

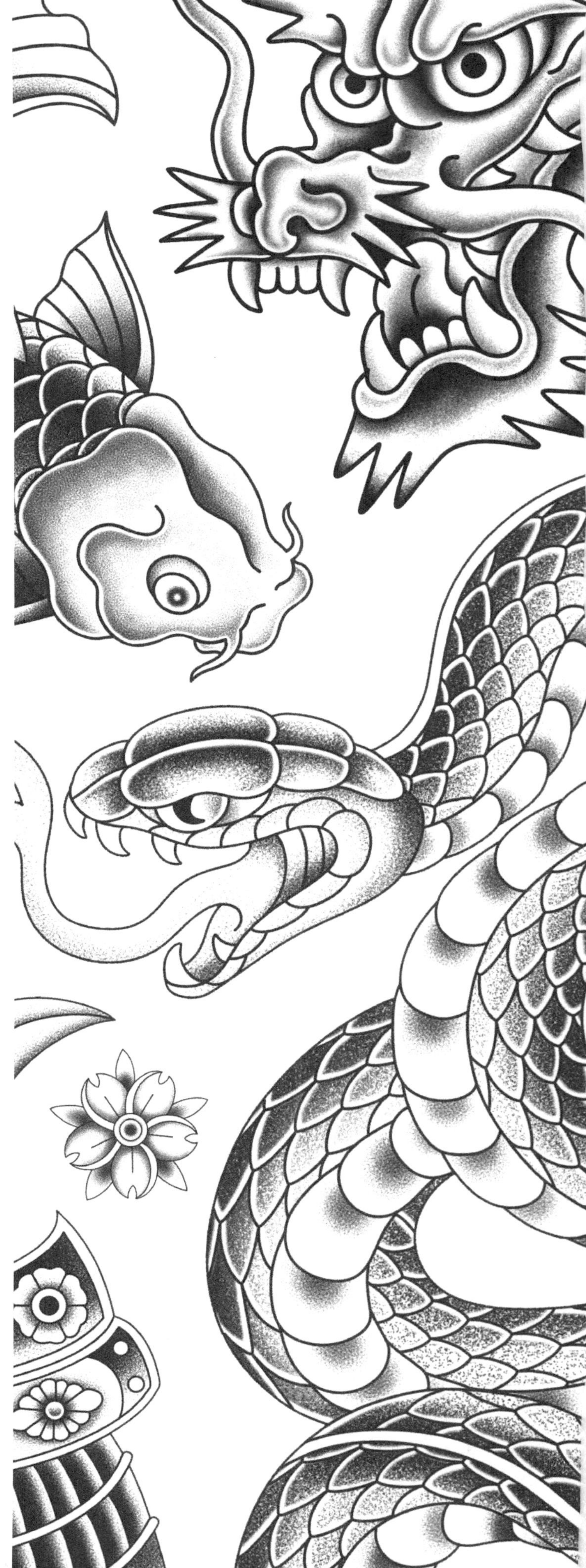

04

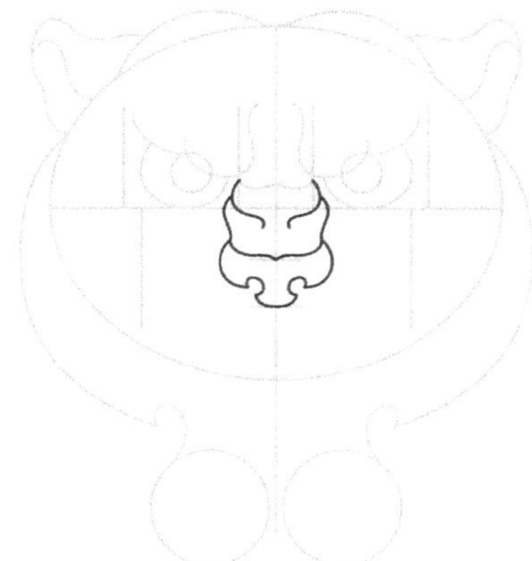

05

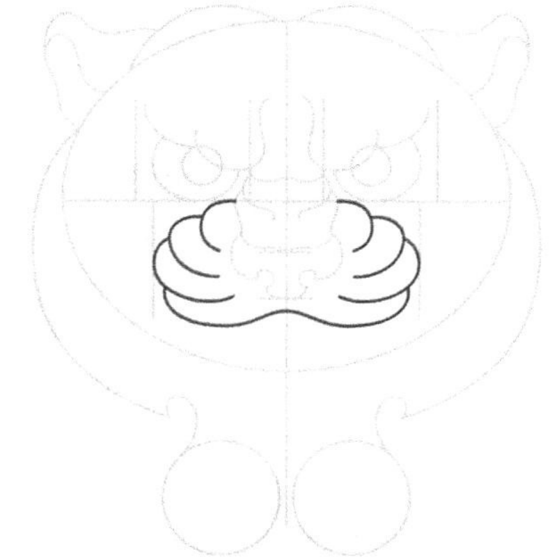

06

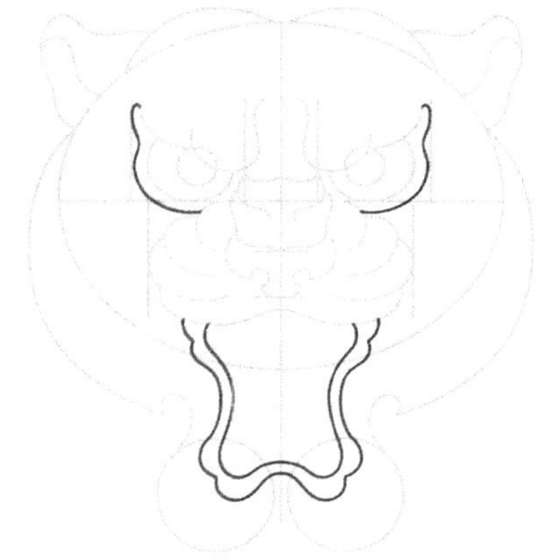

07

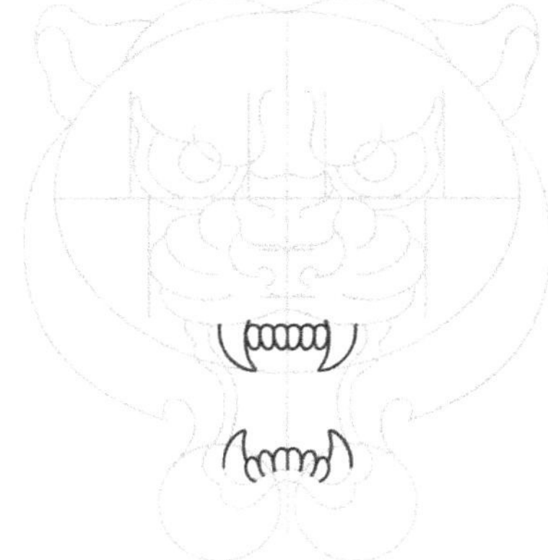

08

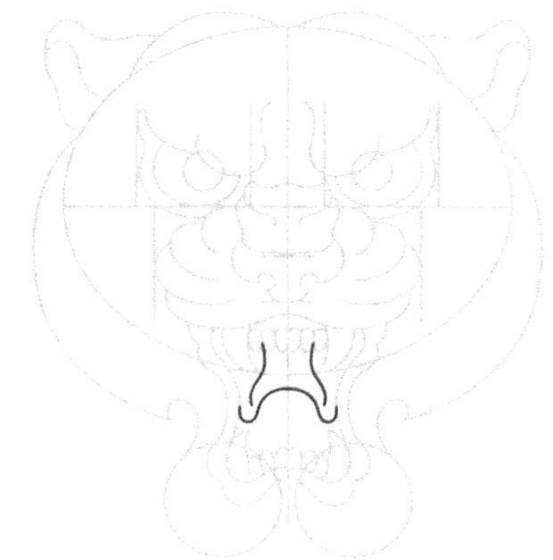

09

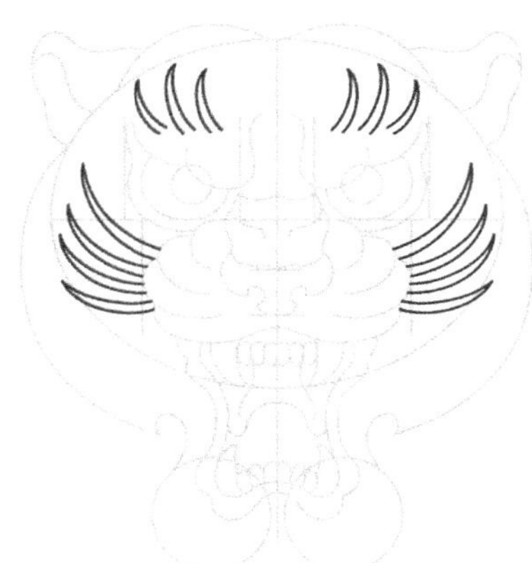

10

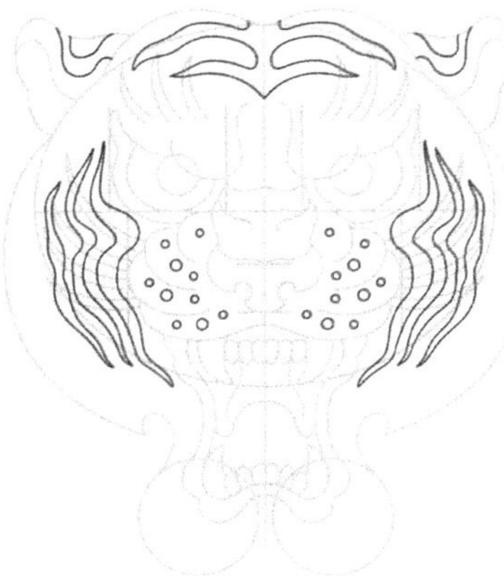

11

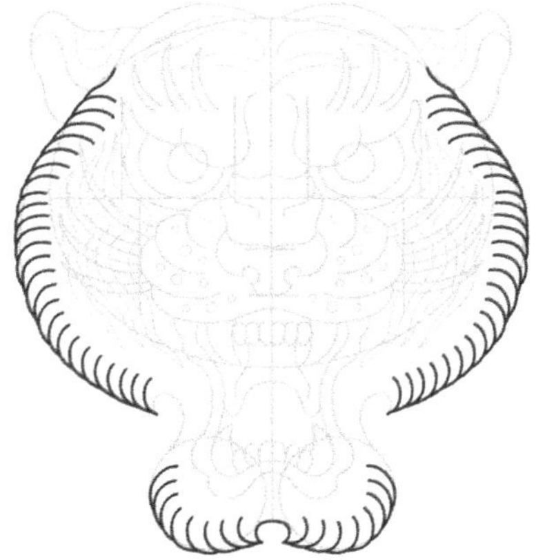

12

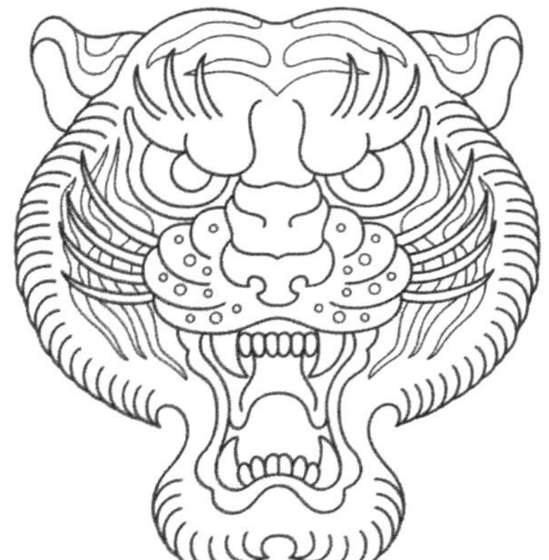

JAPANESE TATTOOS

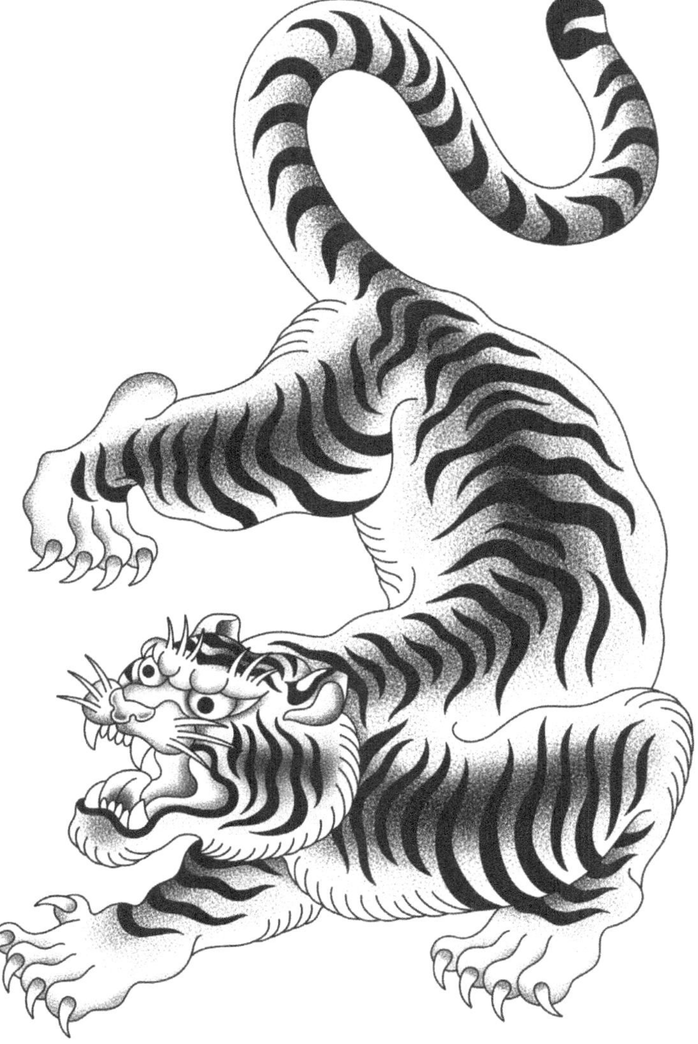

TIGER

The tiger symbolises strength, protection, and courage in Japanese tattooing. It is often associated with warding off evil and overcoming life's challenges.

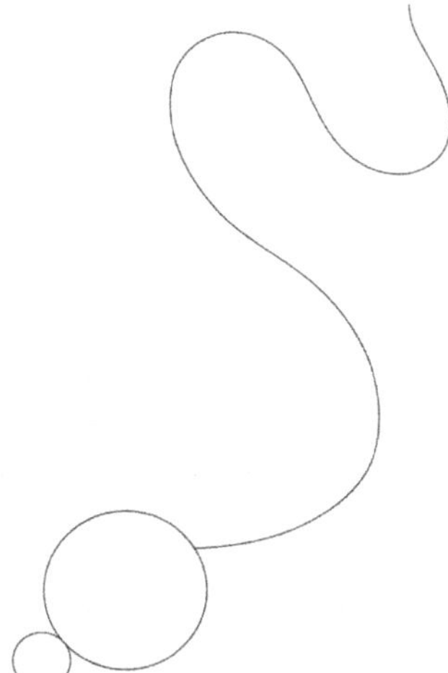

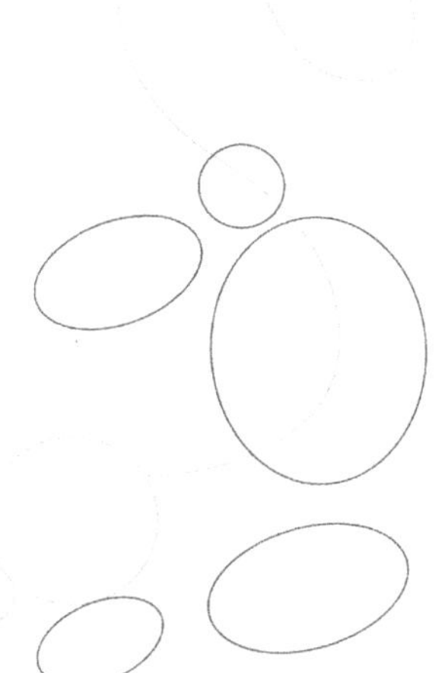

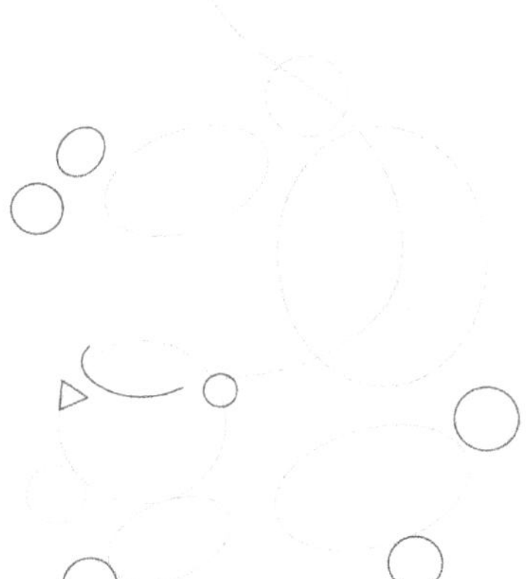

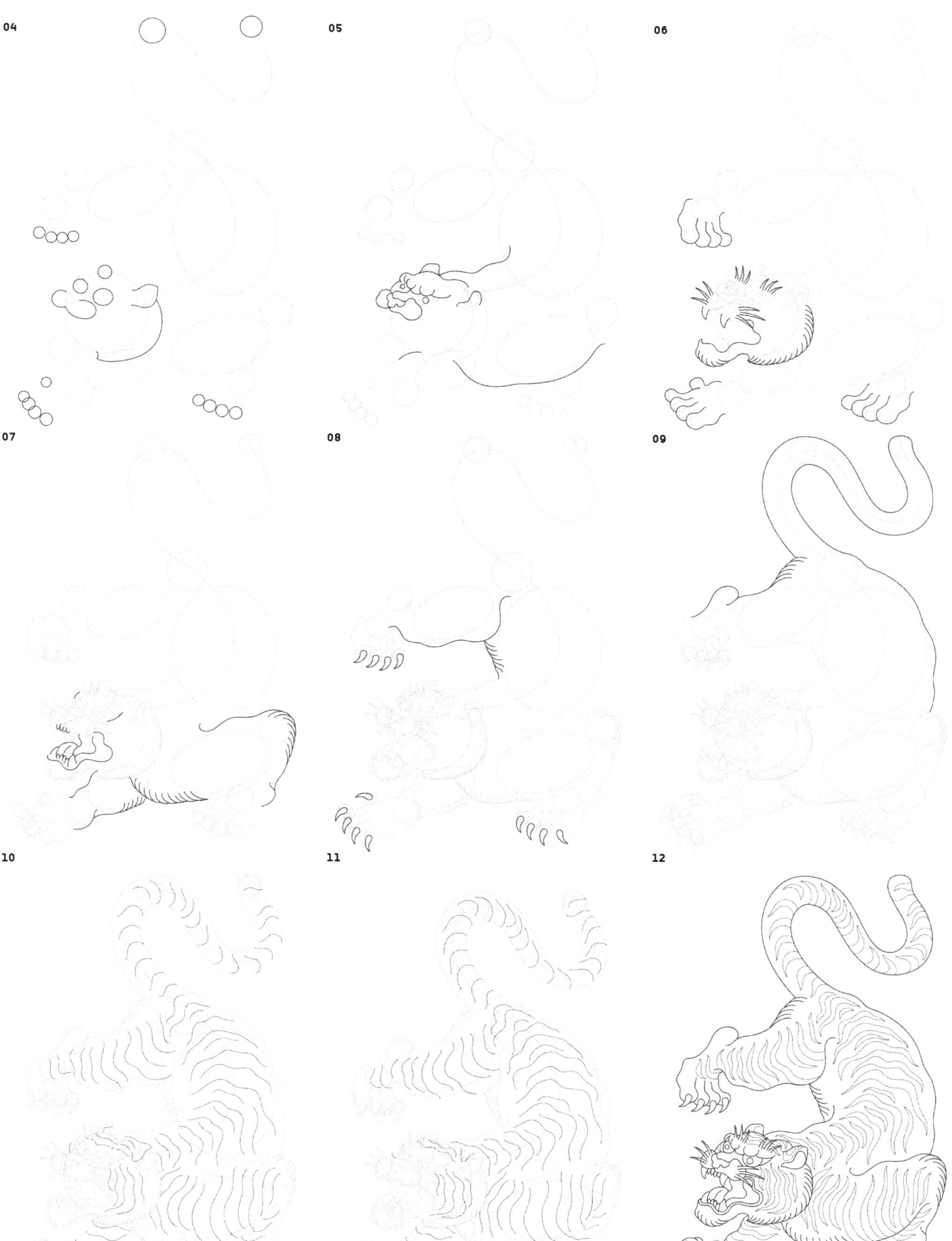

04
05
06
07
08
09
10
11
12
JAPANESE TATTOOS

TENGU

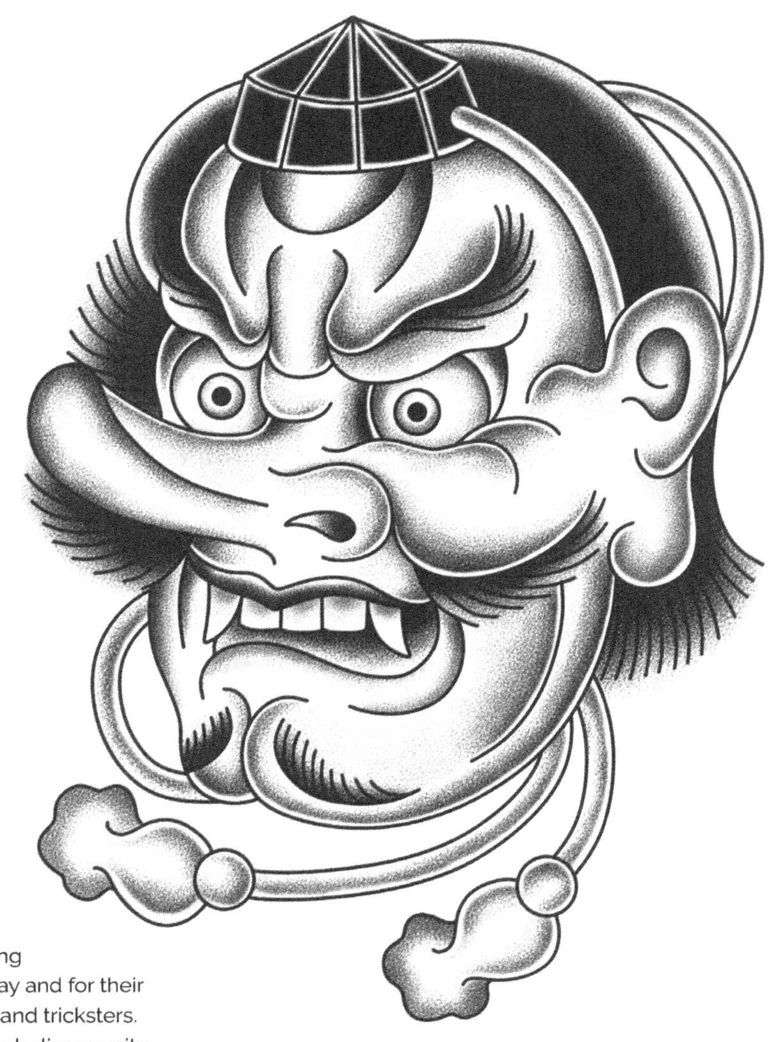

Tengus are known for being accomplished at swordplay and for their dual nature as protectors and tricksters. The tengu's long nose symbolises vanity in Japanese culture.

01

02

03

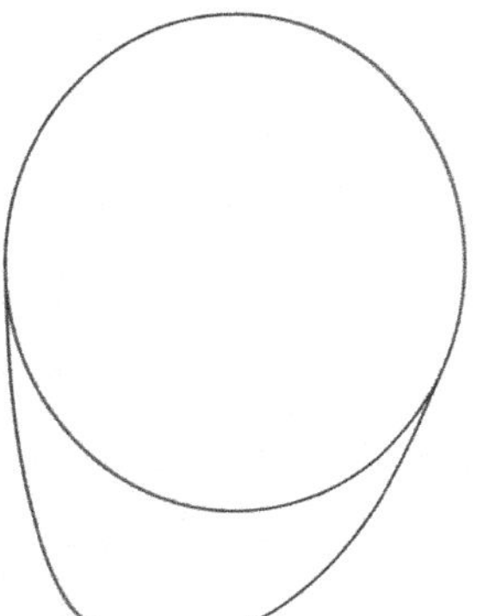

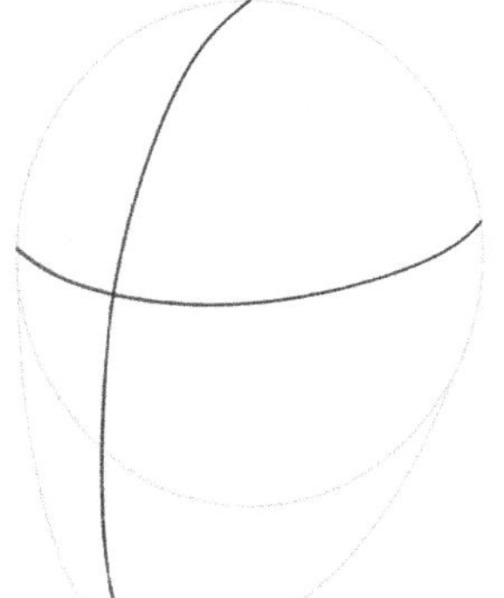

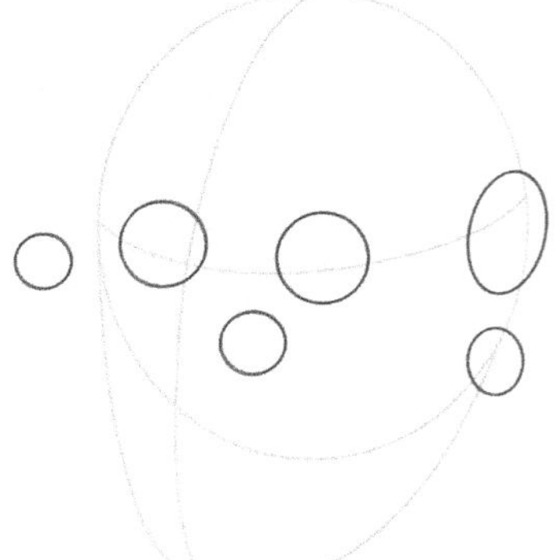

04

05

06

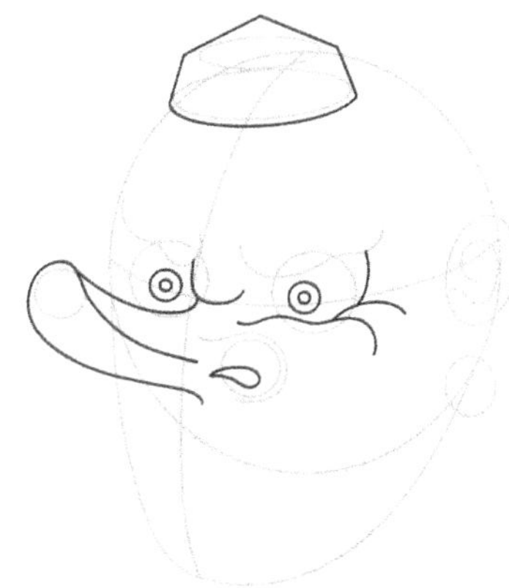

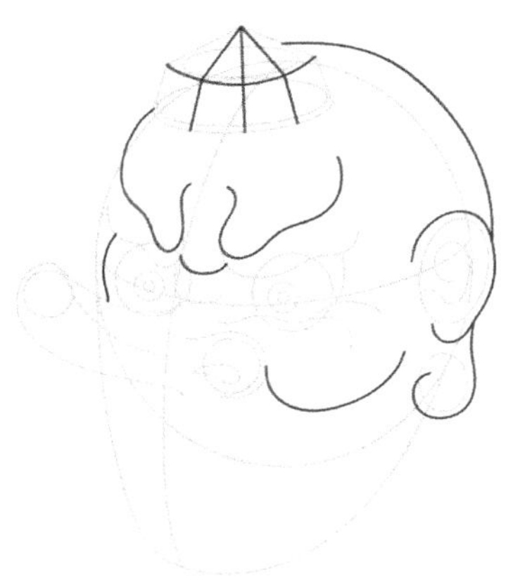

07

08

09

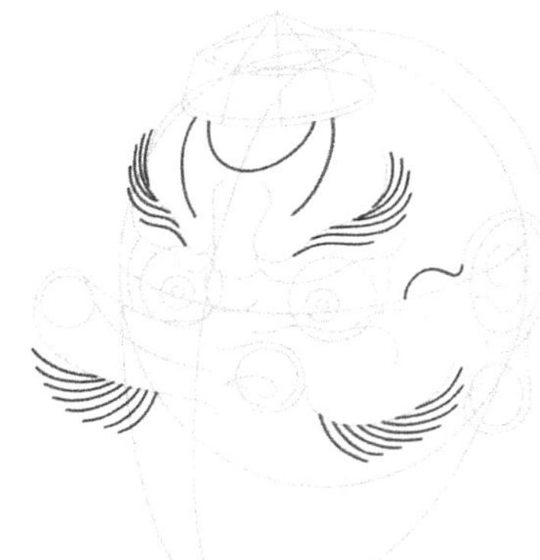

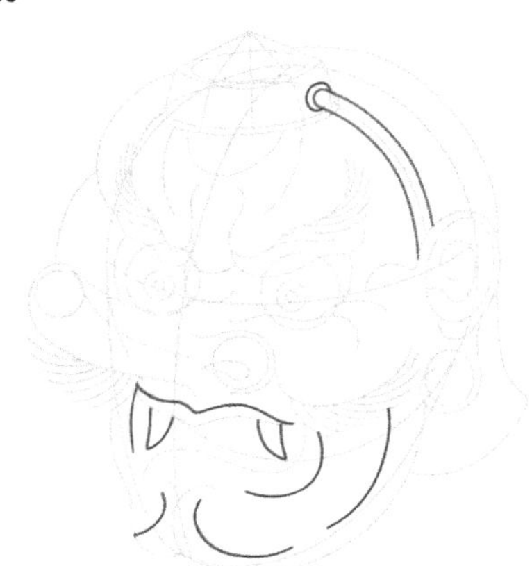

JAPANESE TATTOOS

10

11

12

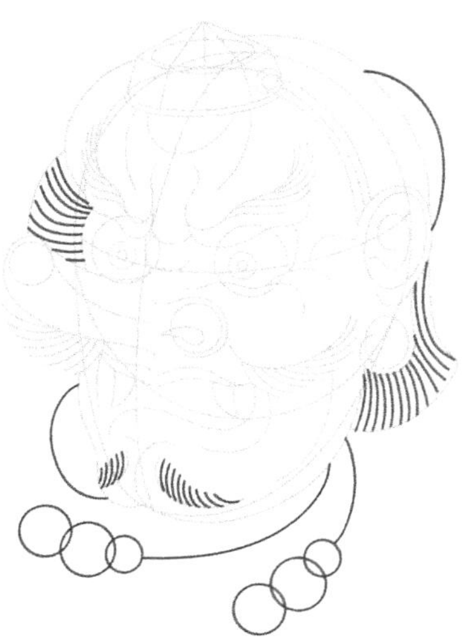

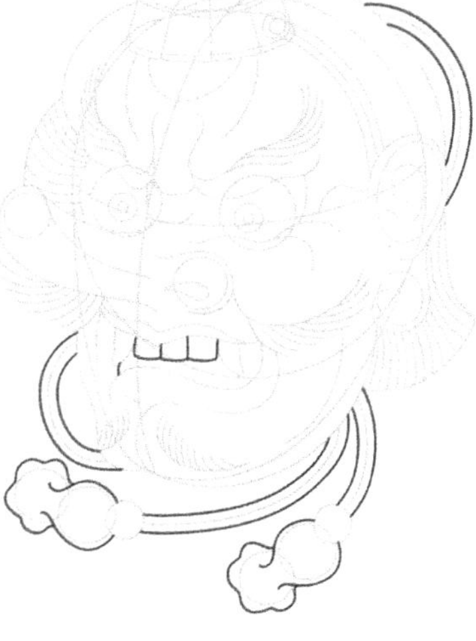

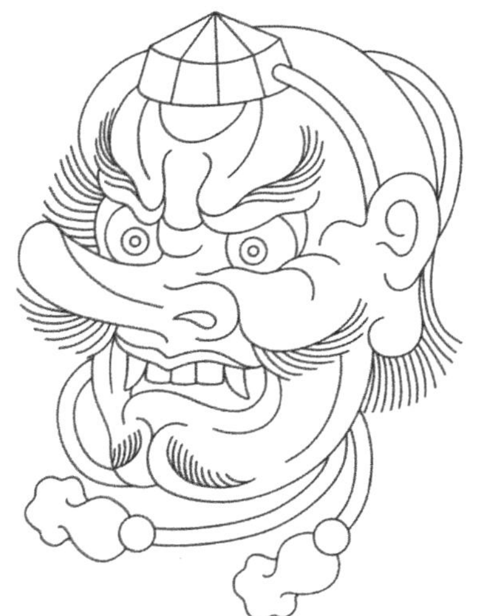

TSUCHIGUMO

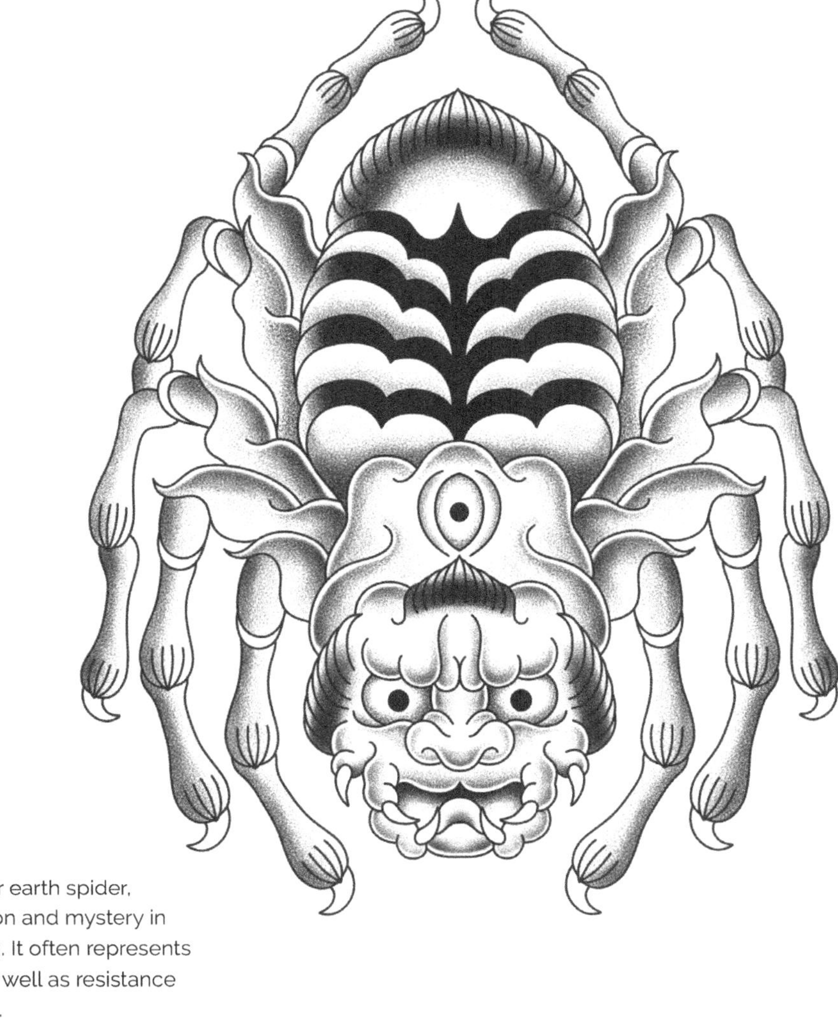

The tsuchigumo, or earth spider, symbolises rebellion and mystery in Japanese tattooing. It often represents hidden strength as well as resistance against oppression.

01 02 03

04

05

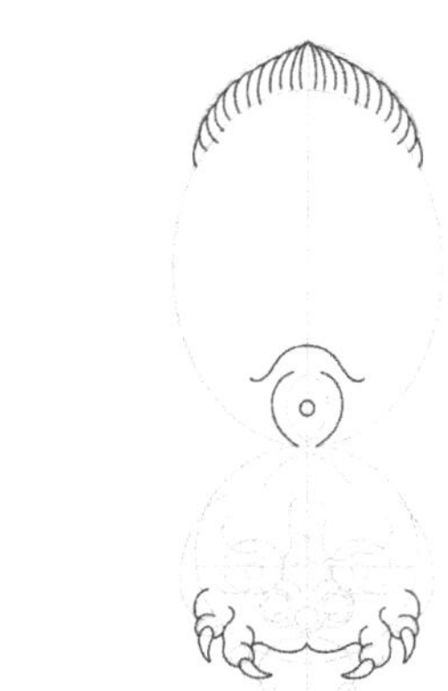

06

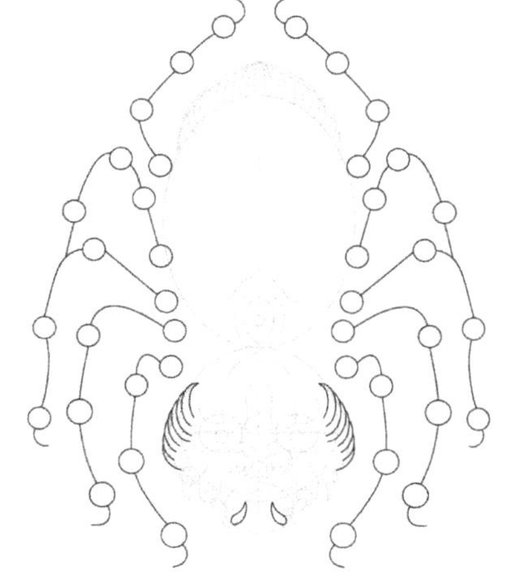

07

08

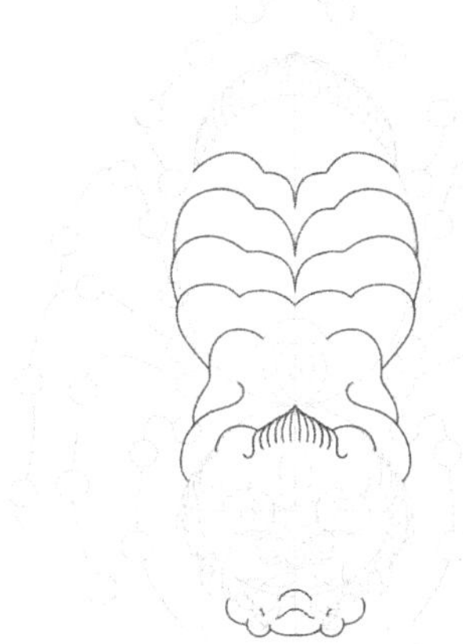

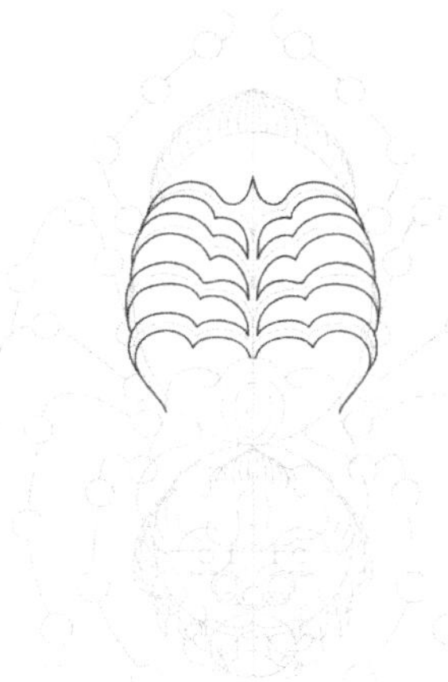

09

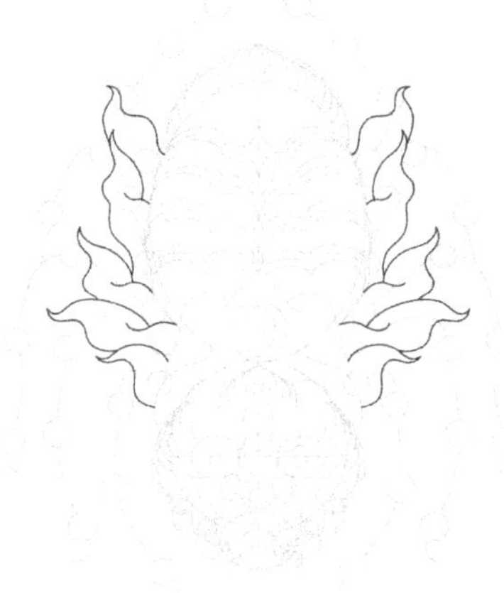

10

11

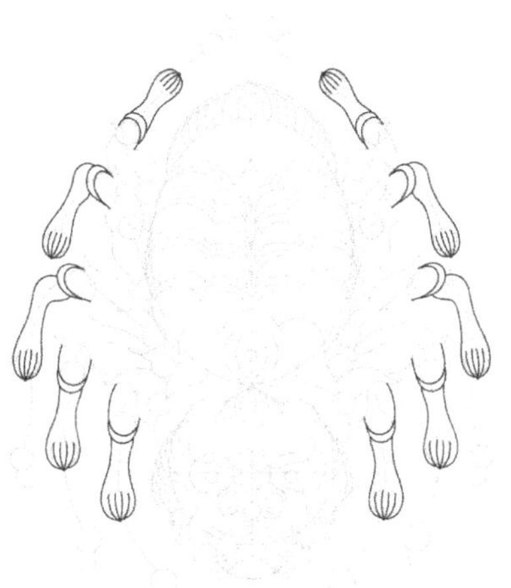

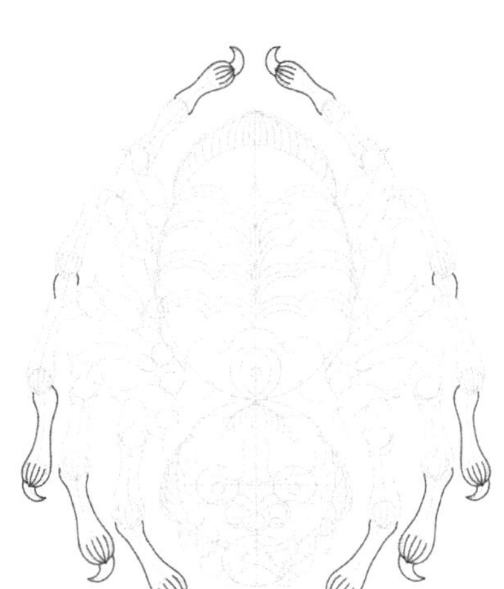

12

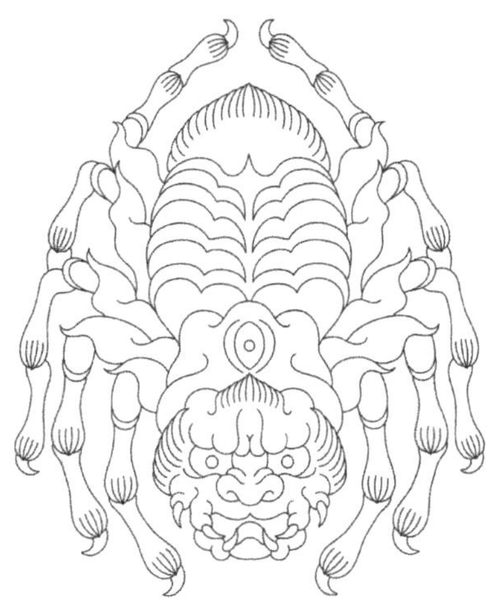

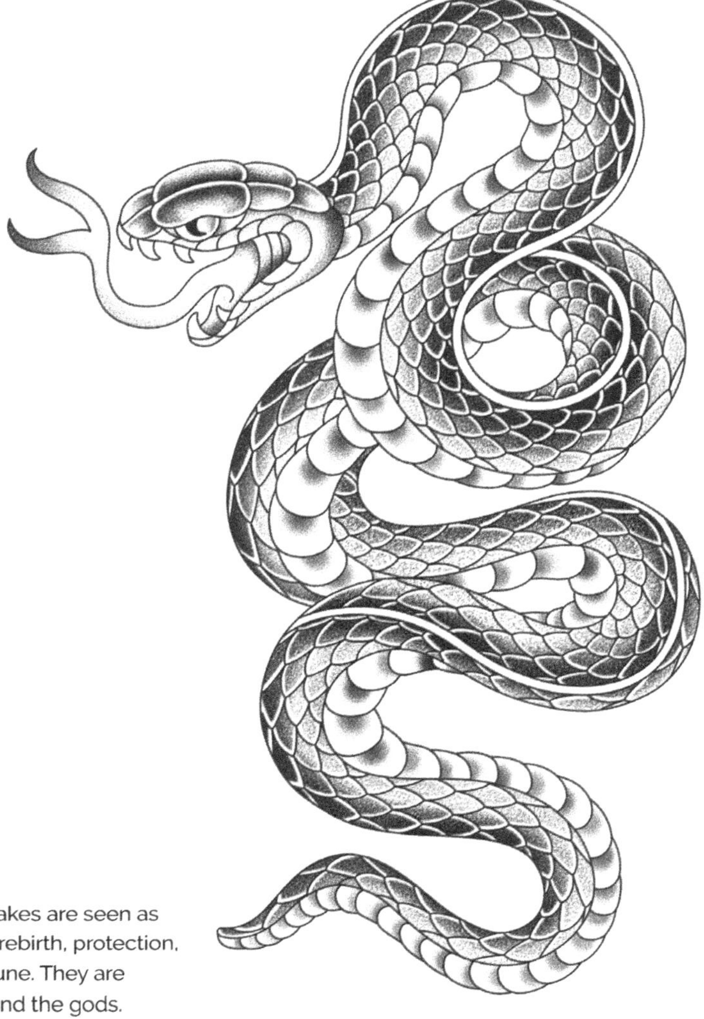

SNAKE | HEBI

In Japanese culture, snakes are seen as mysterious symbols of rebirth, protection, wisdom, and good fortune. They are associated with water and the gods.

01

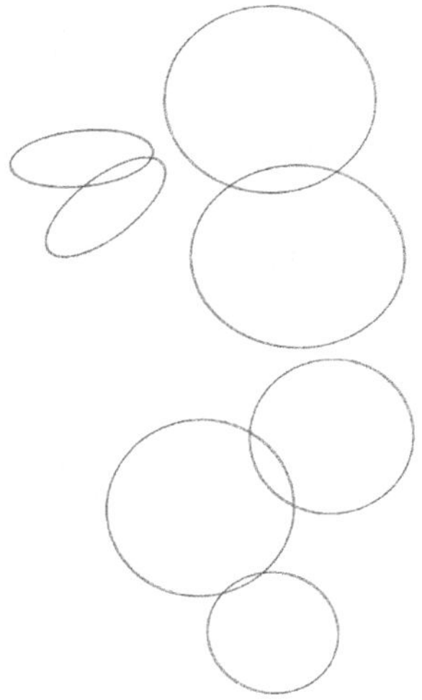

02

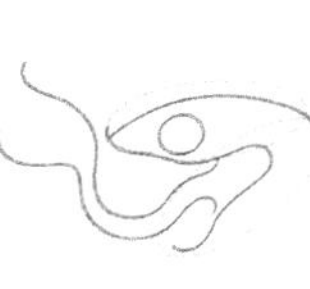

03

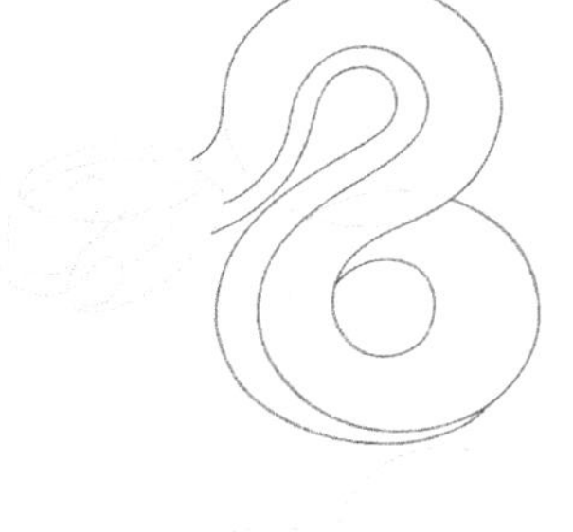

04

05

06

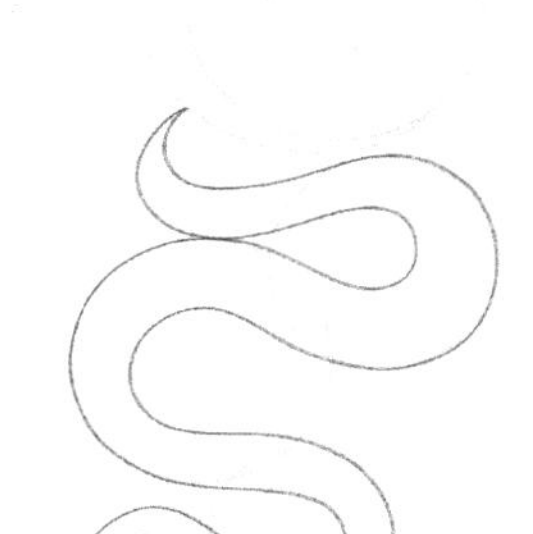
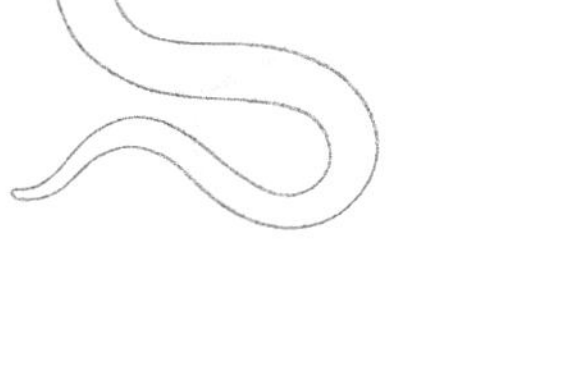
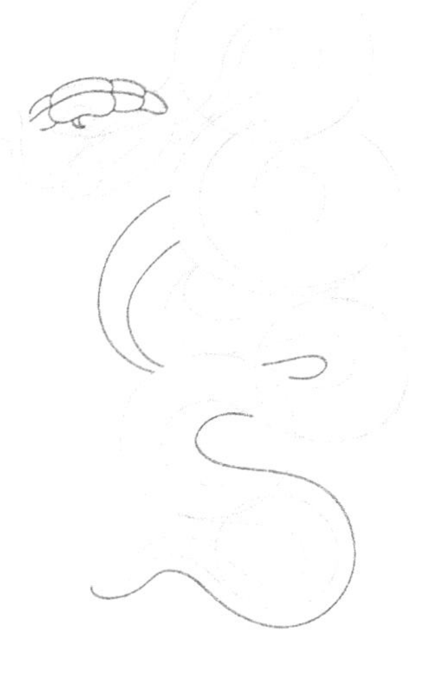

07

08

09

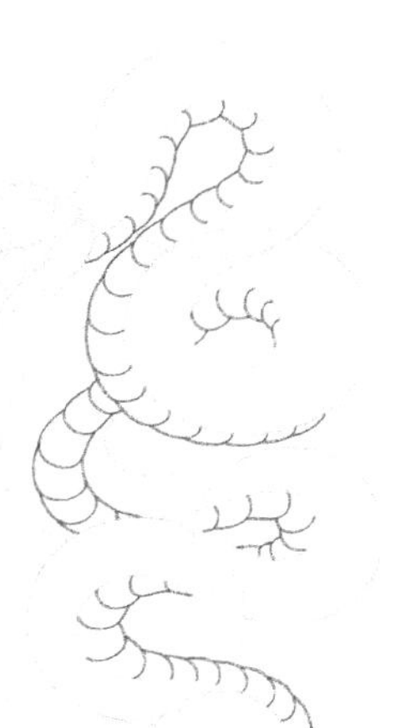
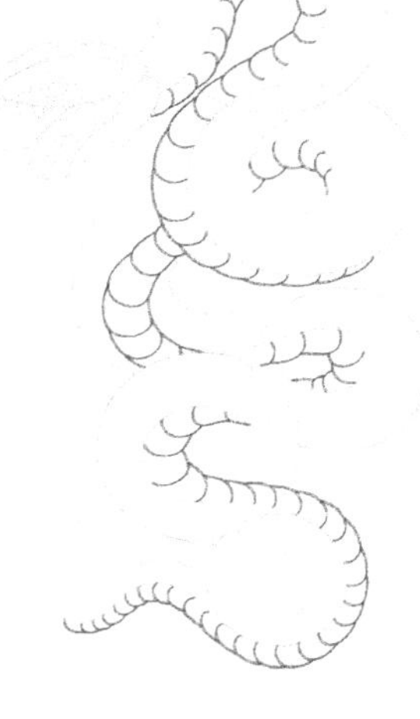
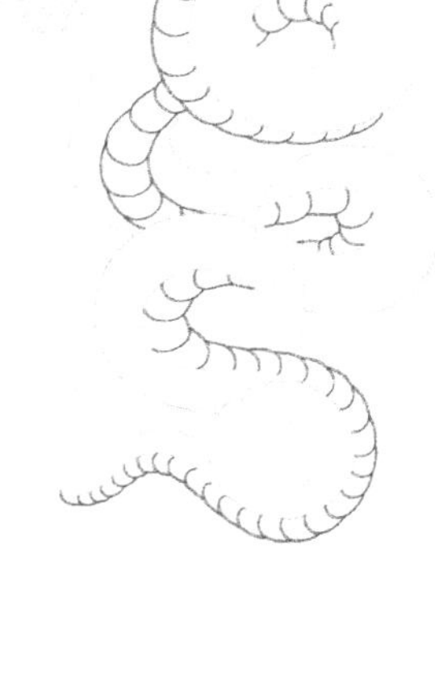
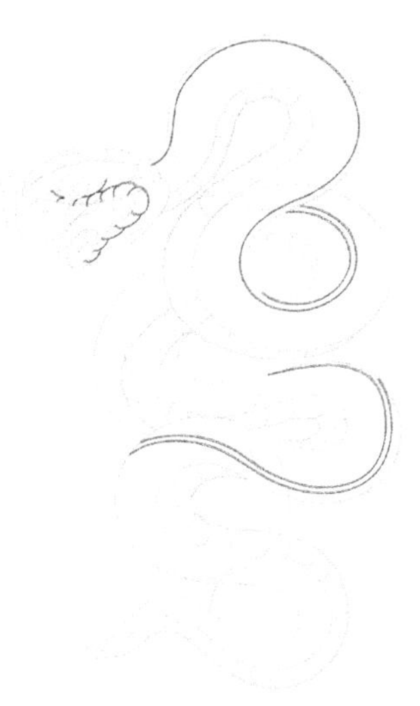
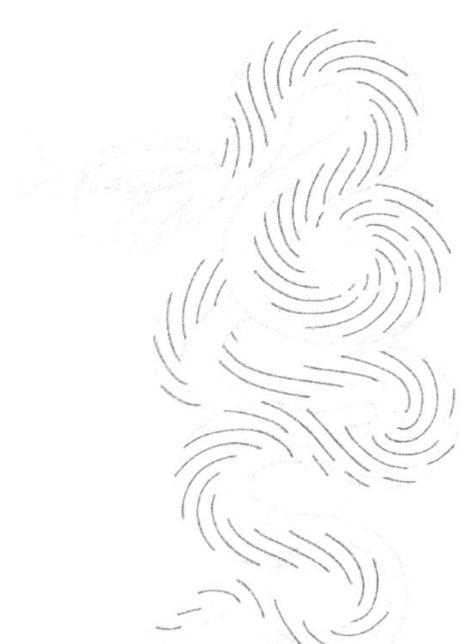

10

11

12

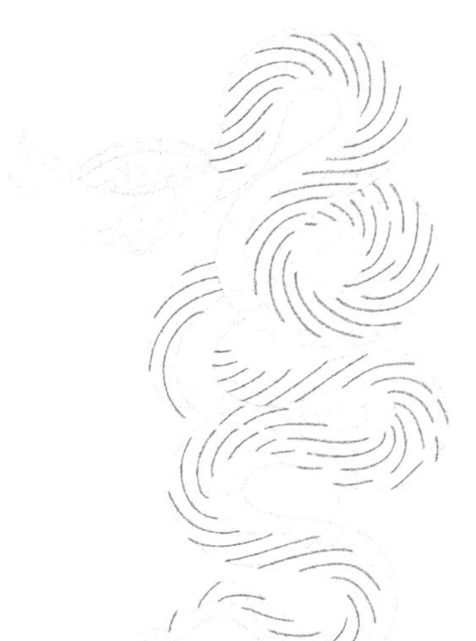
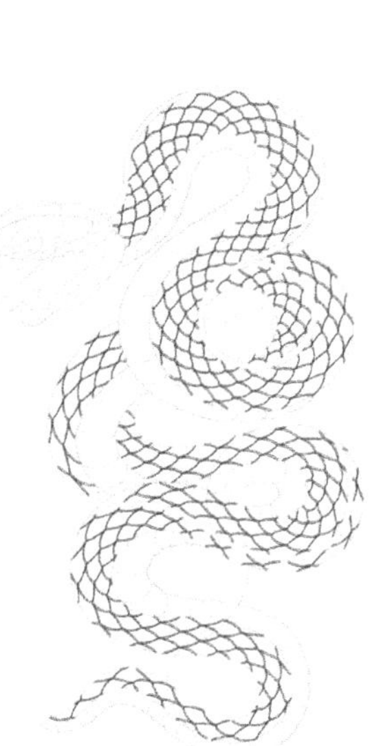
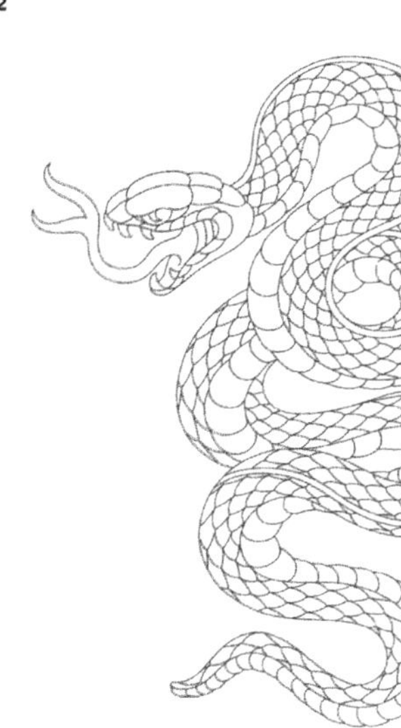

JAPANESE TATTOOS

FROG | KAERU

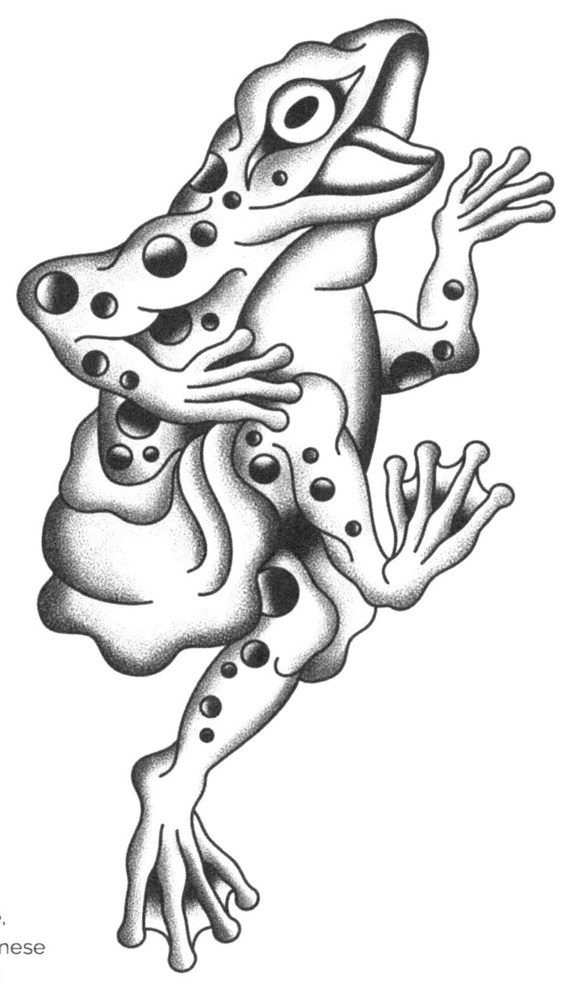

The frog can symbolise good fortune, longevity, and transformation in Japanese tattooing. It is often linked to mystical knowledge and the supernatural.

01

02

03

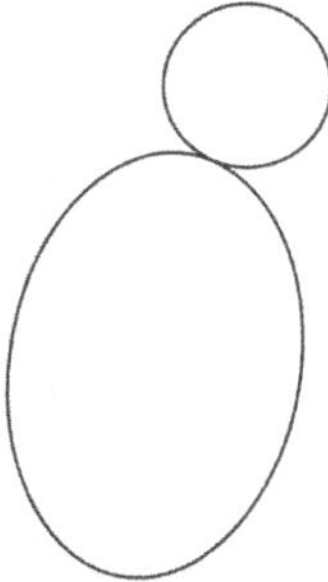

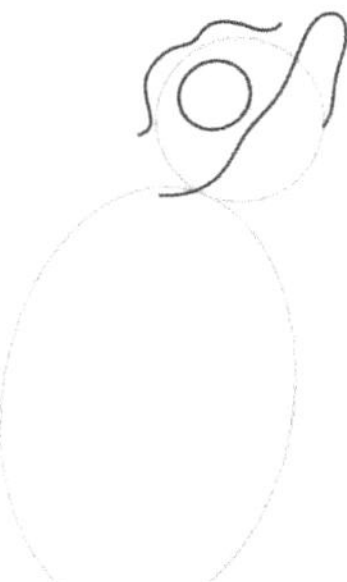

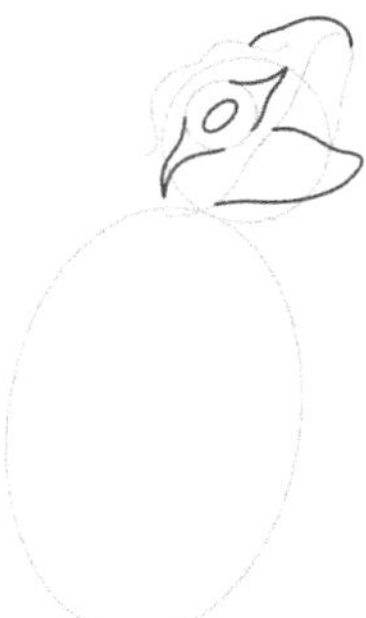

04

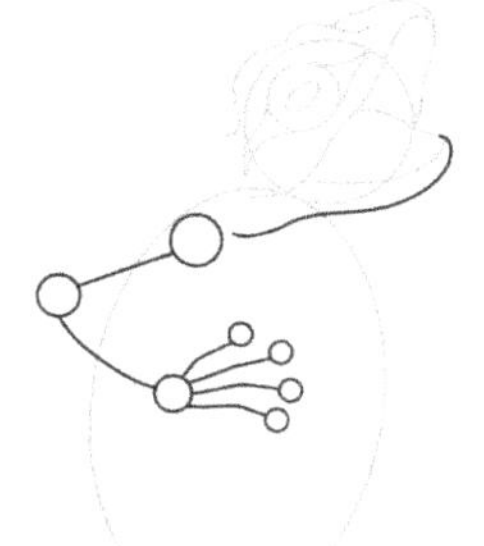

05

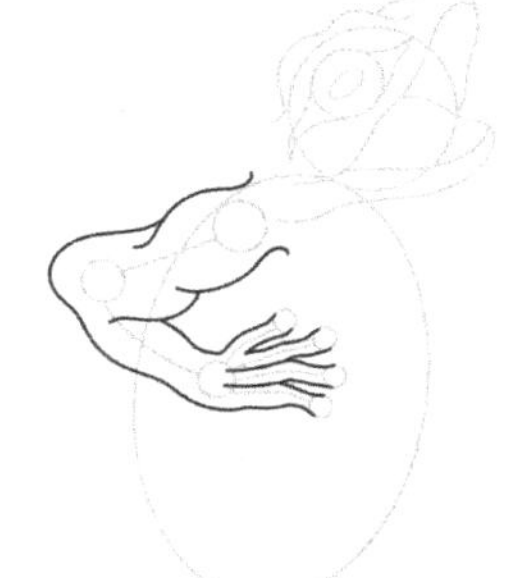

06

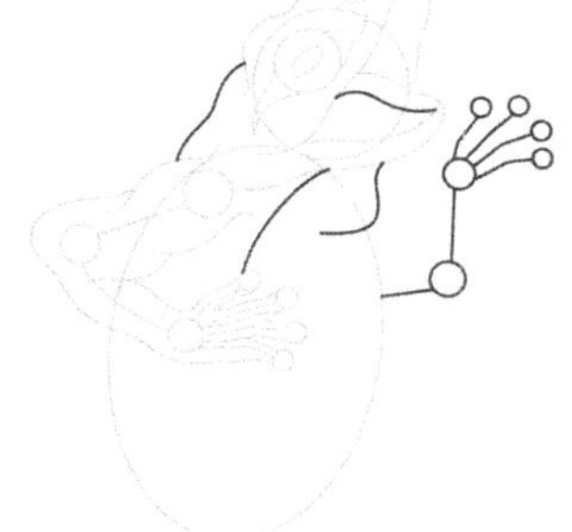

07

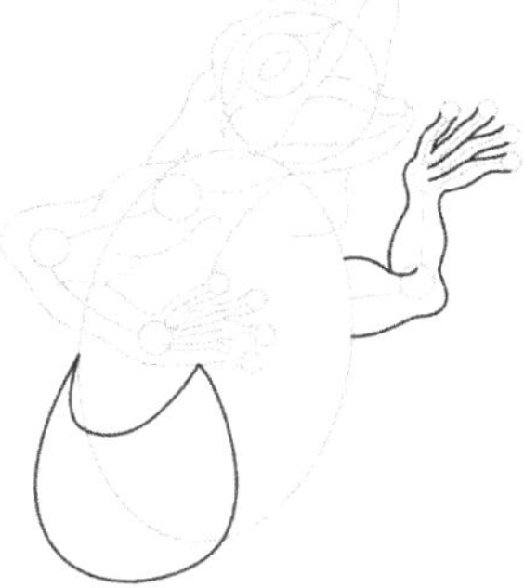

08

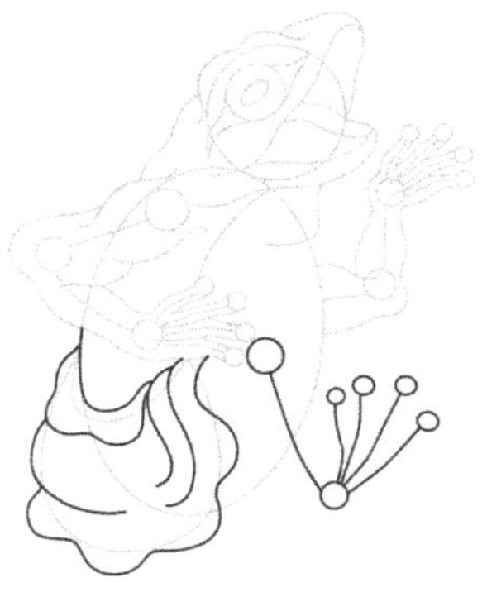

09

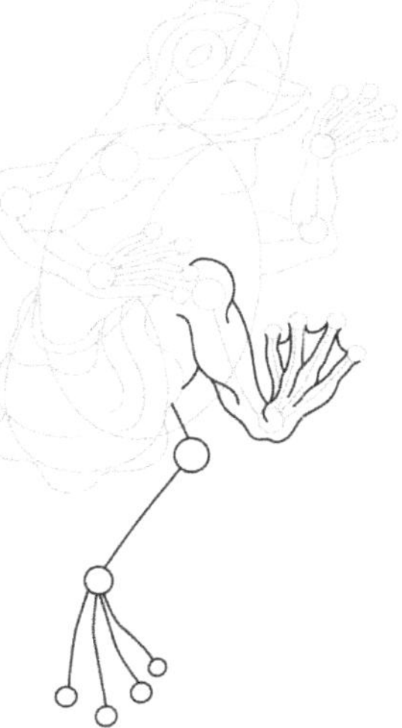

10

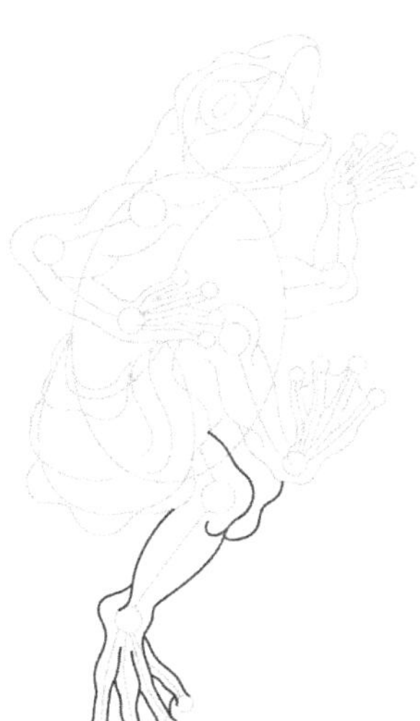

11

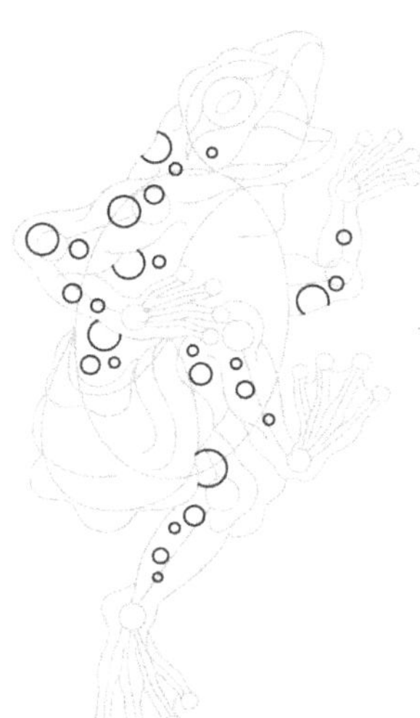

12

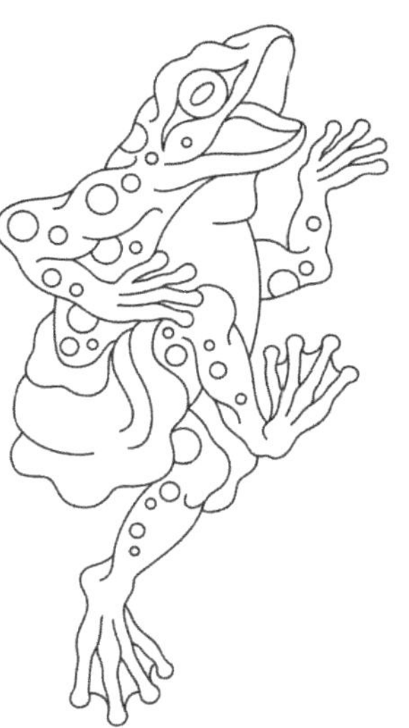

JAPANESE TATTOOS

KOI FISH | NISHIKIGOI

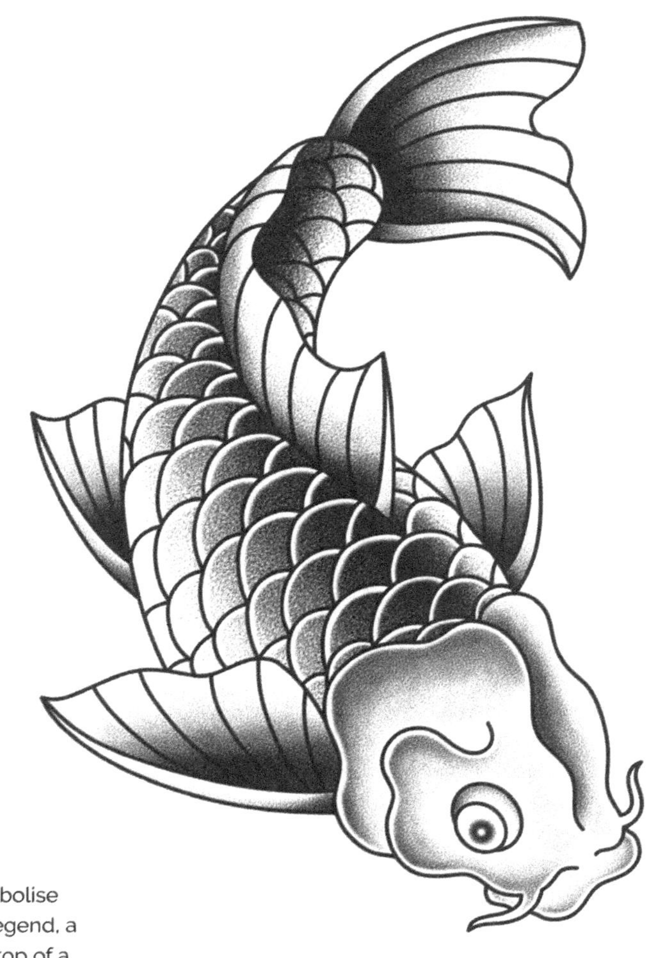

In Japanese culture koi fish symbolise courage and perseverance. In legend, a koi that swims upstream to the top of a waterfall transforms into a mighty dragon.

01   02   03

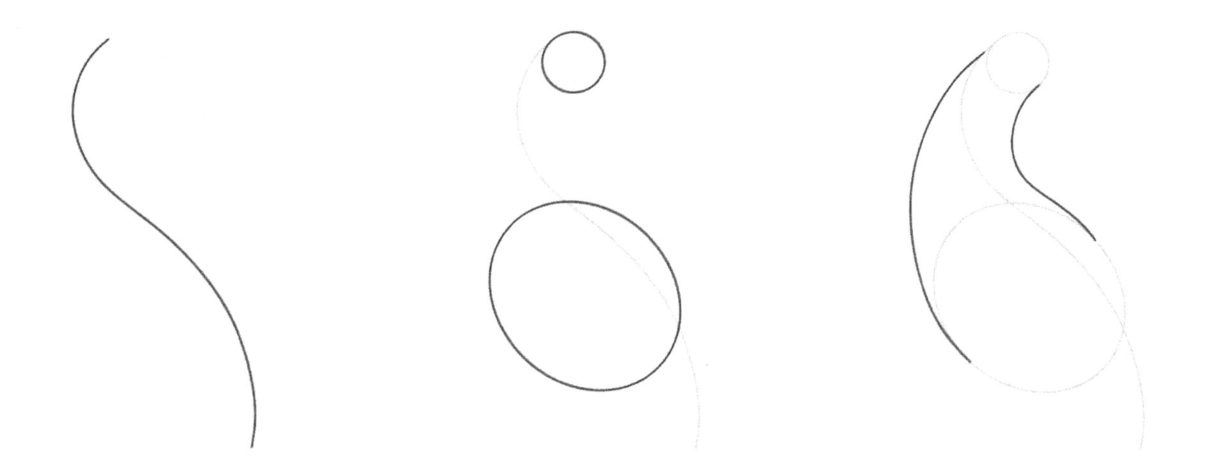

04

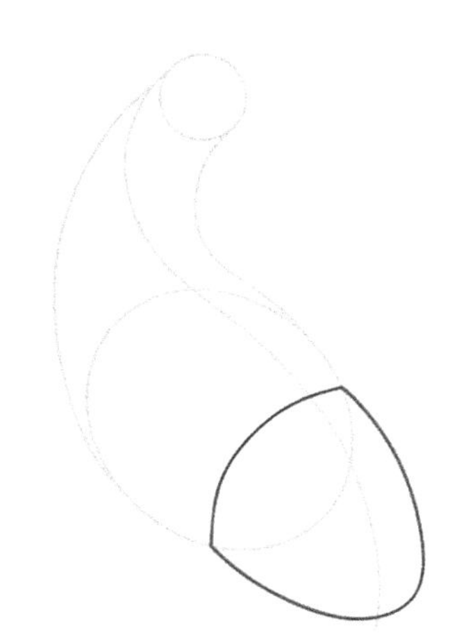

05

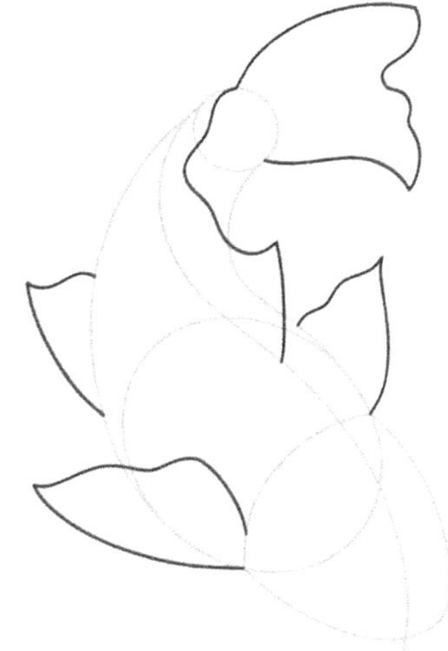

06

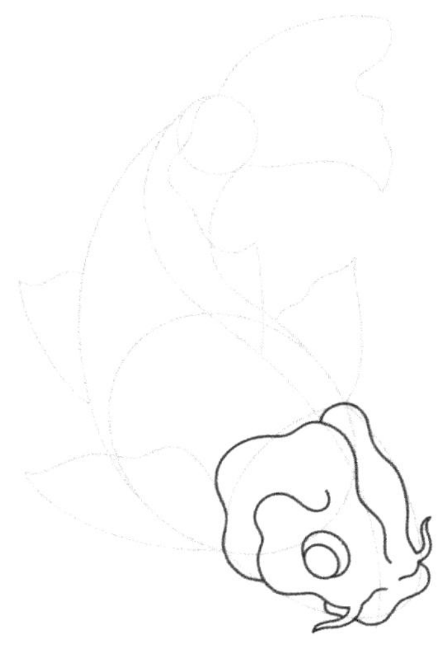

07

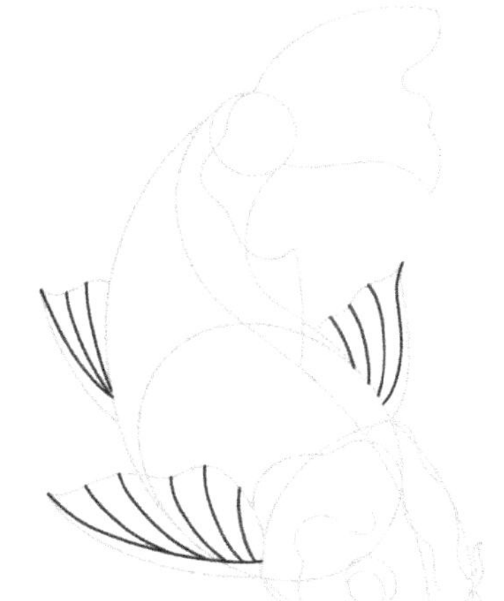

08

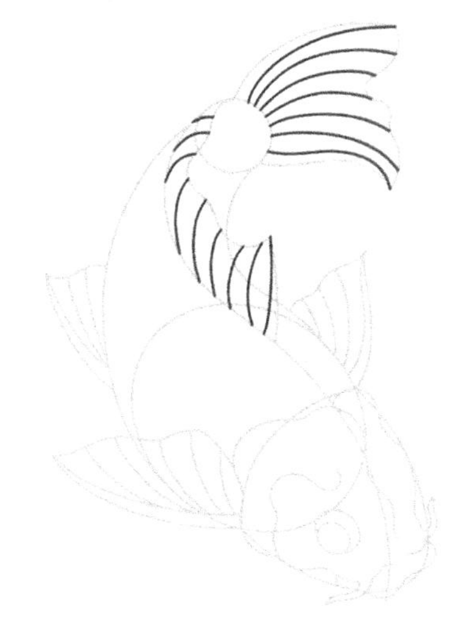

09

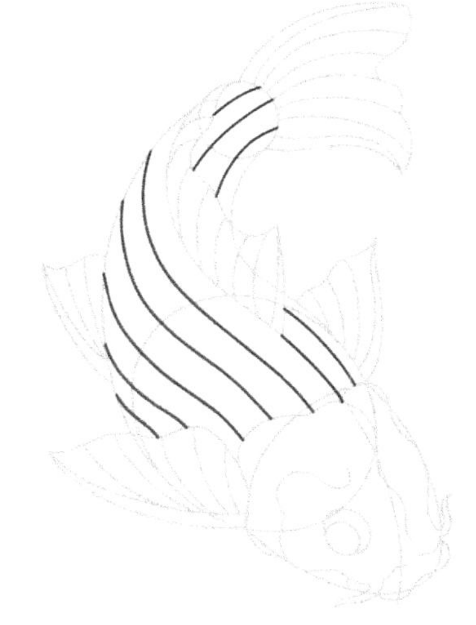

10

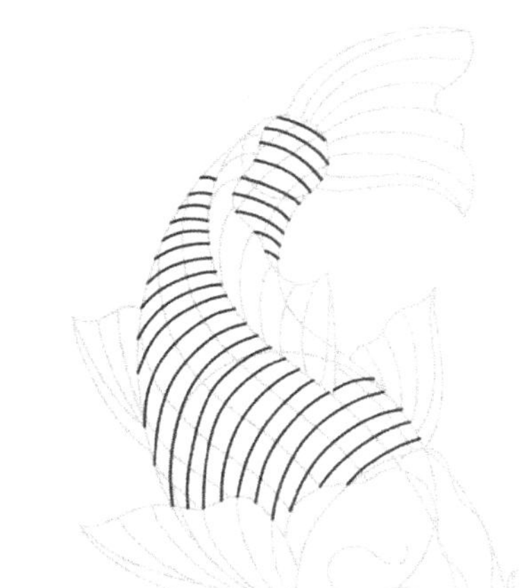

11

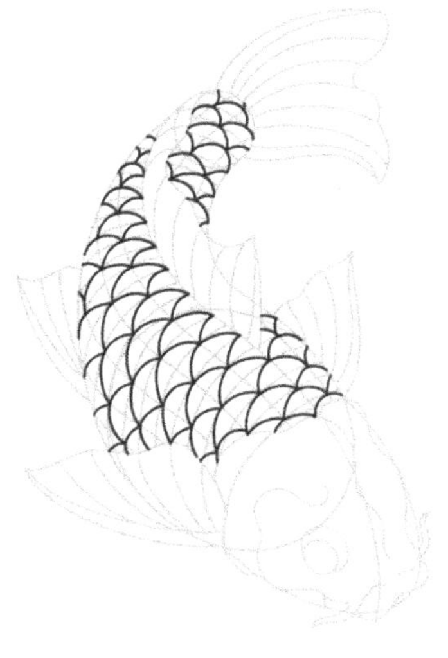

12

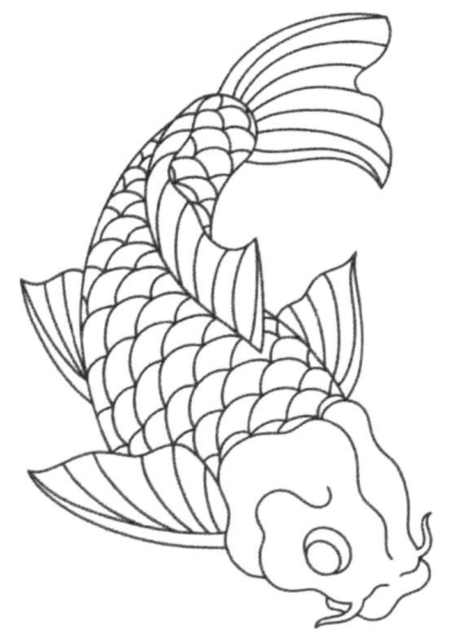

JAPANESE TATTOOS

PHOENIX | HOU-OU

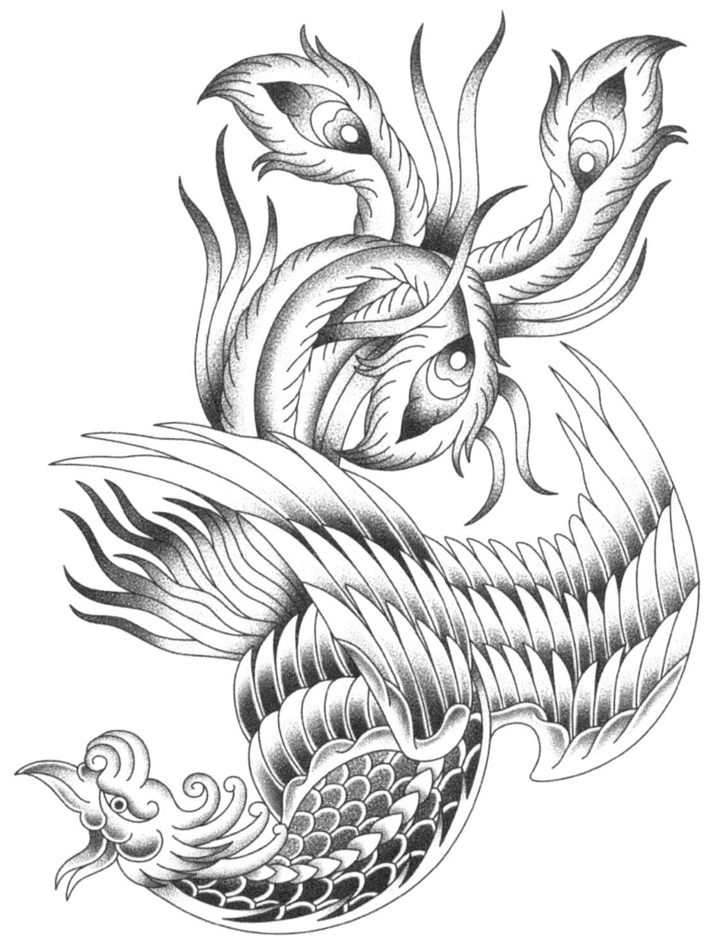

The phoenix symbolises both hope and renewal. In Japanese myth, it represents peace and appears during harmonious and prosperous periods.

01

02

03

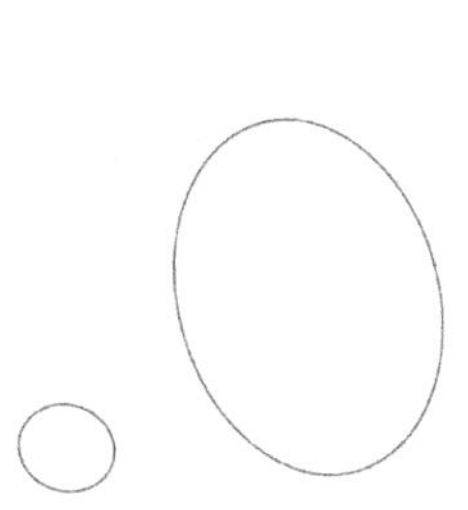

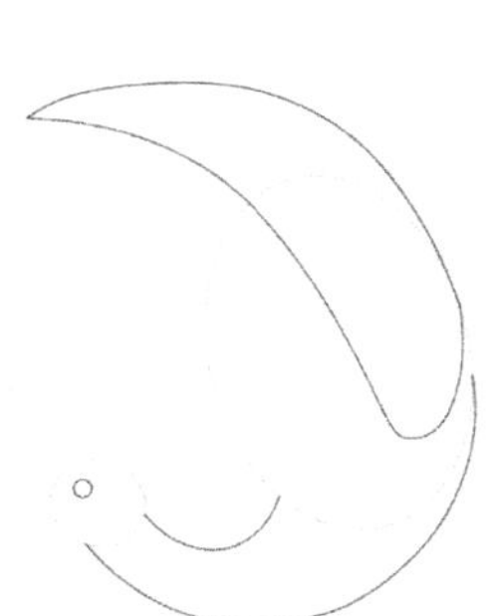

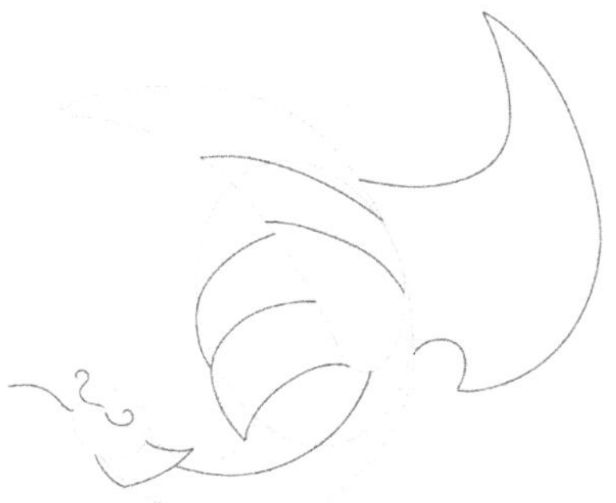

04

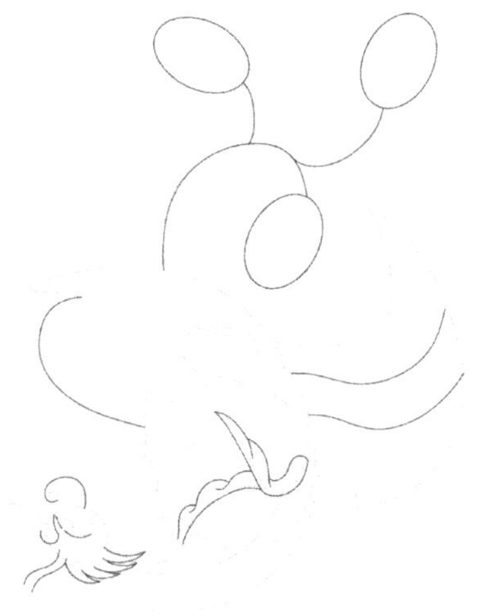

05

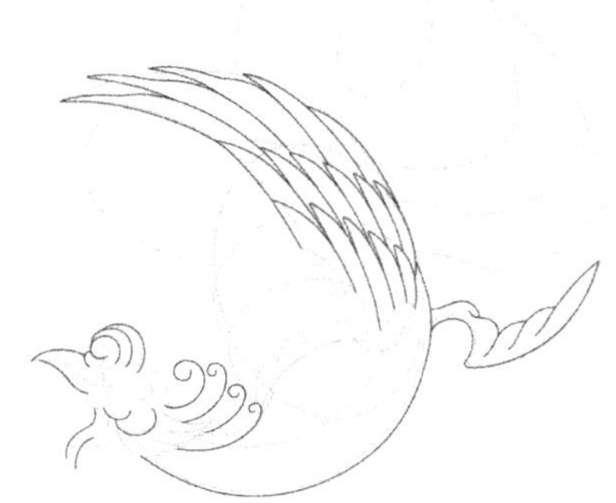

06

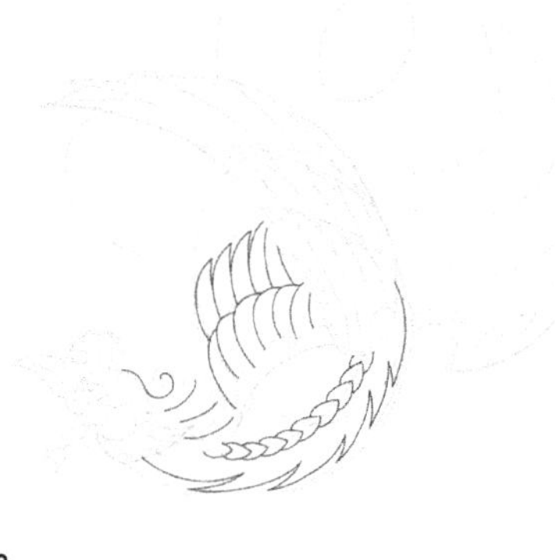

07

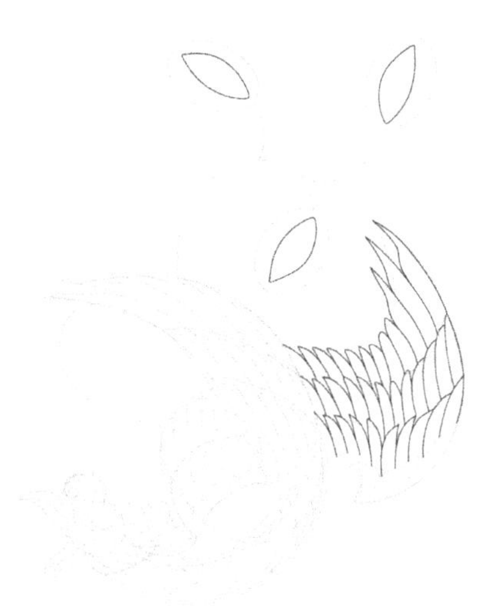

08

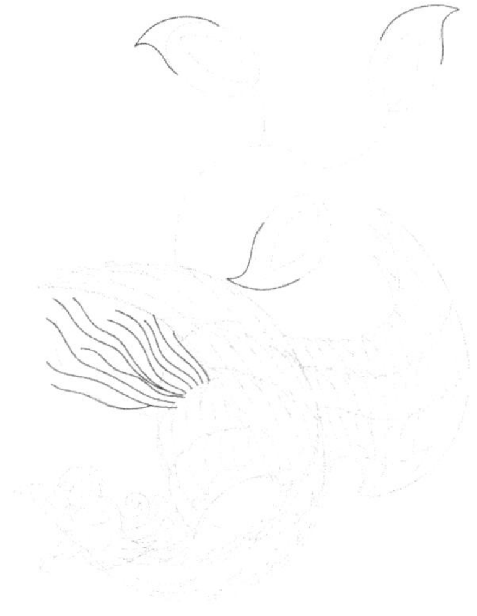

09

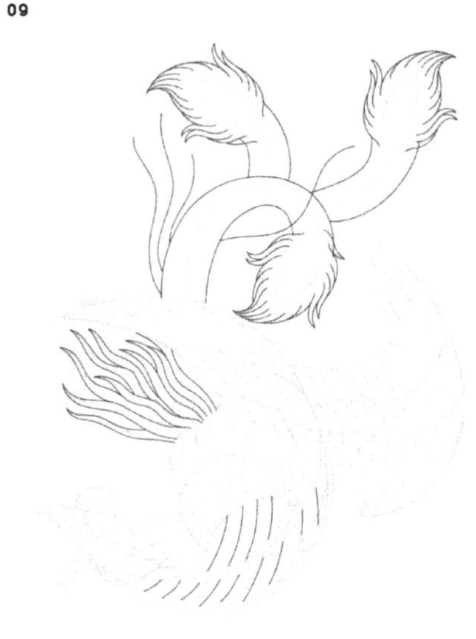

10

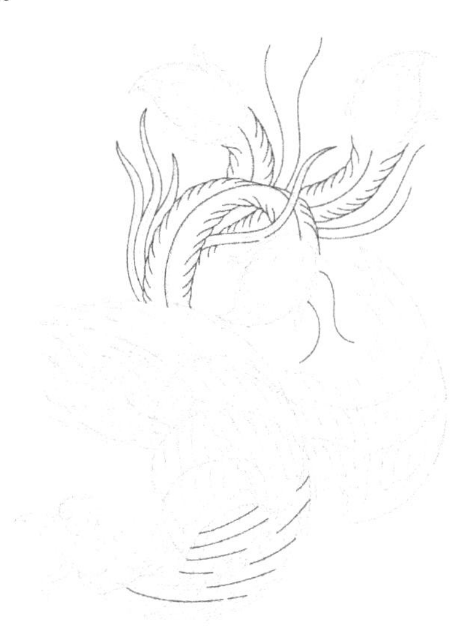

11

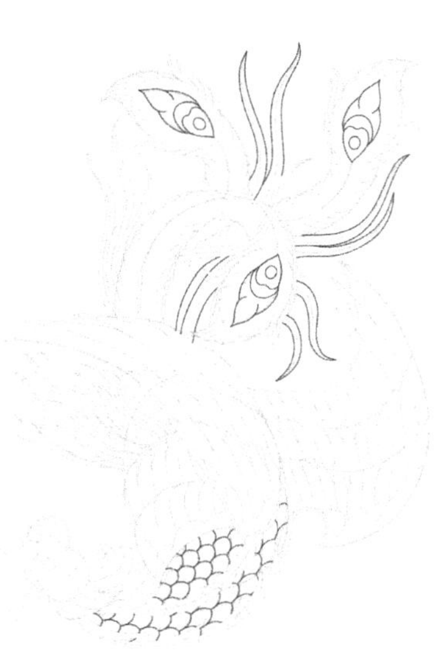

12

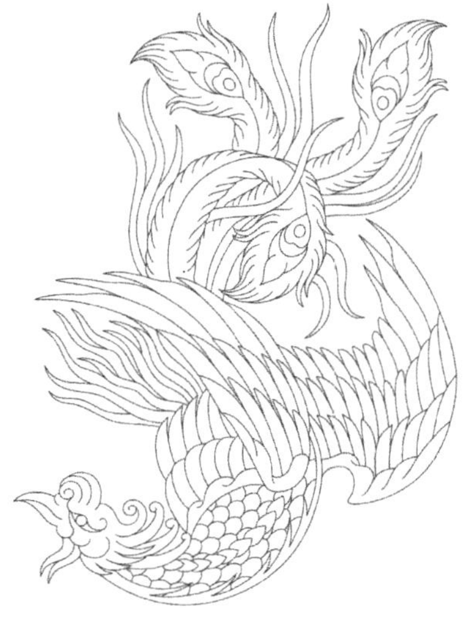

JAPANESE TATTOOS

DRAGON | RYU

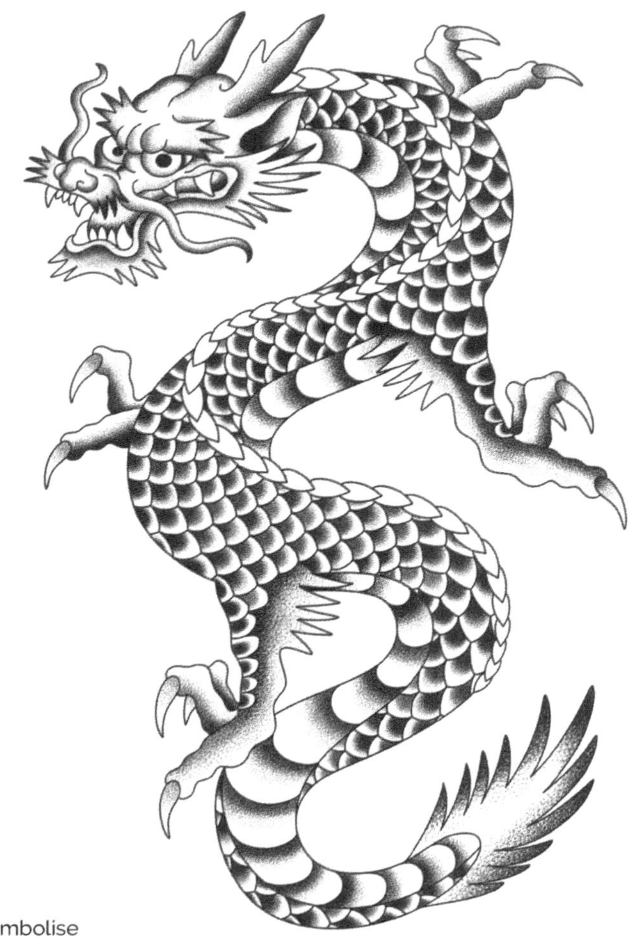

In Japanese culture, dragons symbolise power, wisdom, wealth, longevity, and good fortune.

01

02

03

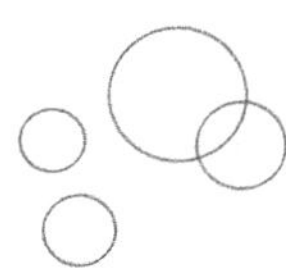

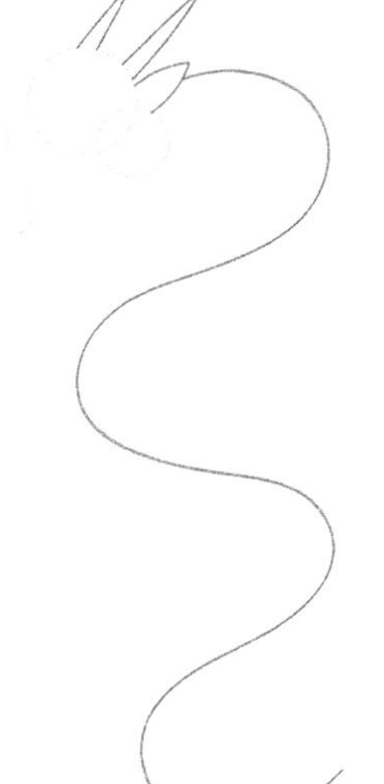

04

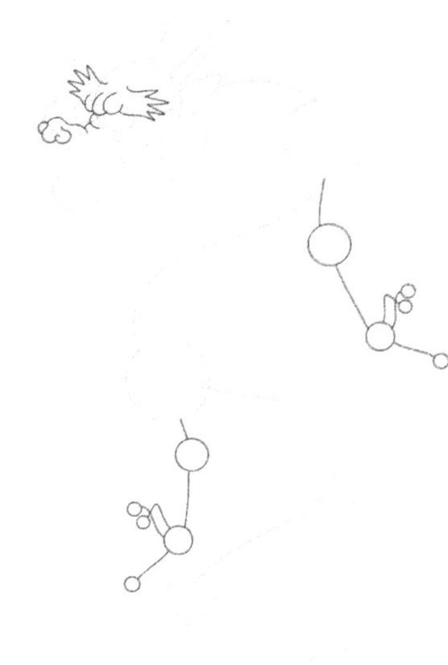

05

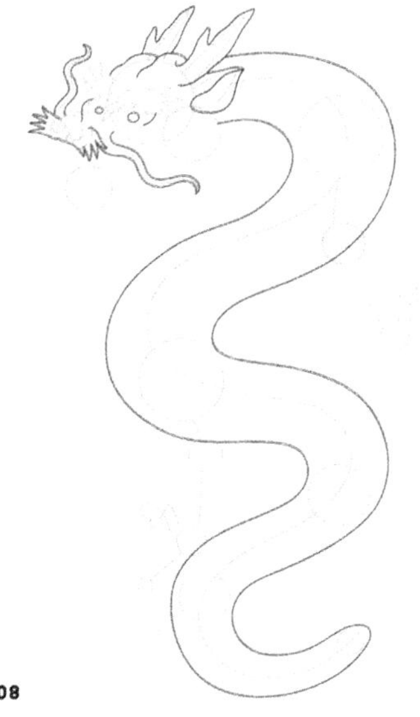

06

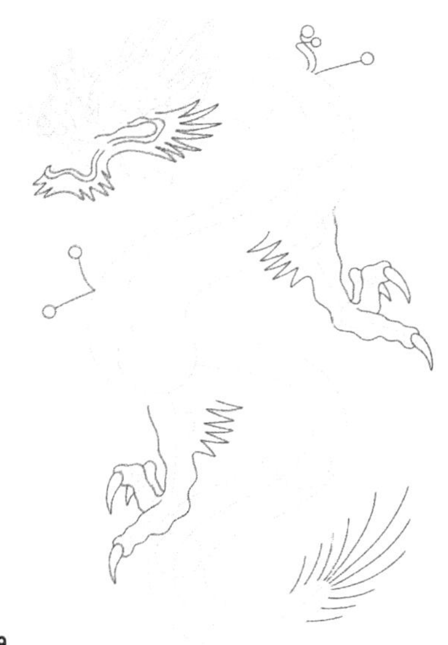

07

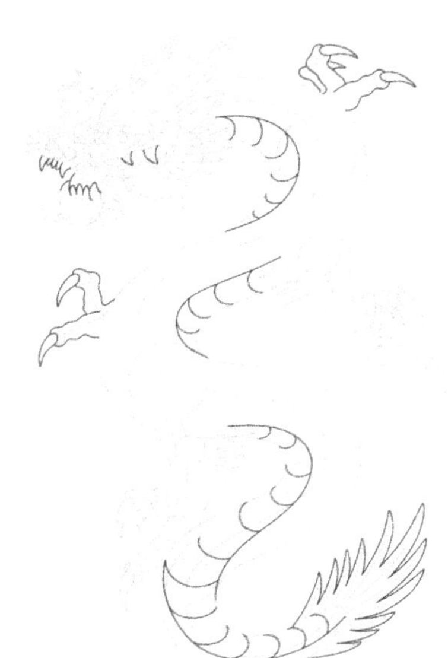

08

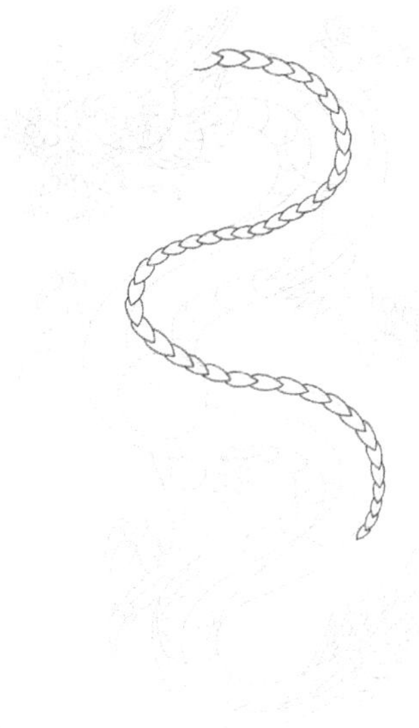

09

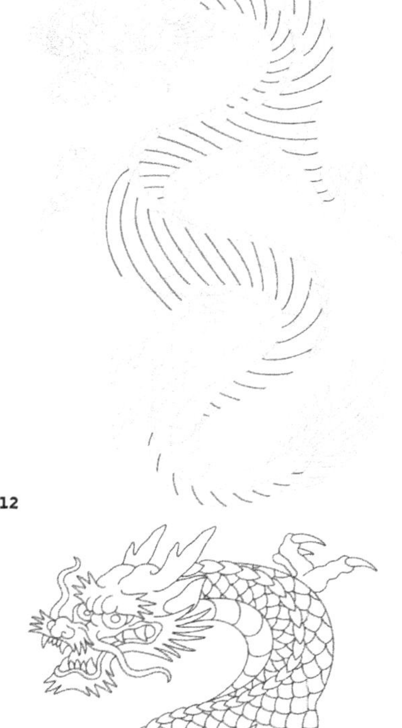

10

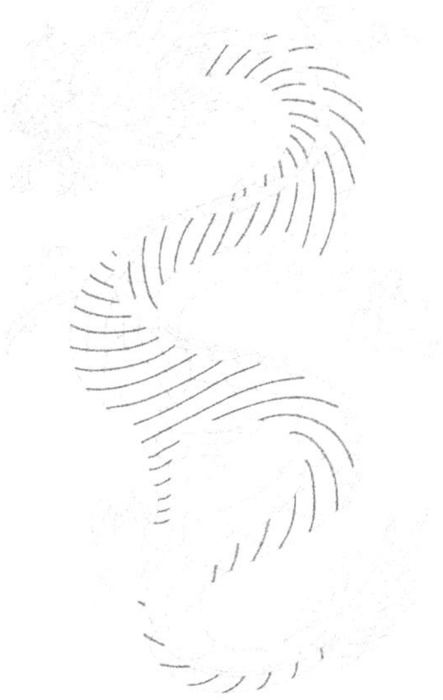

11

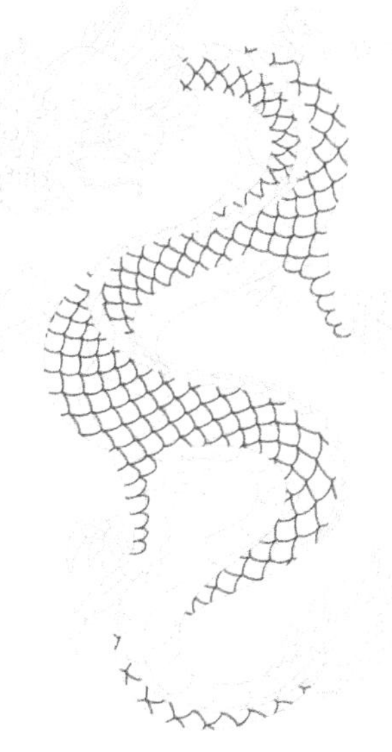

12

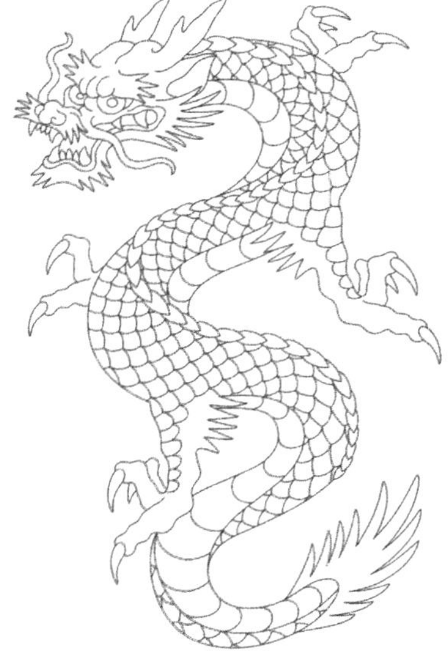

DRAGON HEAD | RYU

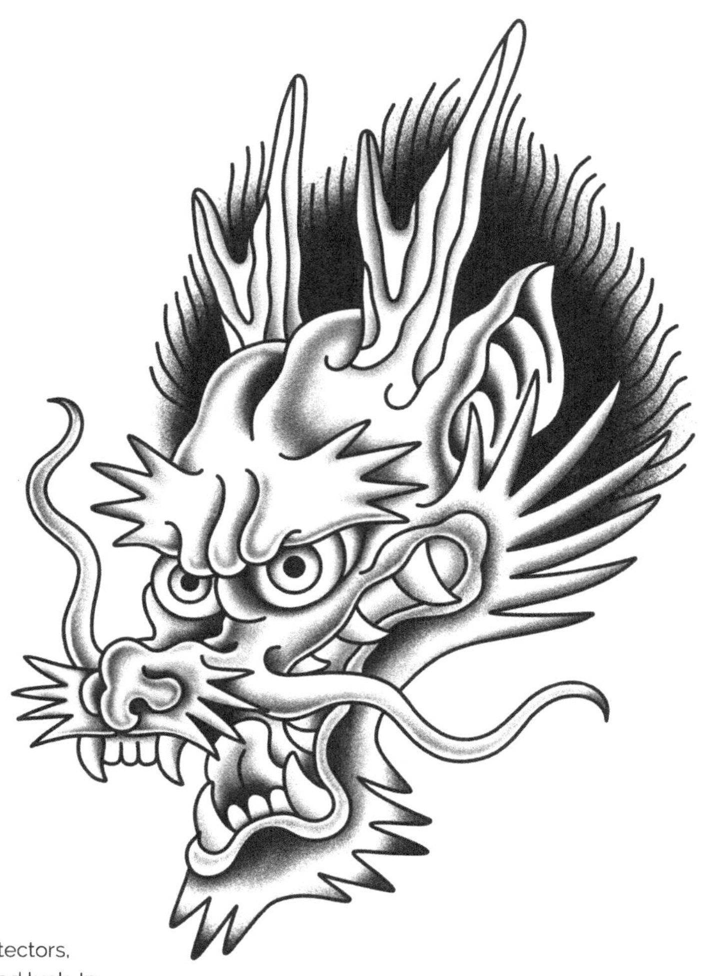

Dragons are wise, strong protectors, symbolising courage and good luck. In Japanese culture, they are revered as powerful water deities.

01

02

03

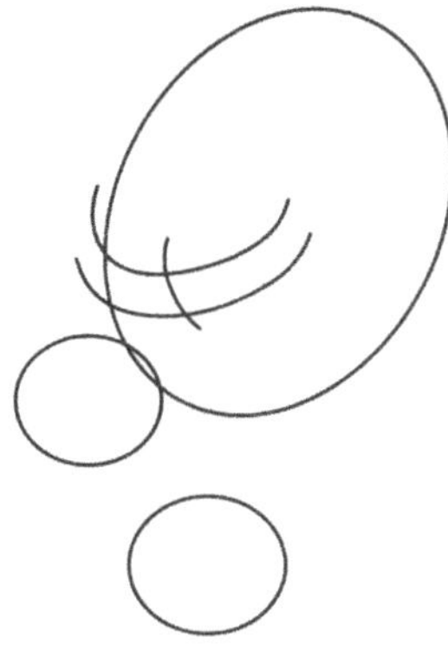

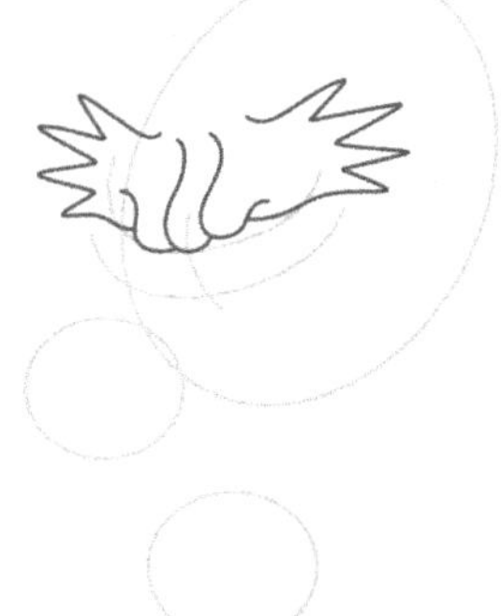

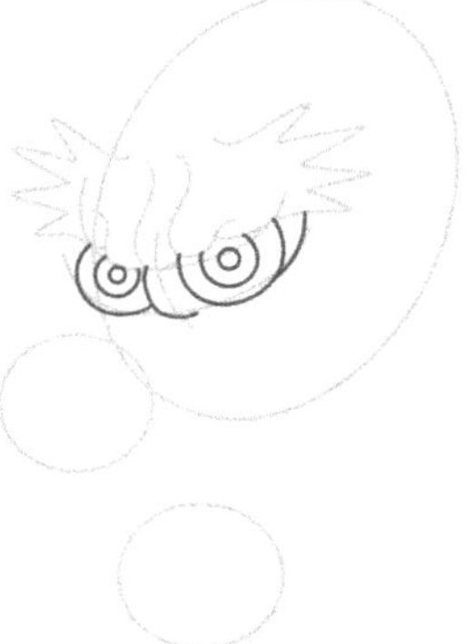

04

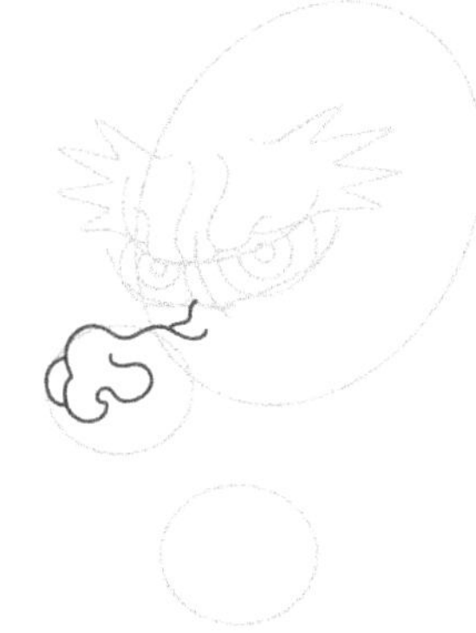

05

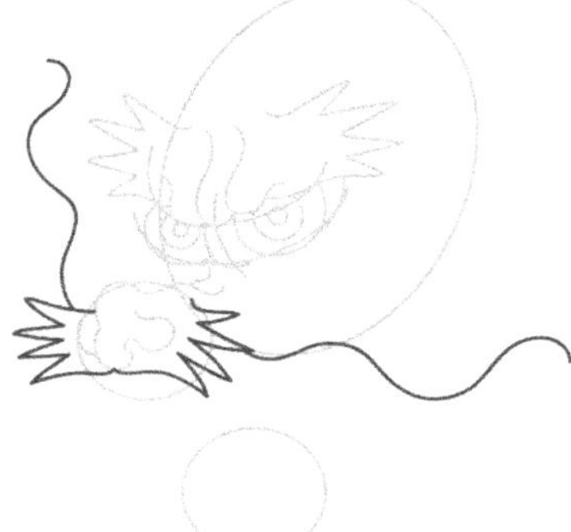

06

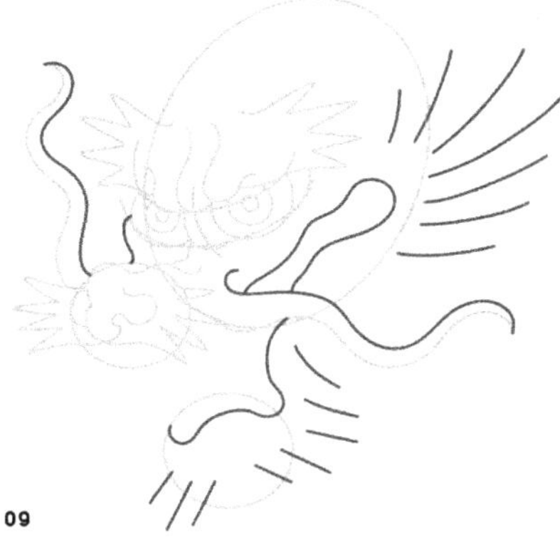

07

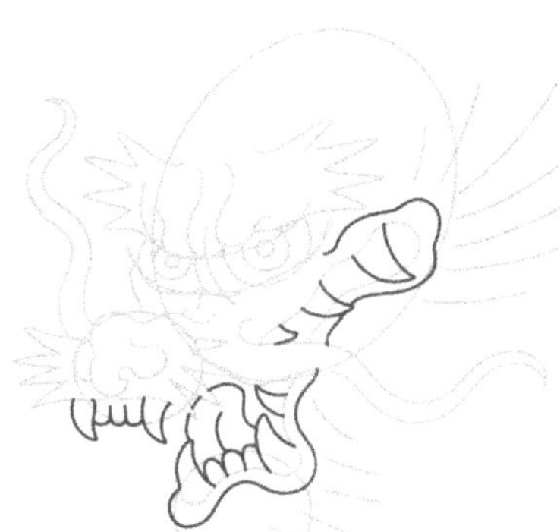

08

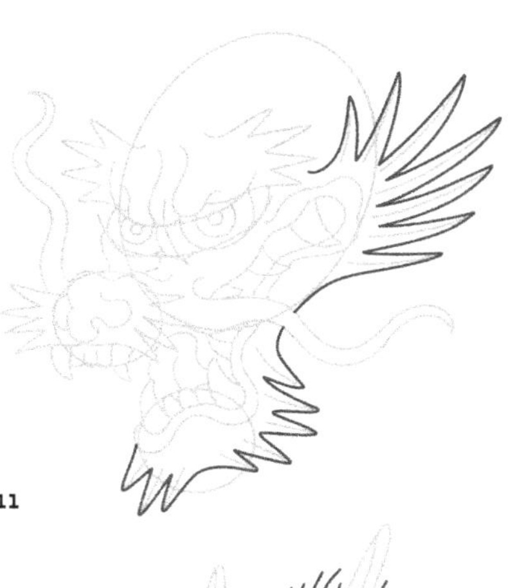

09

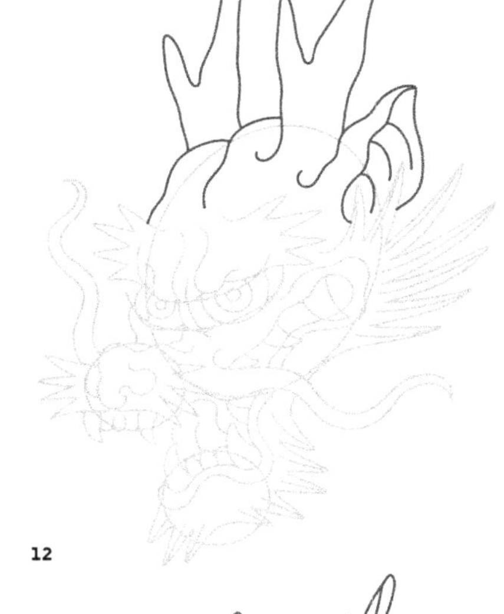

10

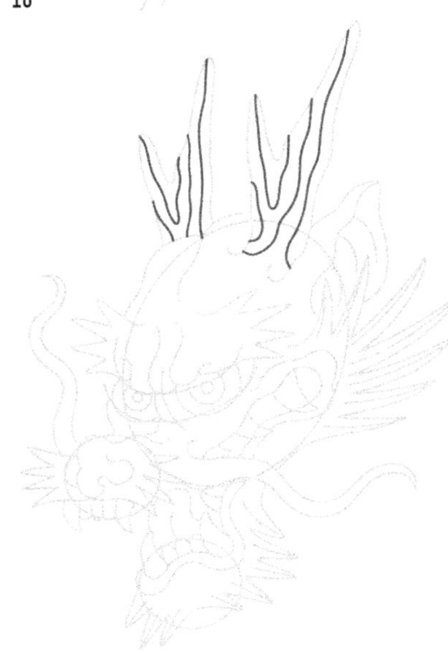

11

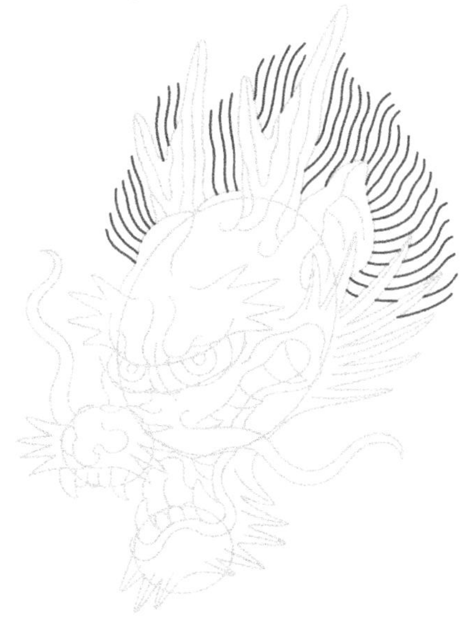

12

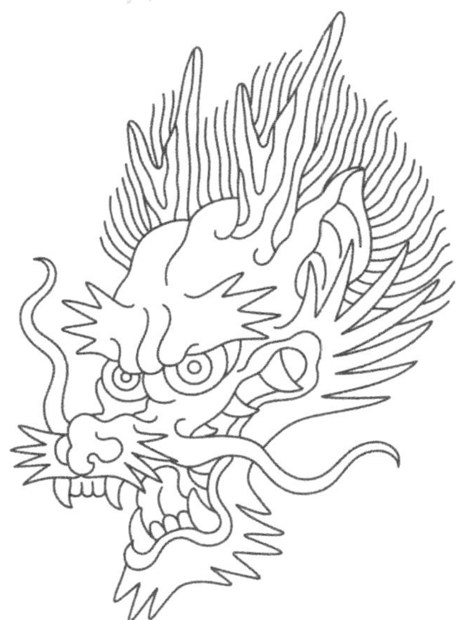

JAPANESE TATTOOS

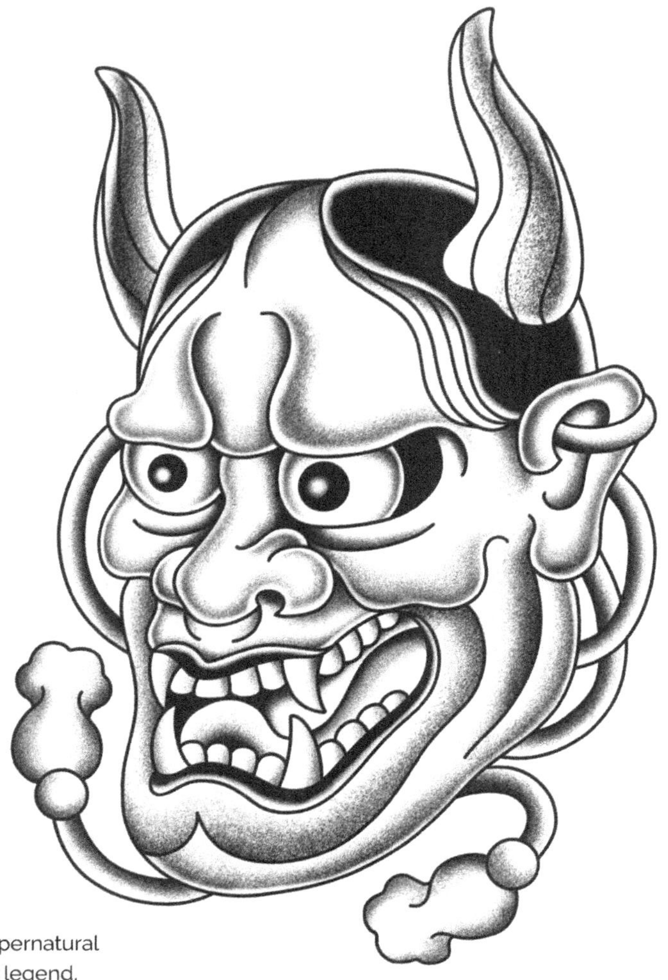

DEMON | ONI

Oni are very strong, horned, supernatural beings. According to Japanese legend, they are cruel and malicious but can also ward off bad luck when used in rituals and festivals.

01

02

03

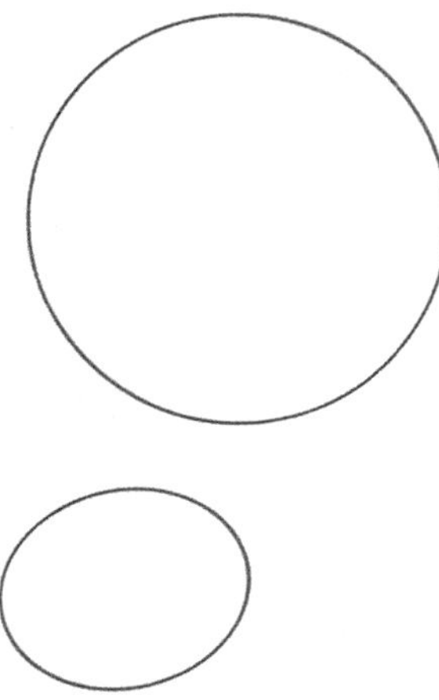

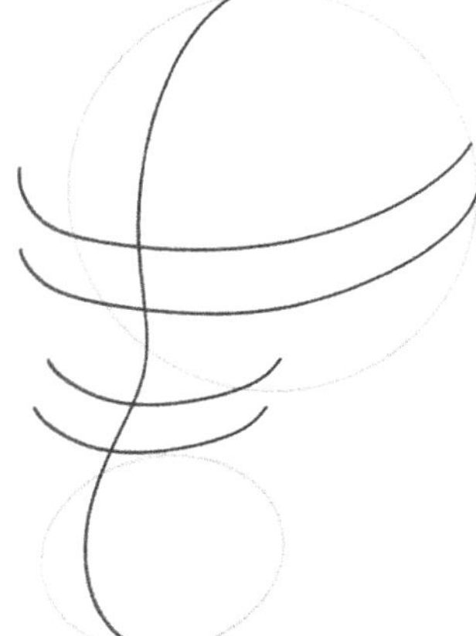

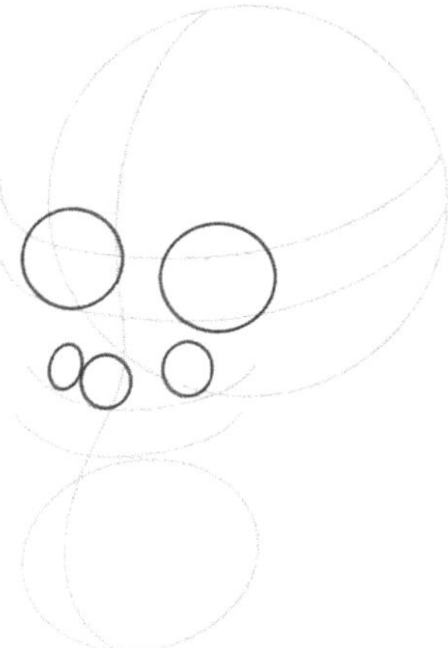

04

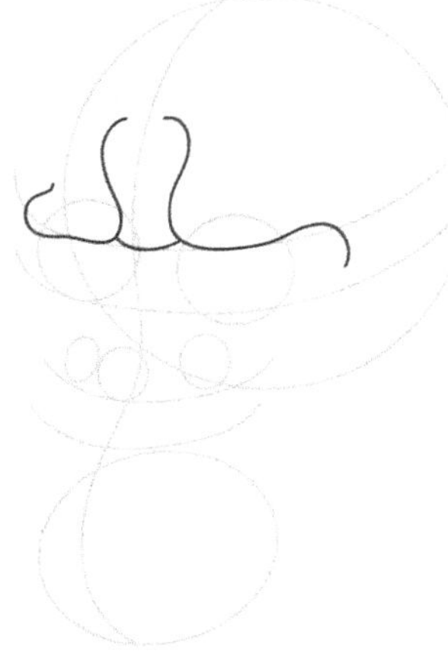

05

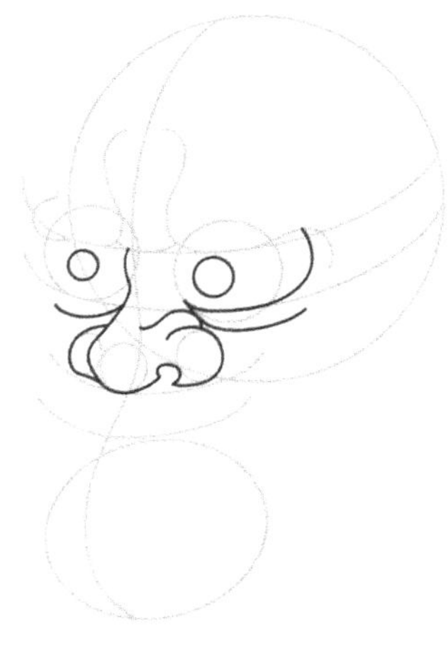

06

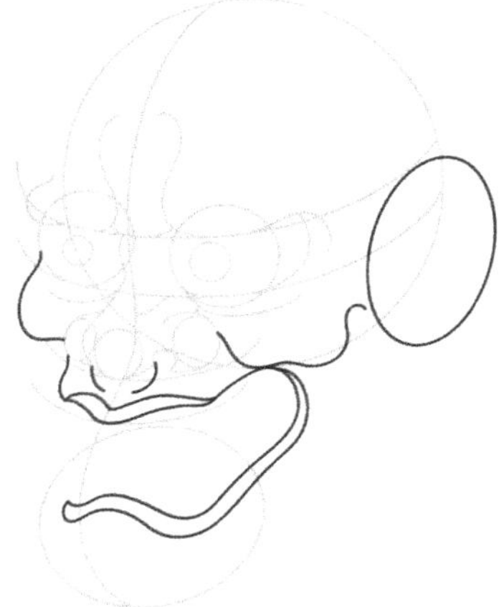

07

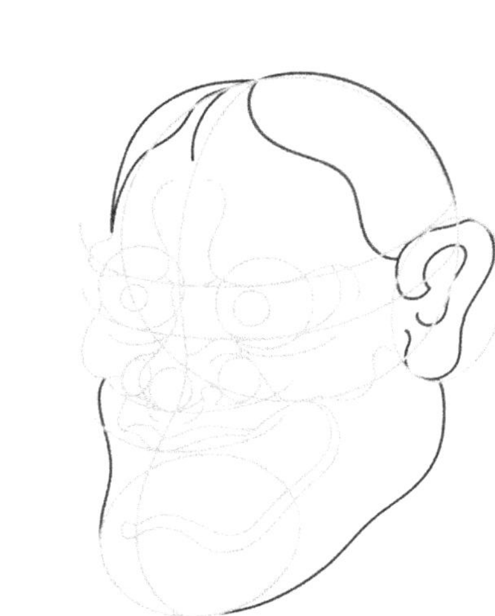

08

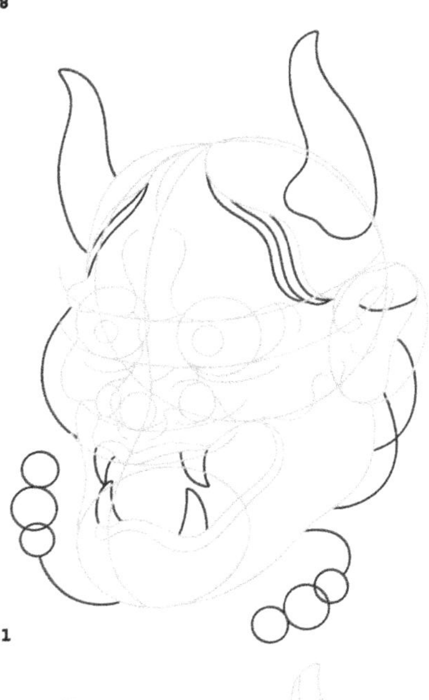

09

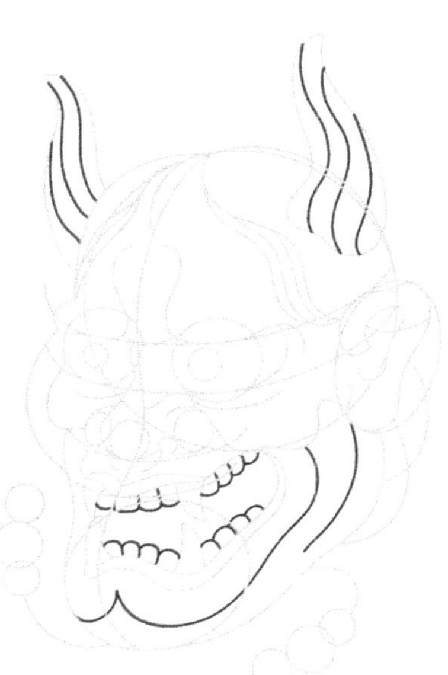

10

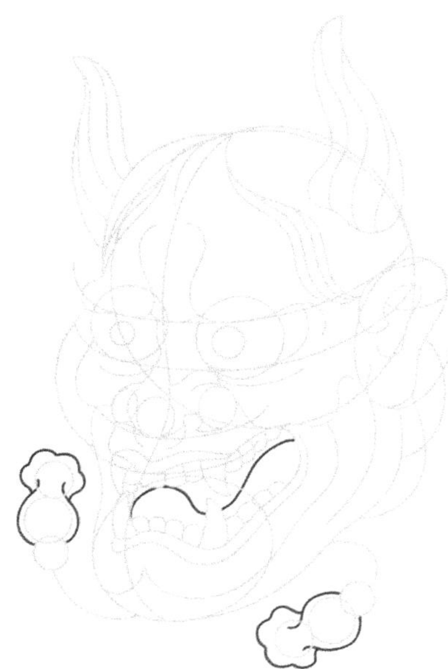

11

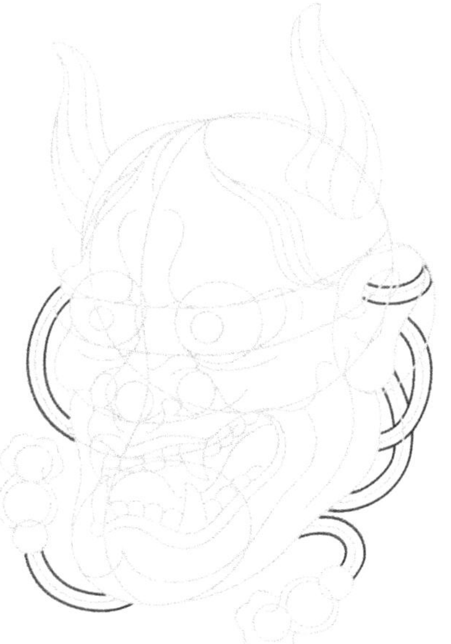

12

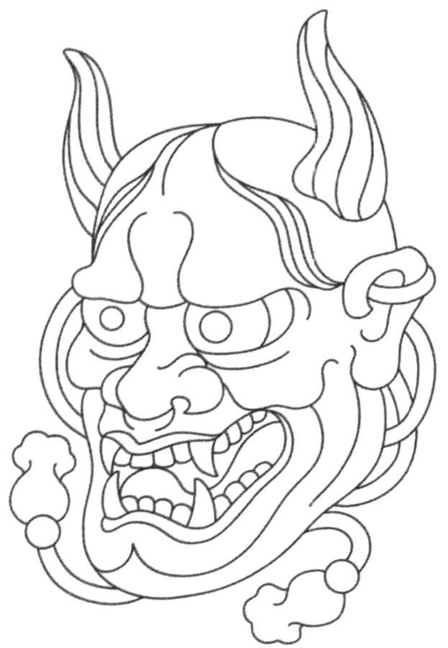

JAPANESE TATTOOS

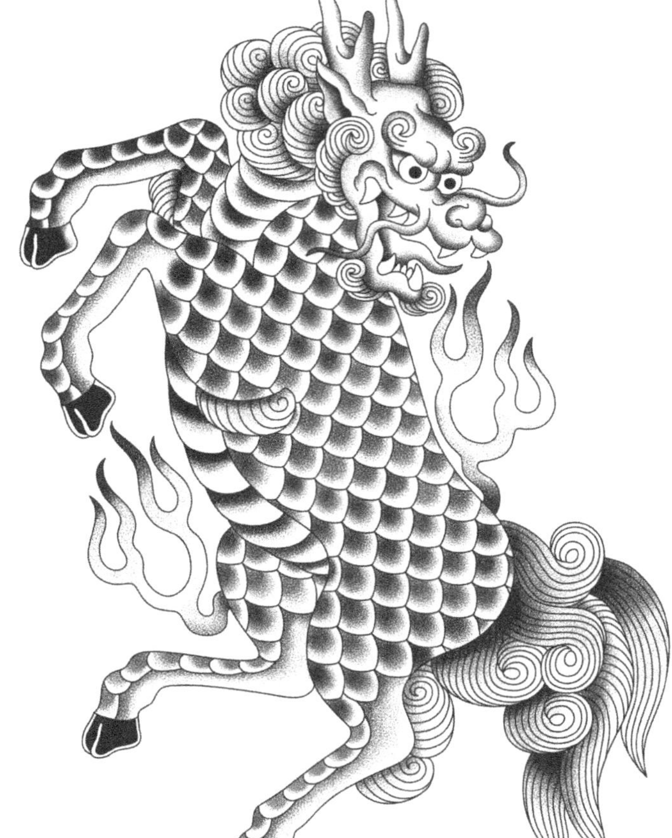

KIRIN

Kirin is a mythical beast symbolising peace and prosperity. Its appearance signals the presence of wisdom, purity, and just rule.

01

02

03

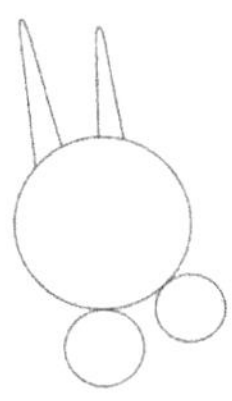

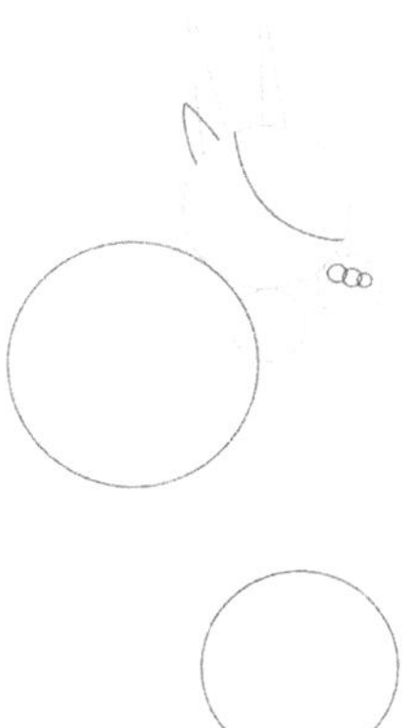

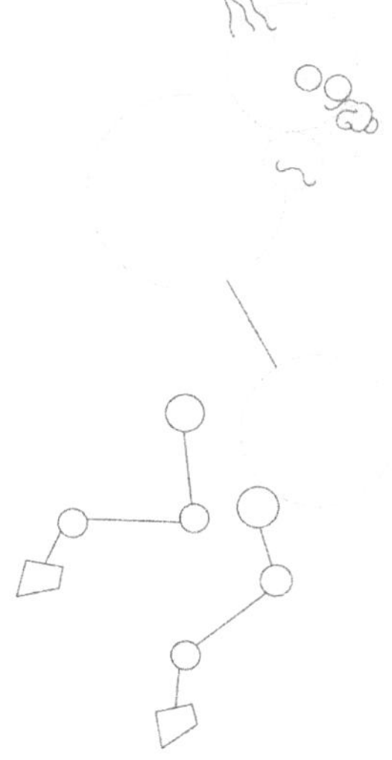

04

05

06

07

08

09

10

11

12

THREE-LEGGED CROW
YATAGARASU

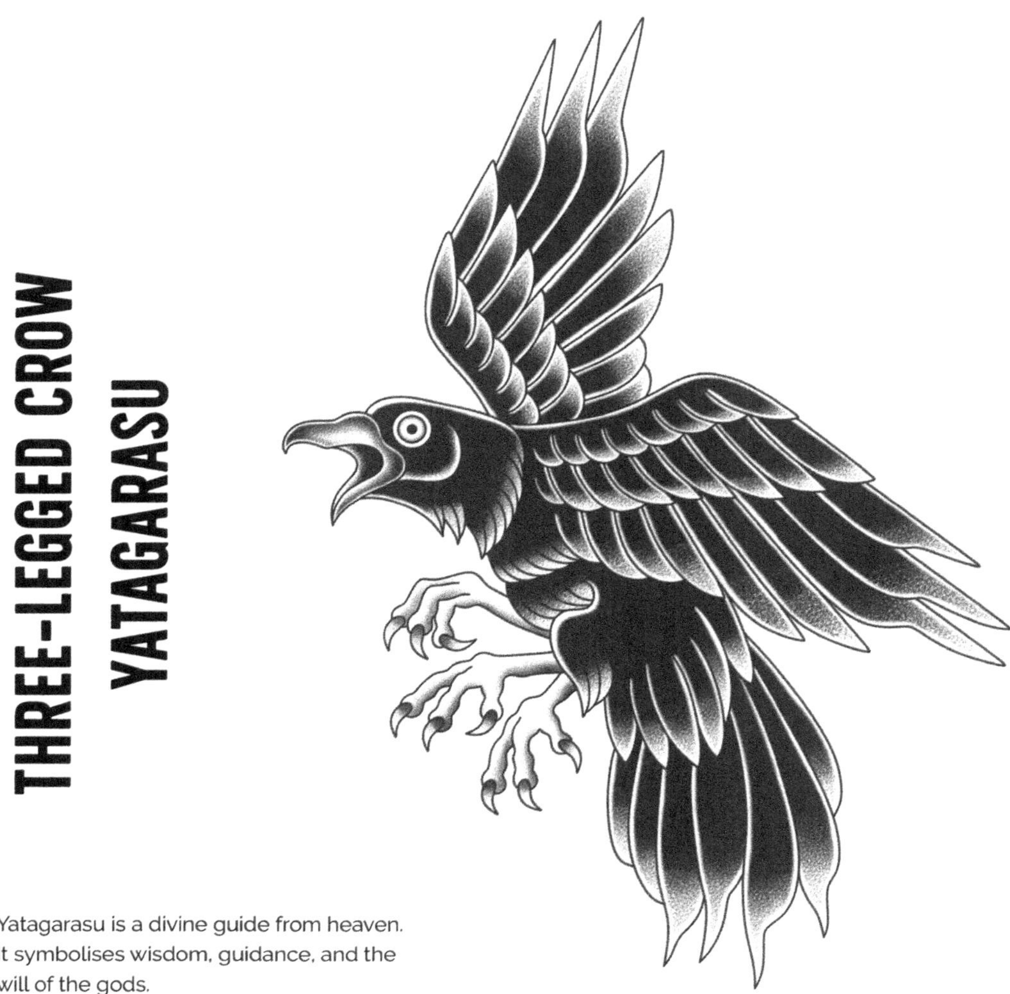

Yatagarasu is a divine guide from heaven.
It symbolises wisdom, guidance, and the
will of the gods.

01

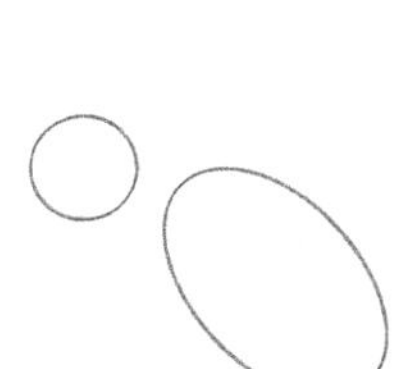

02

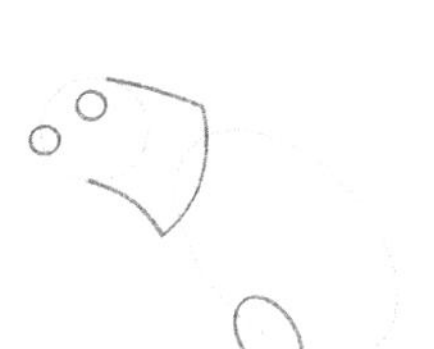

03

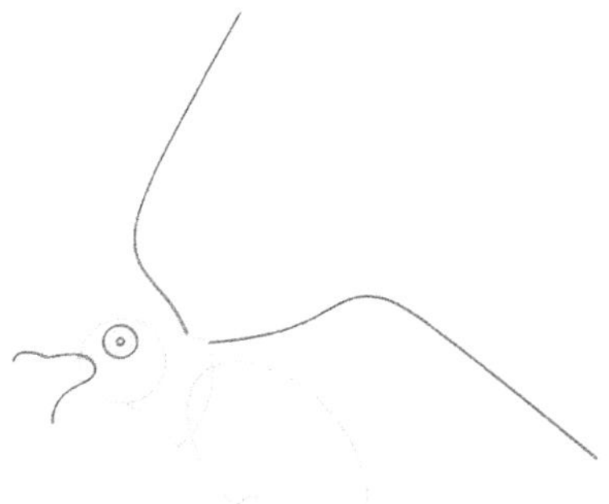

04

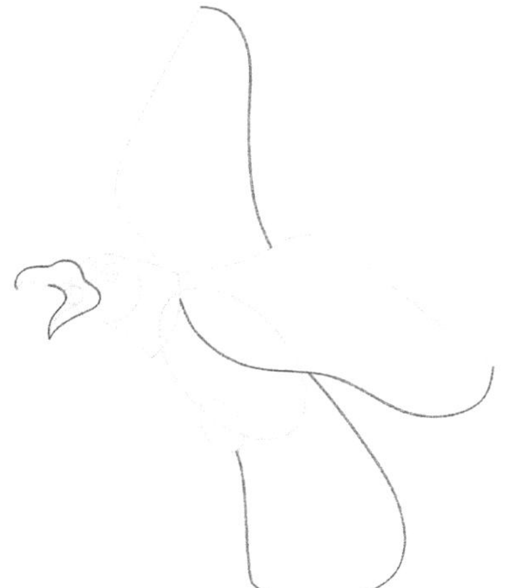

05

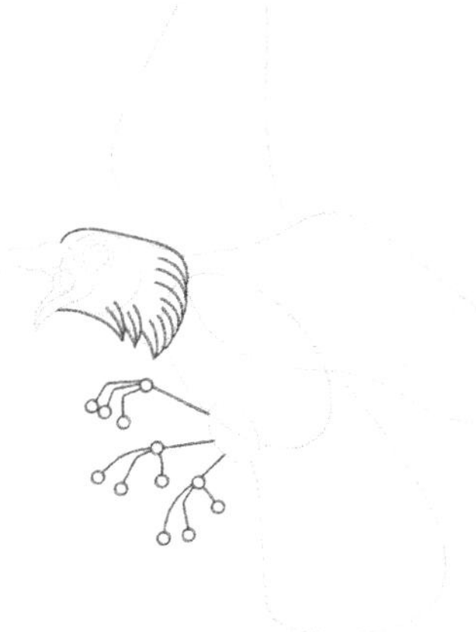

06

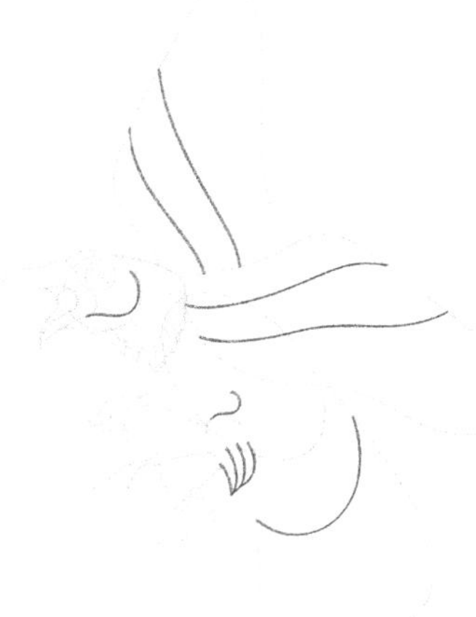

07

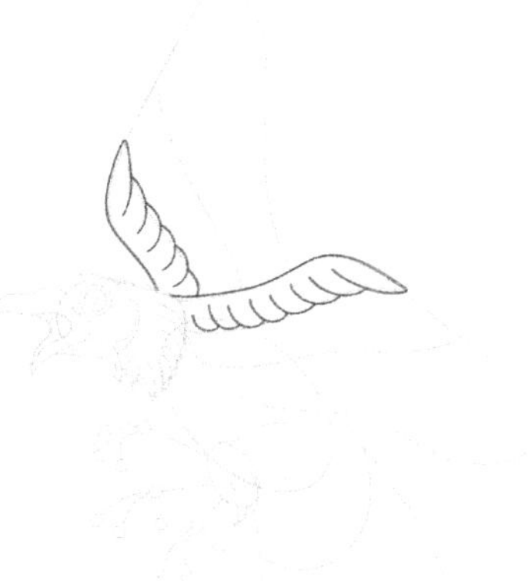

08

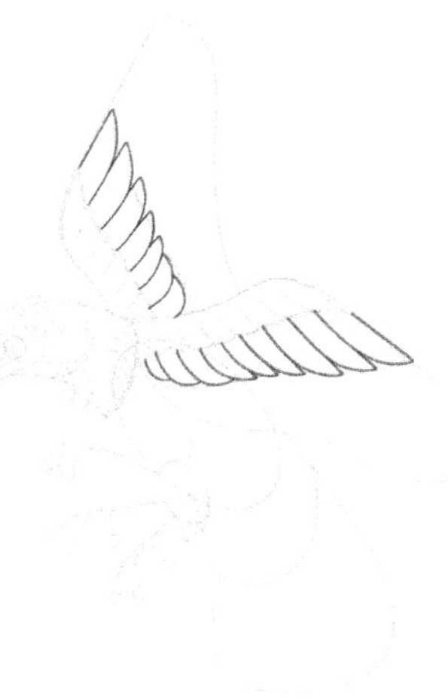

09

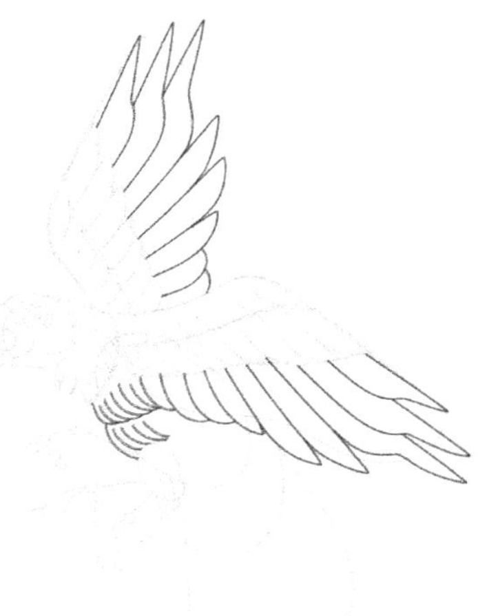

10

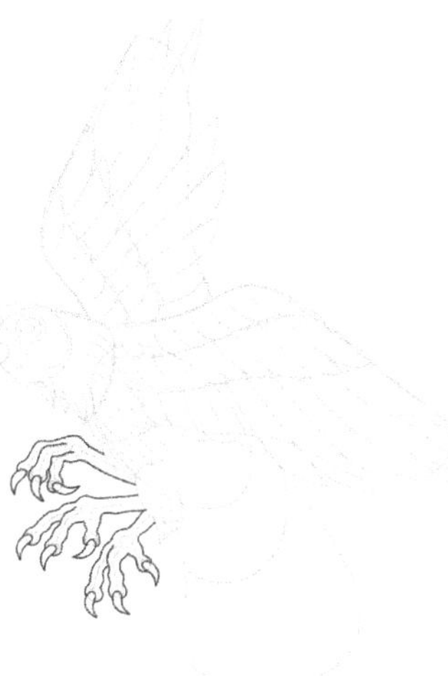

11

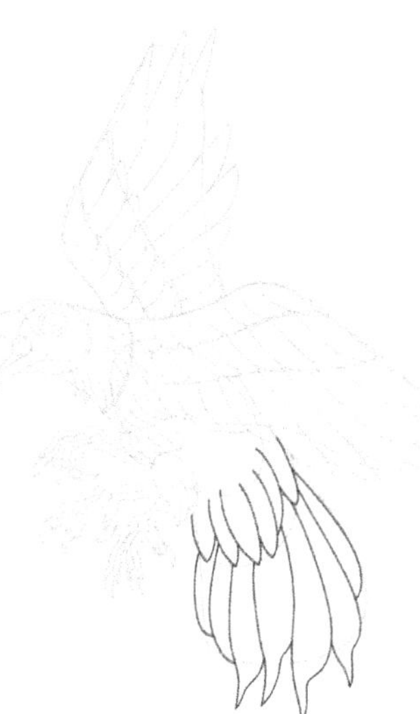

12

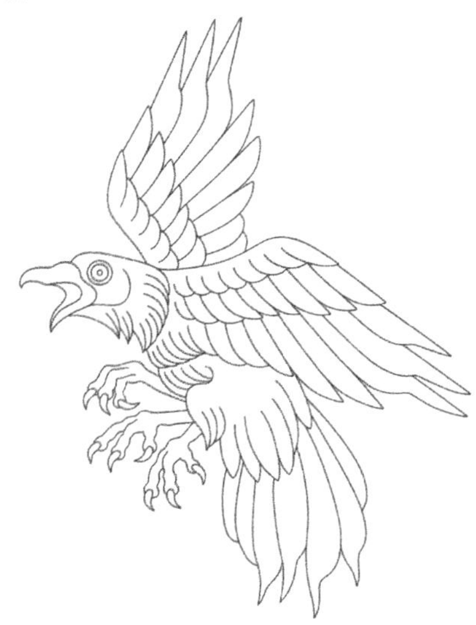

JAPANESE TATTOOS

CHERRY BLOSSOMS SAKURA

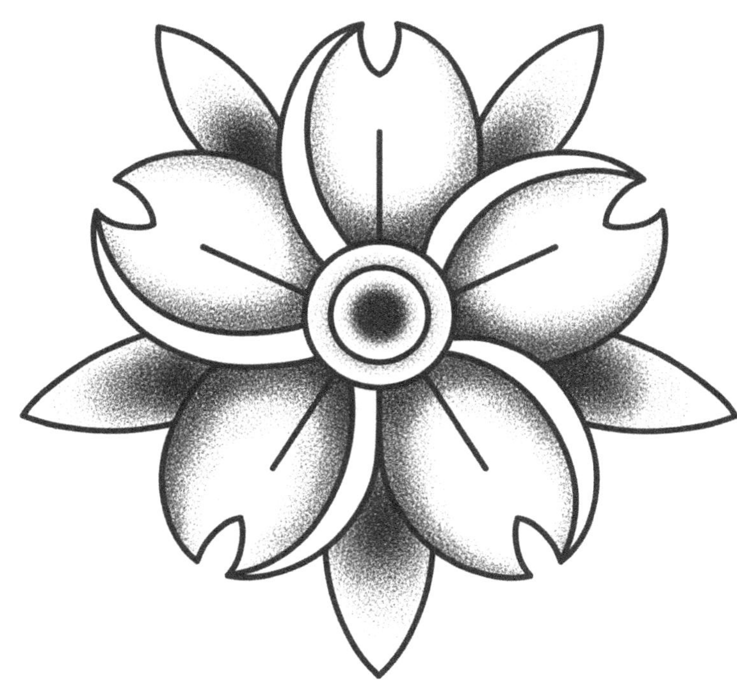

Sakura symbolises both life and death. Their vibrant bloom marks renewal, while their brief life reminds us of beauty's fragility and the fleeting nature of time.

01

02

03

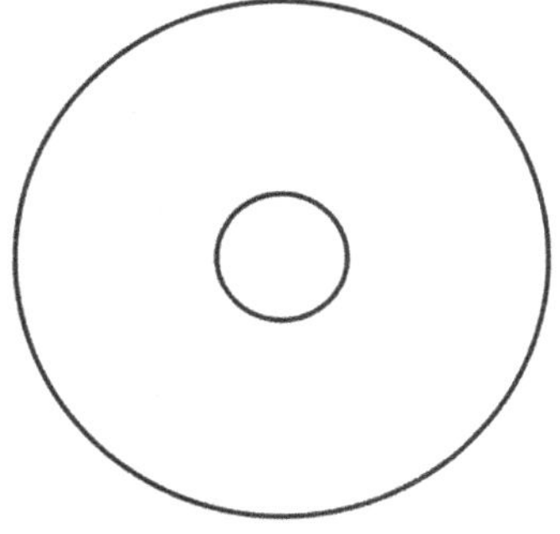

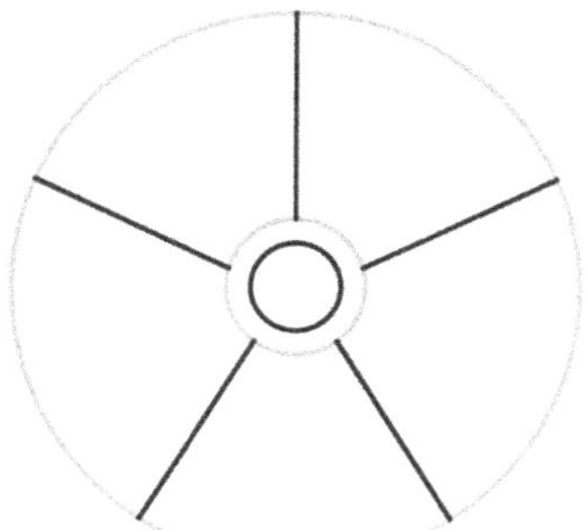

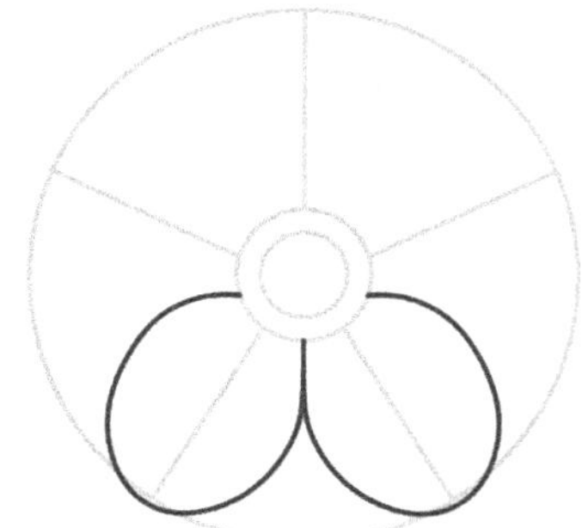

04

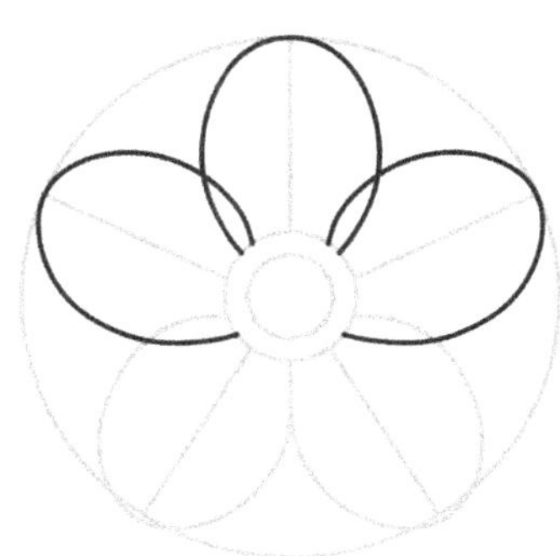

05

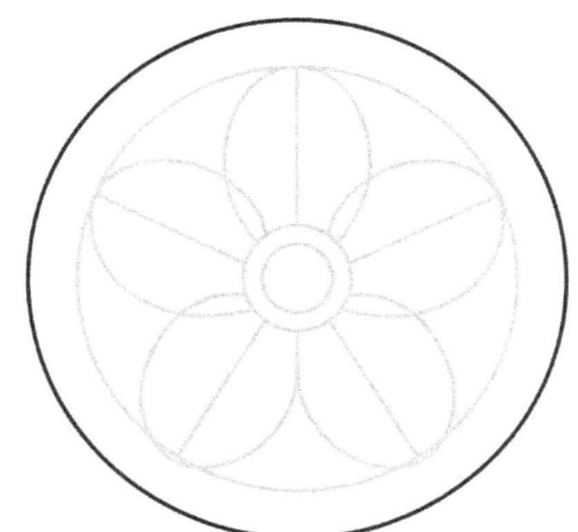

06

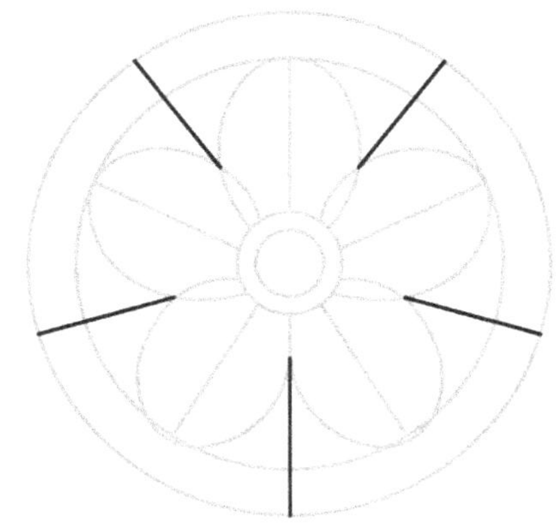

07

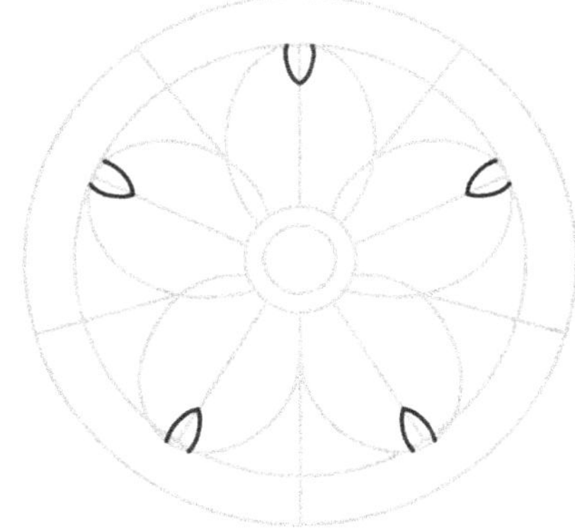

08

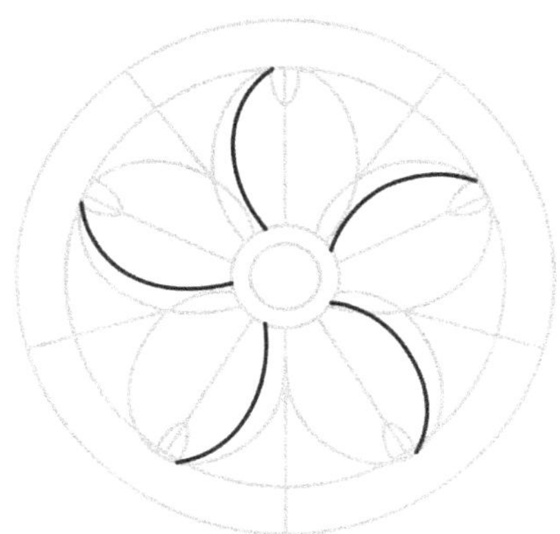

09

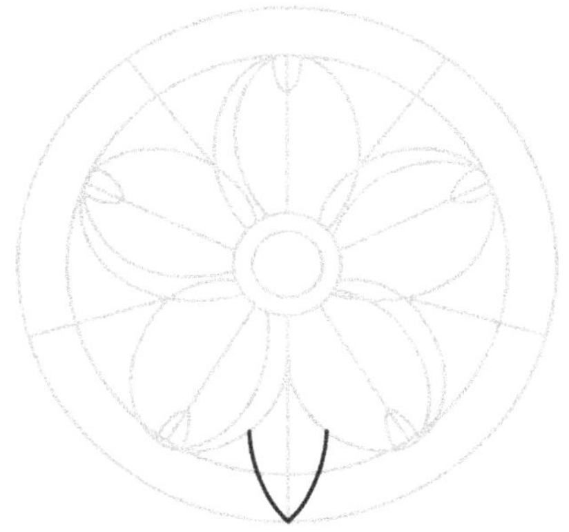

10

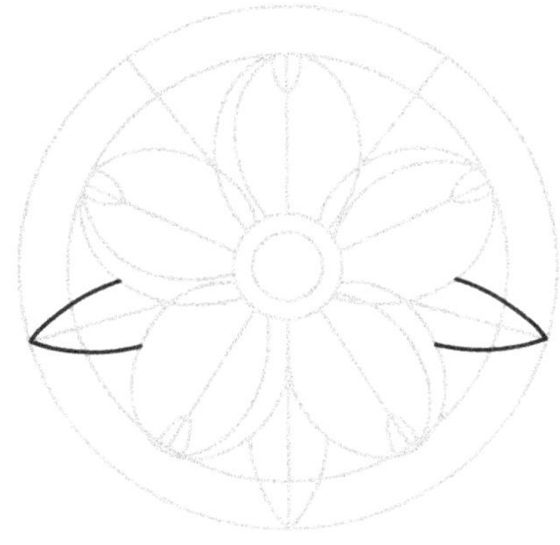

11

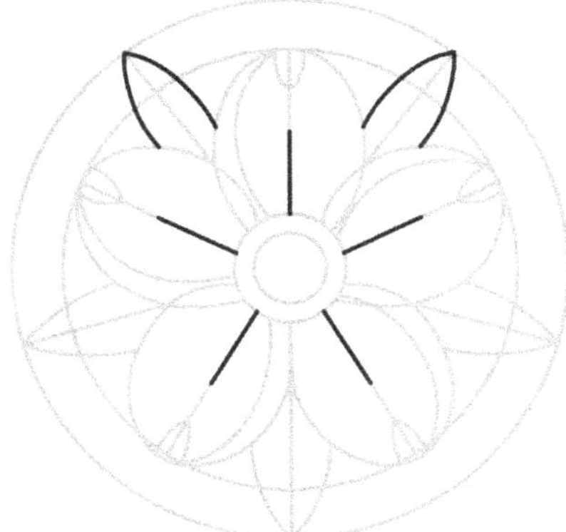

12

JAPANESE TATTOOS

PEONIES | BOTAN

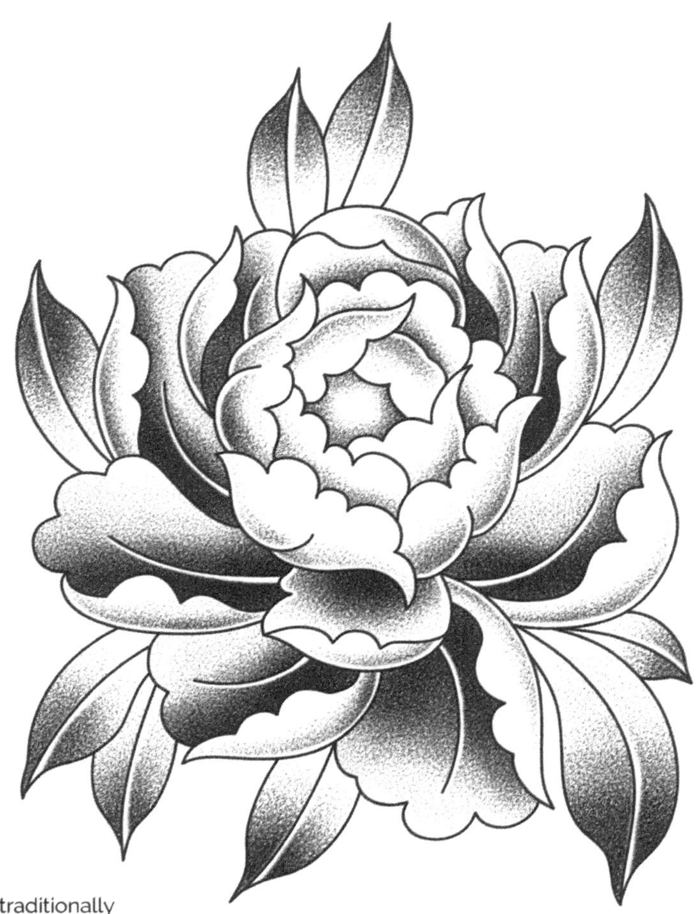

The Japanese Imperial Court traditionally favoured peonies; these lush, blooming flowers symbolise wealth, honour, and nobility in Japanese culture and art.

01

02

03

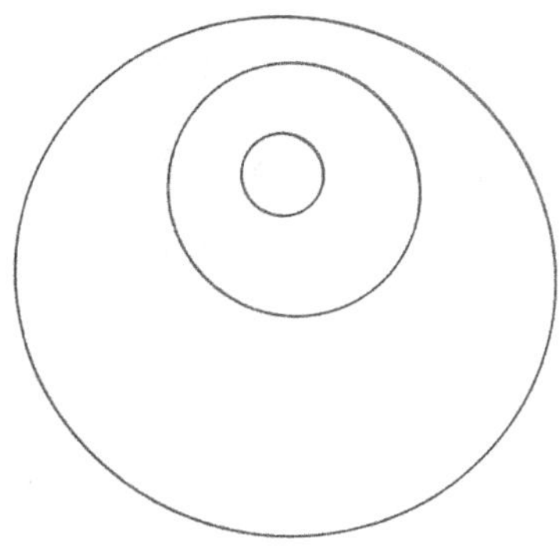

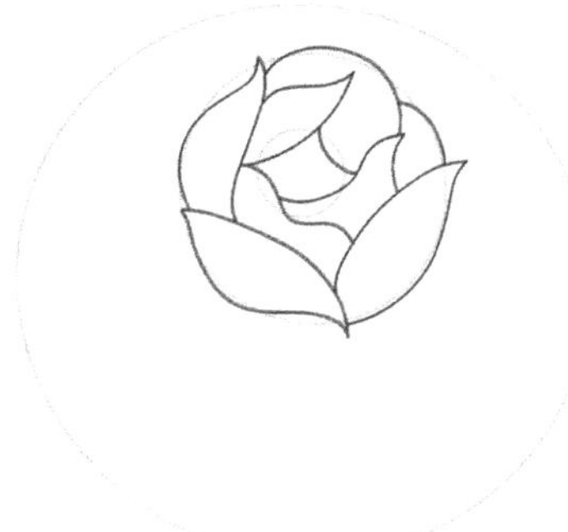

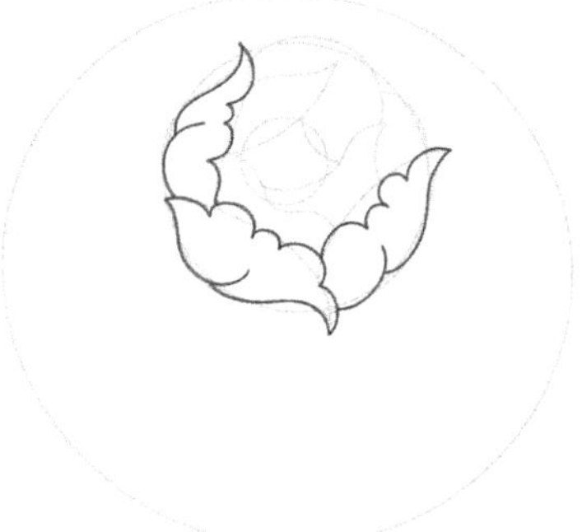

04

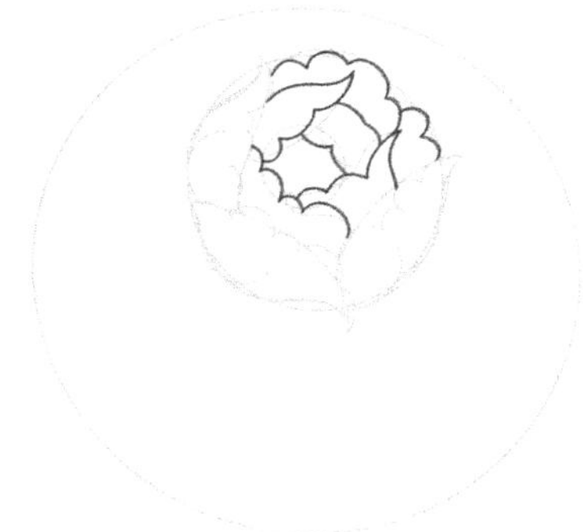

05

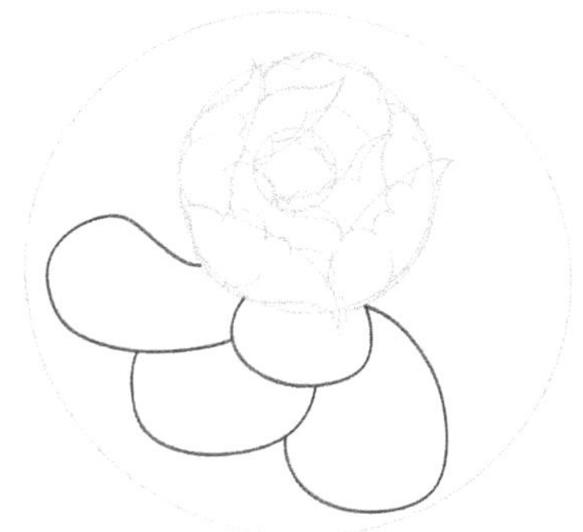

06

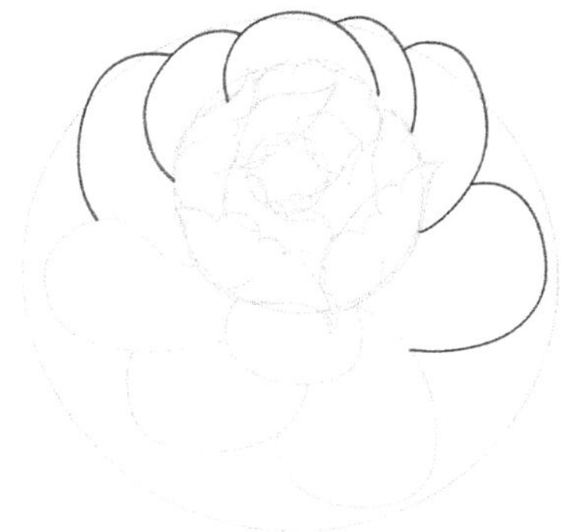

07

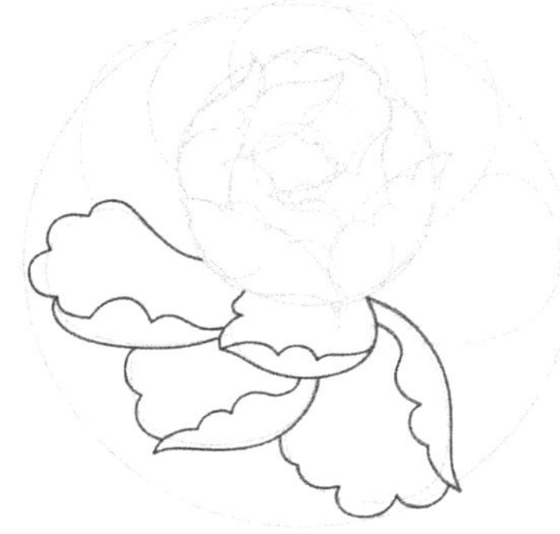

08

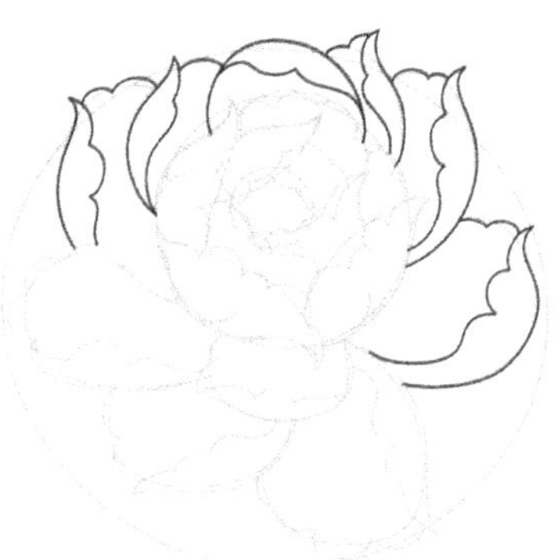

09

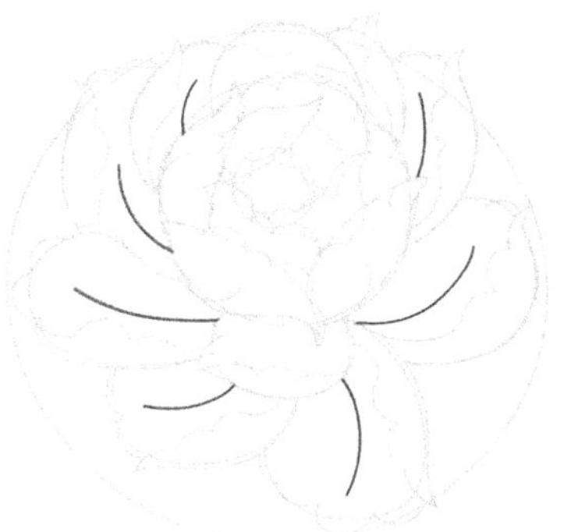

10

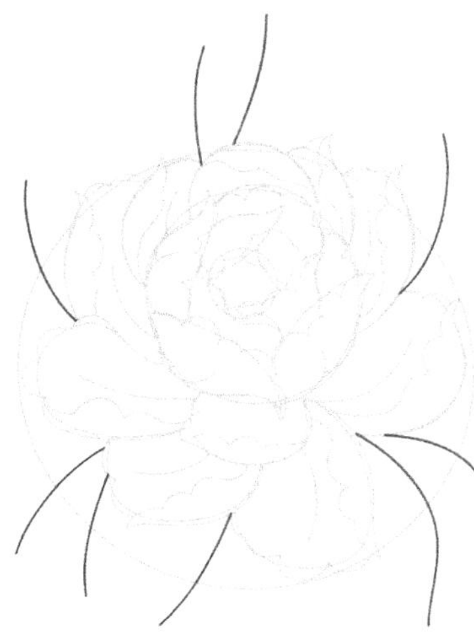

11

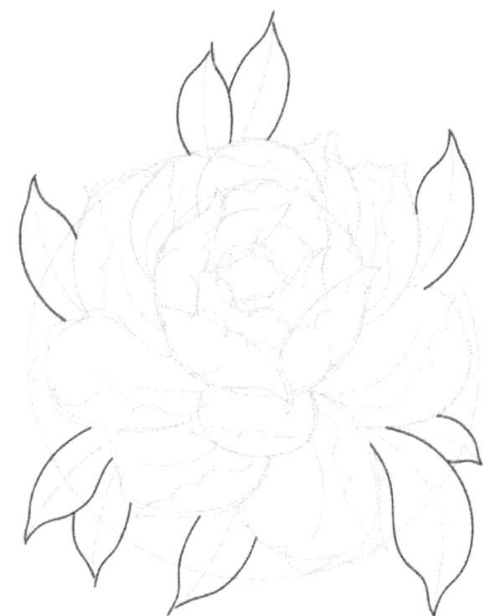

12

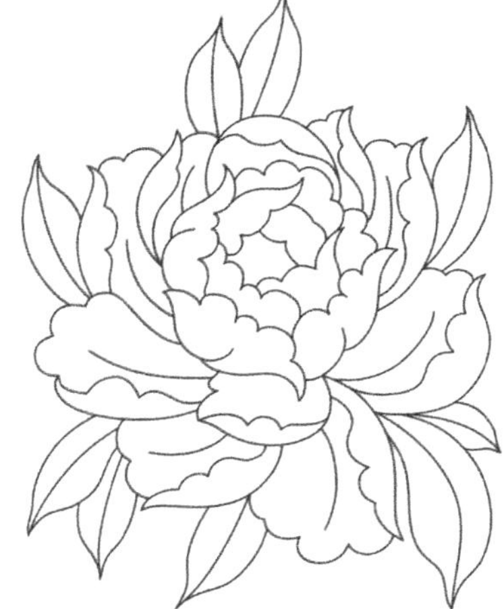

CHRYSANTHEMUMS | KIKU

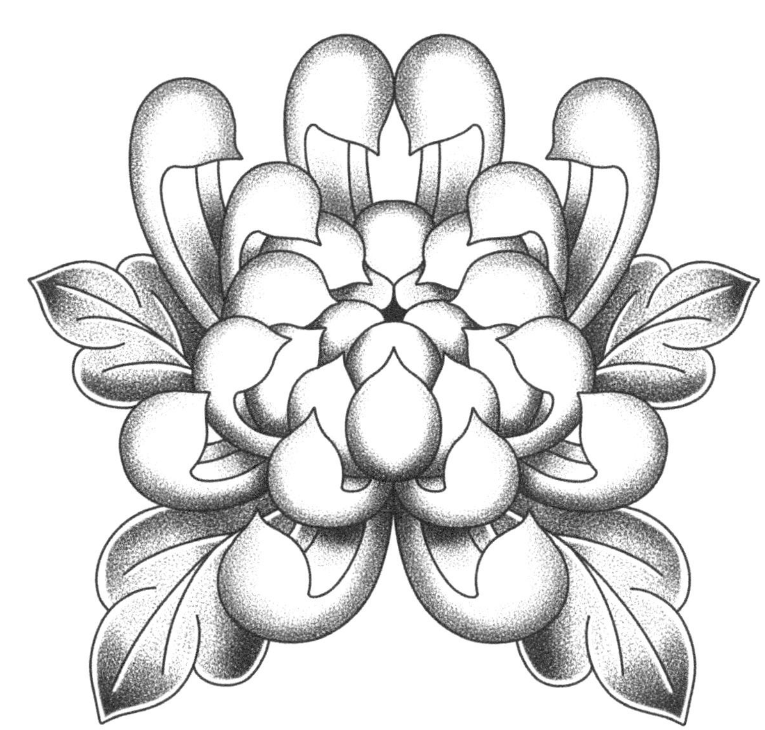

Chrysanthemums are deeply revered, symbolising longevity, rejuvenation, and nobility, and are the emblem of the Japanese Imperial Family.

01

02

03

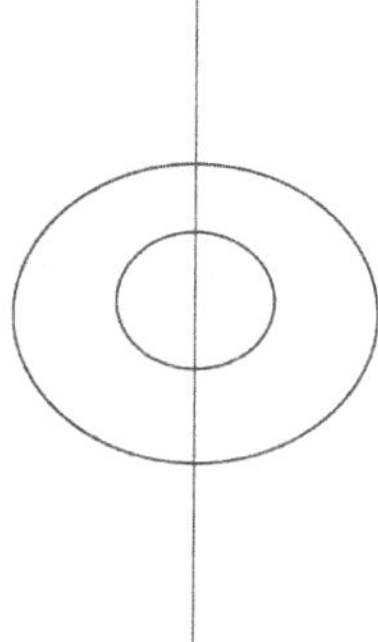

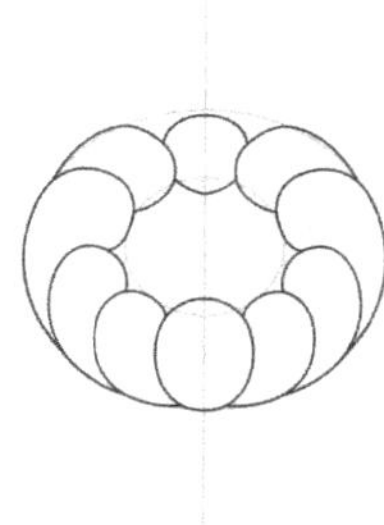

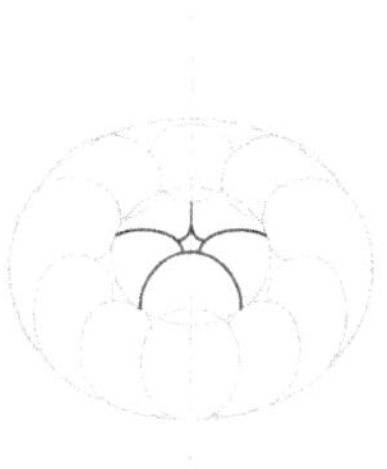

04

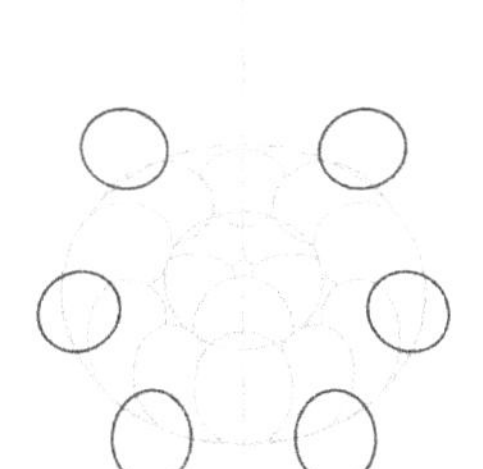

05

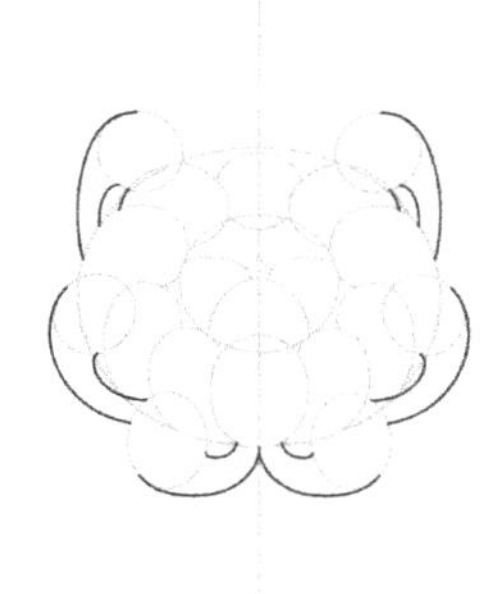

06

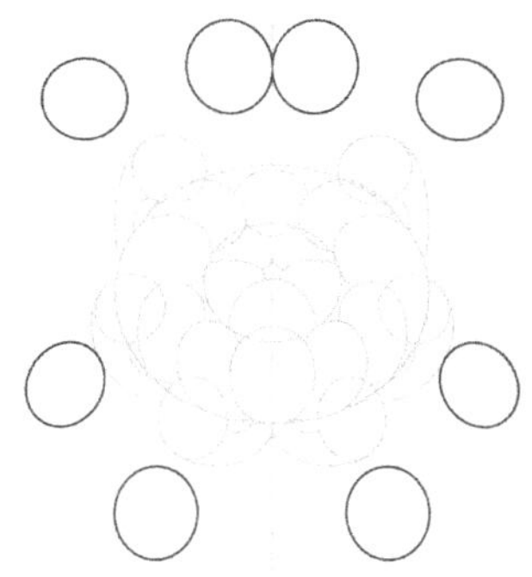

07

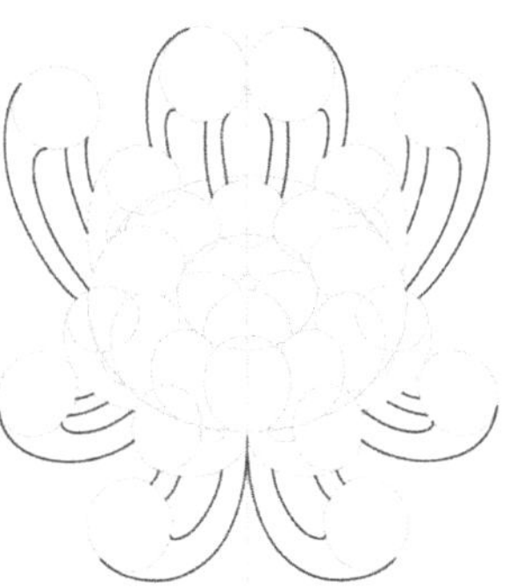

08

09

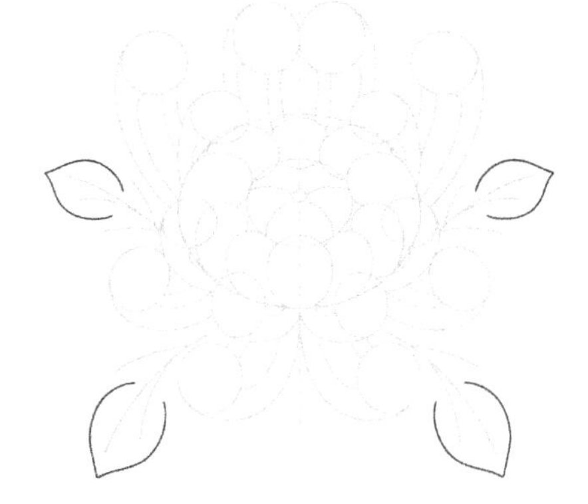

10

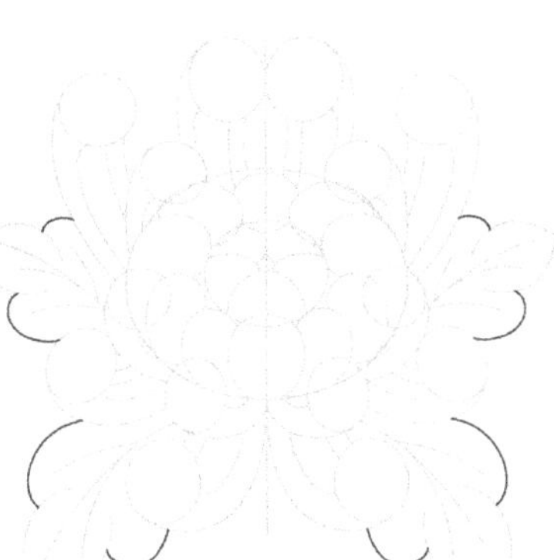

11

12

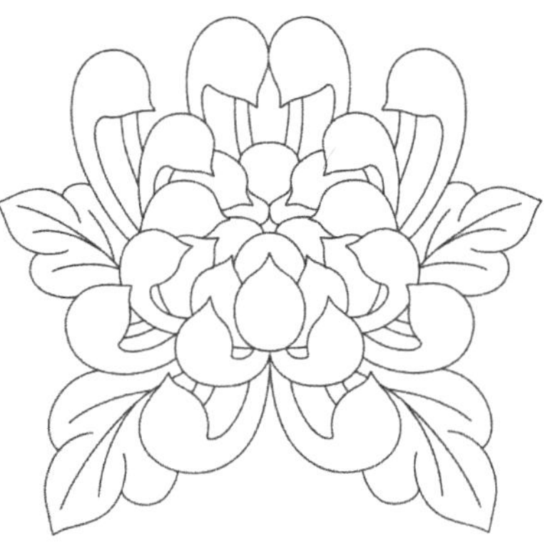

MAPLE LEAVES | MOMIJI

Maple leaves hail the arrival of autumn and is a symbol of seasonal beauty and the fleeting nature of life. They also signify abundant blessings and peace.

01

02

03

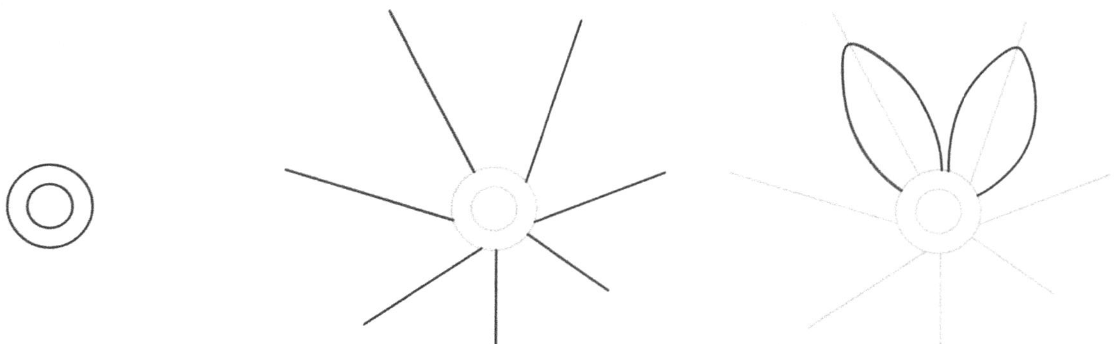

04

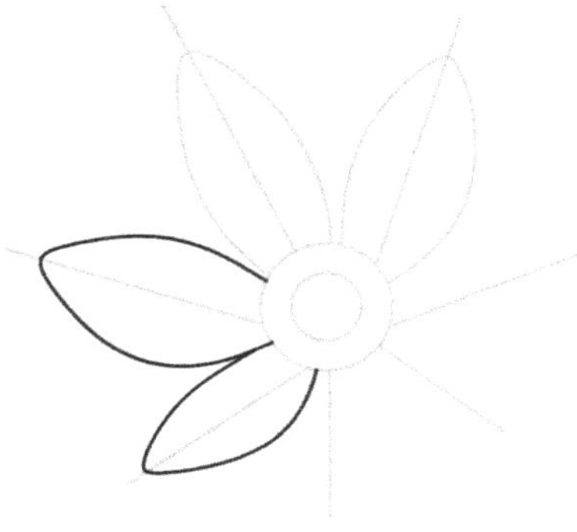

05

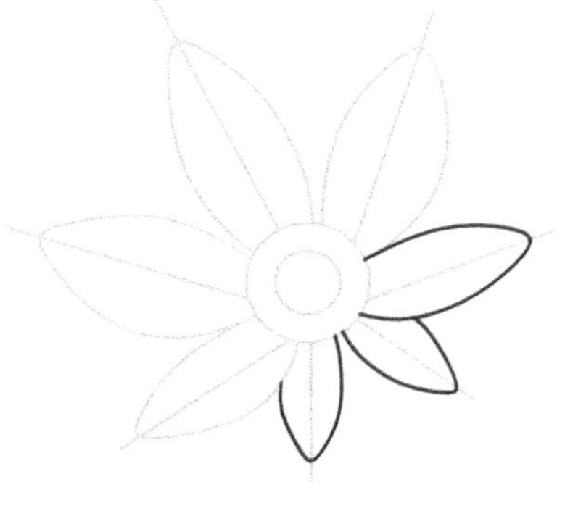

06

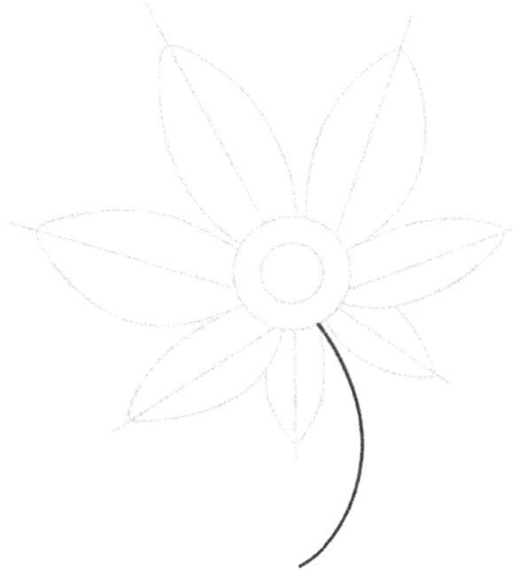

07

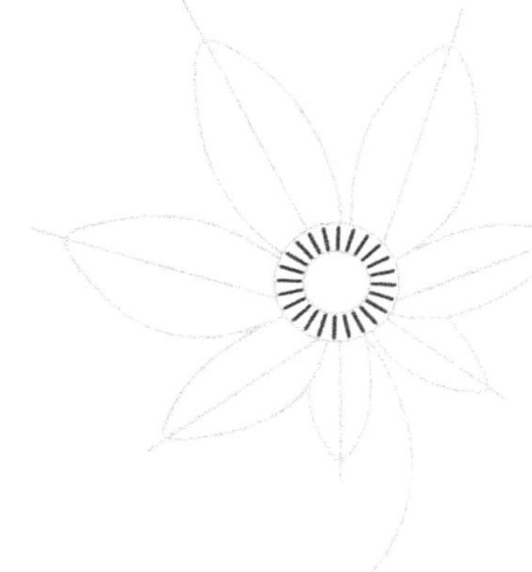

08

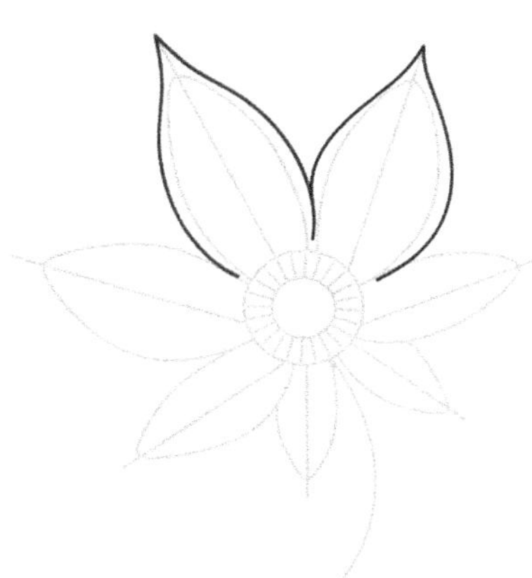

09

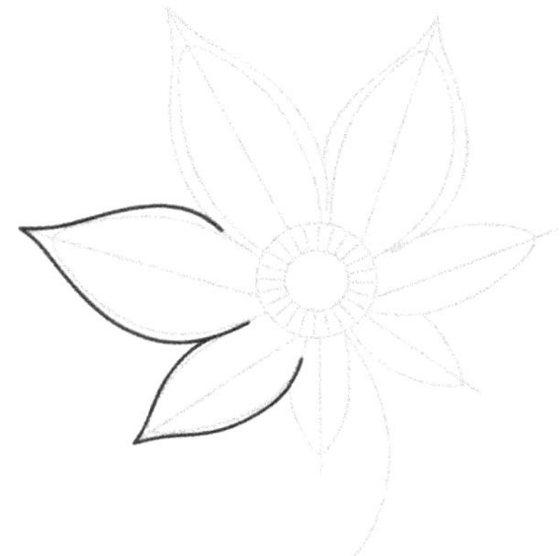

JAPANESE TATTOOS

10

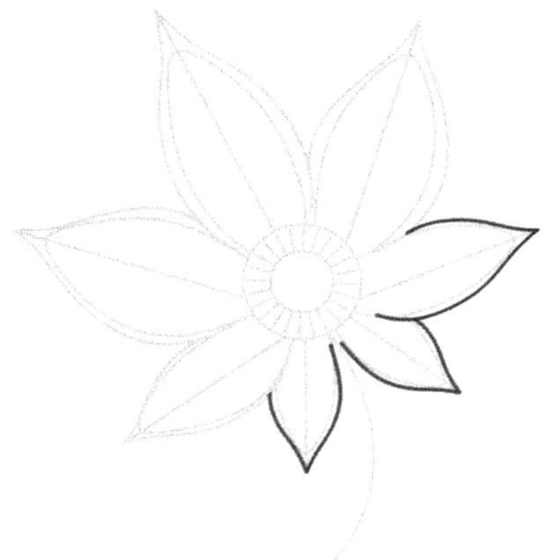

11

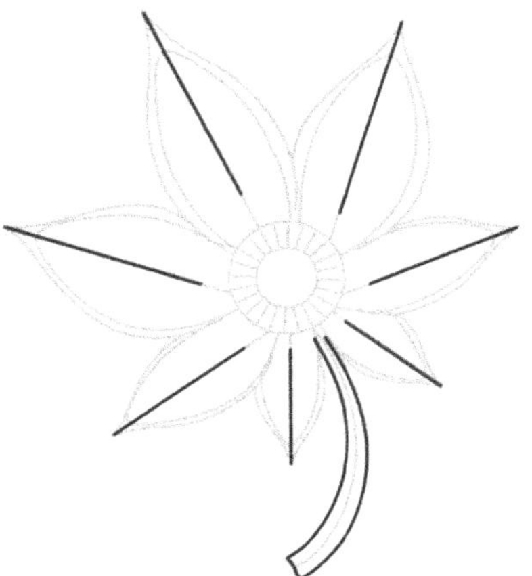

12

LOTUS FLOWER | HASU

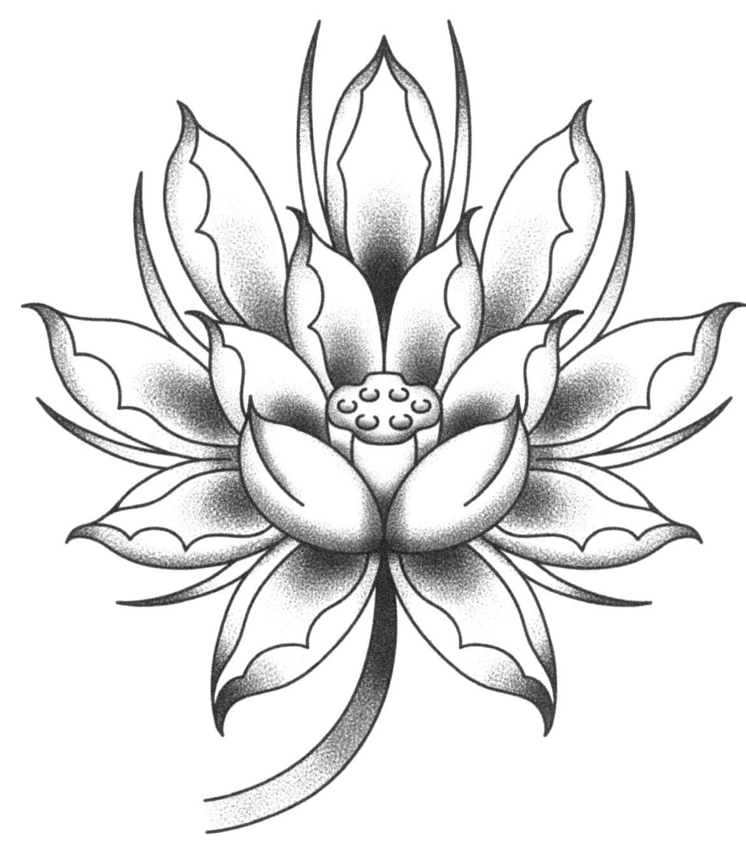

The lotus symbolises purity, rebirth, and enlightenment, rising from muddy water to bloom, it reflects triumph over hardship and spiritual growth.

01

02

03

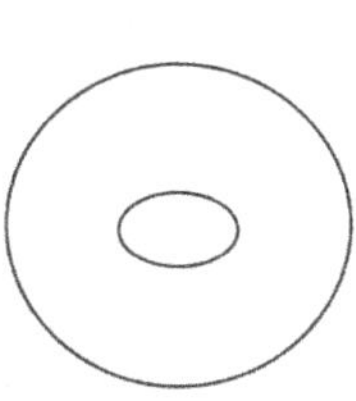

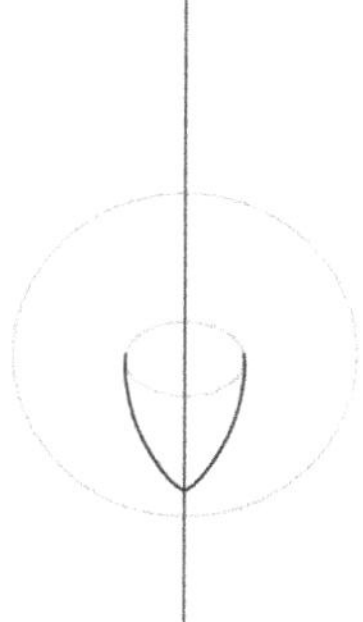

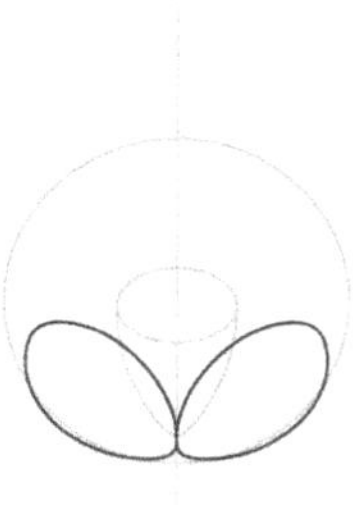

04

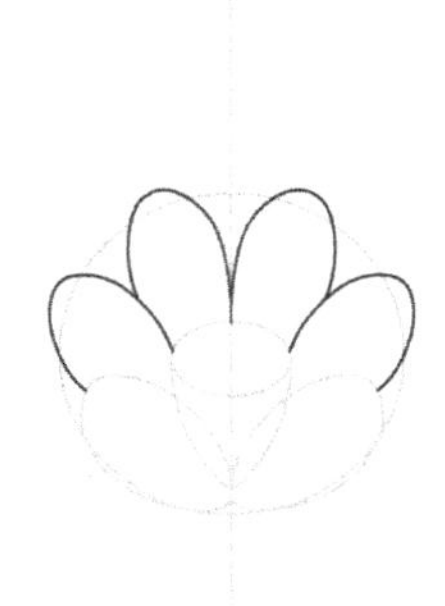

05

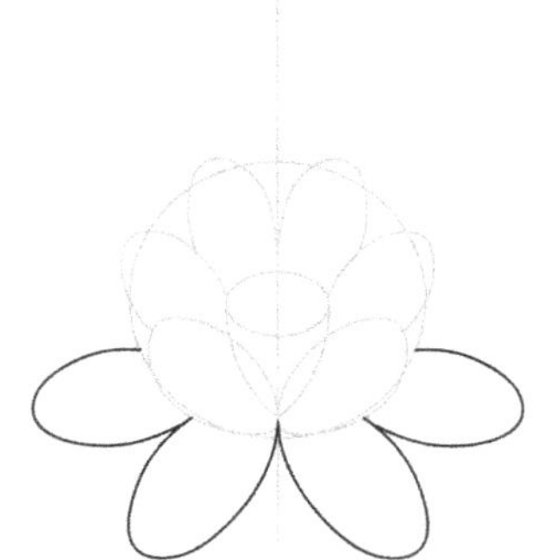

06

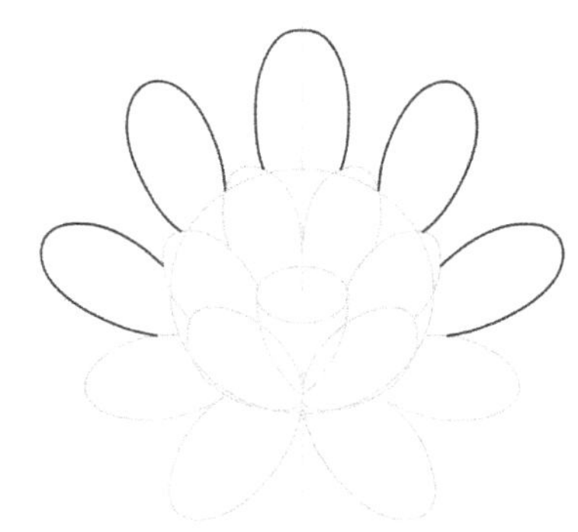

07

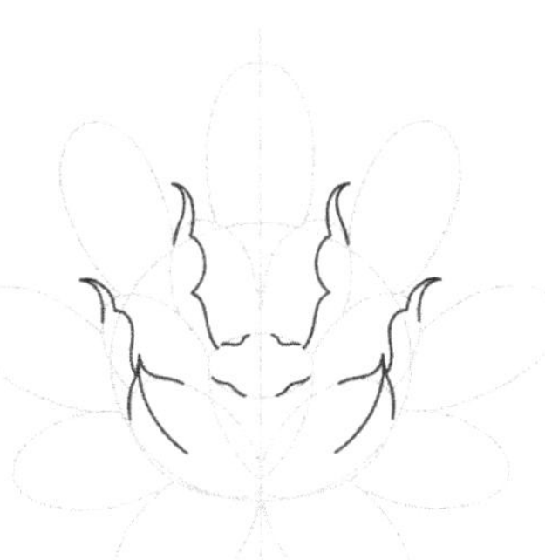

08

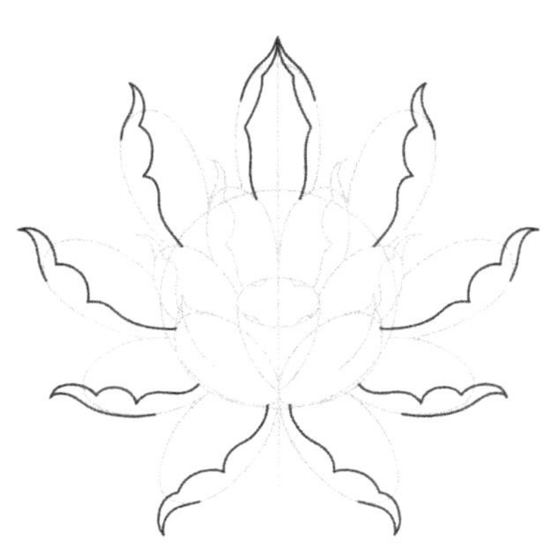

09

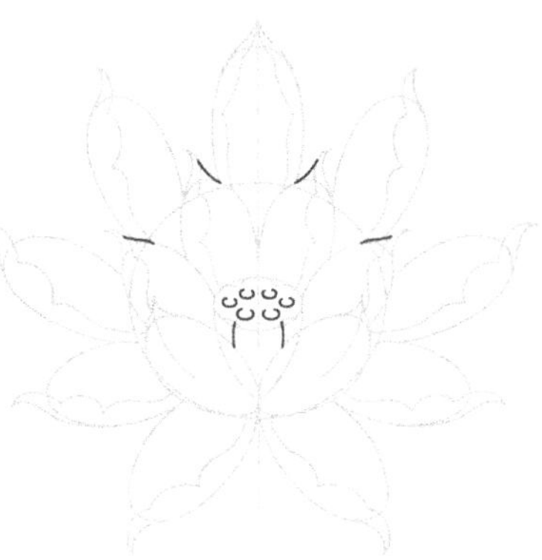

10

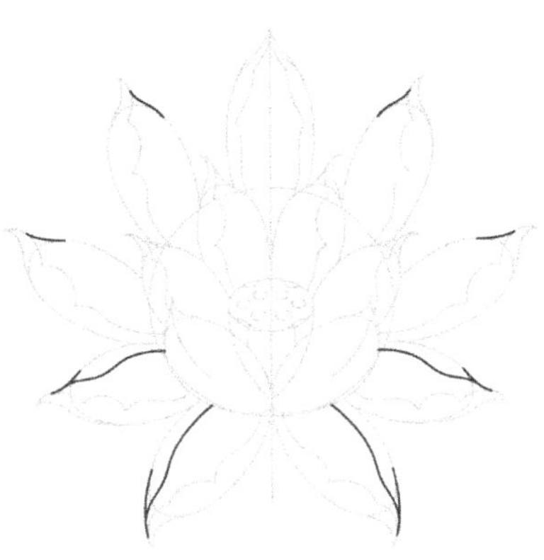

11

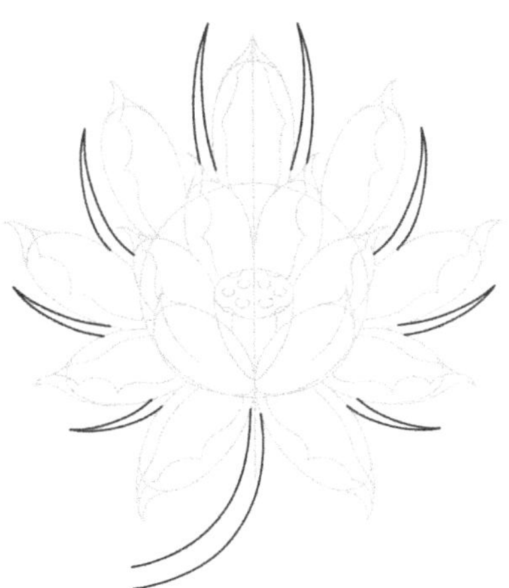

12

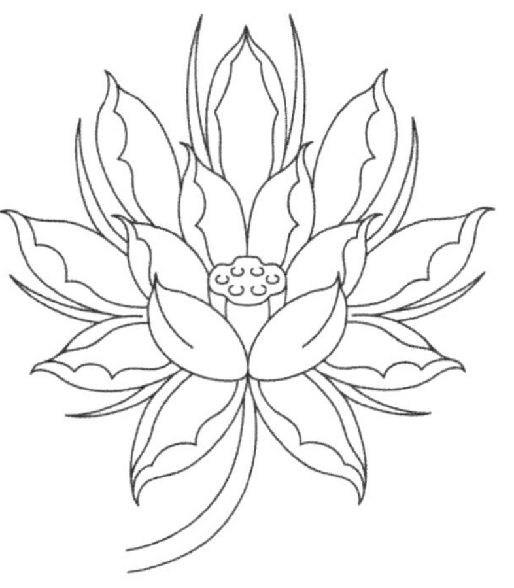

BAMBOO | TAKE

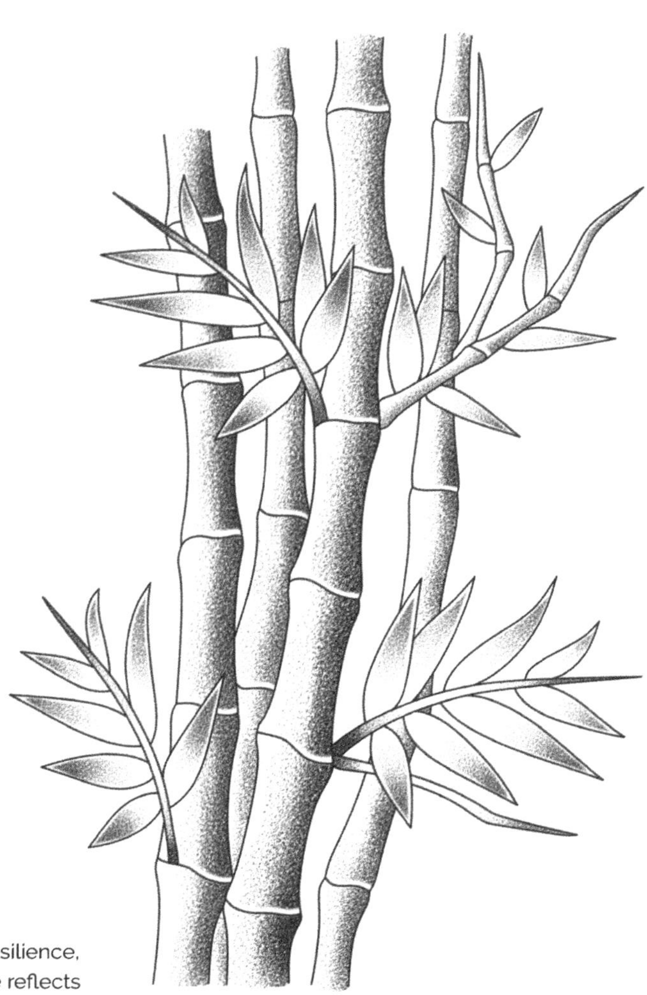

Bamboo symbolises strength, resilience, and prosperity. Its flexible nature reflects the grace to endure hardship, adapt without breaking, and thrive in adversity.

01

02

03

04

05

06

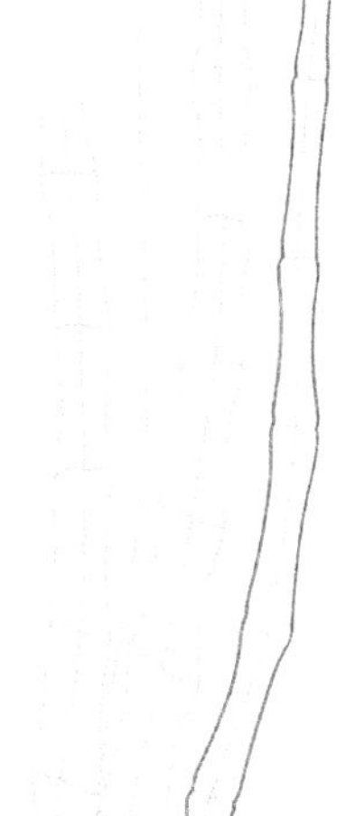

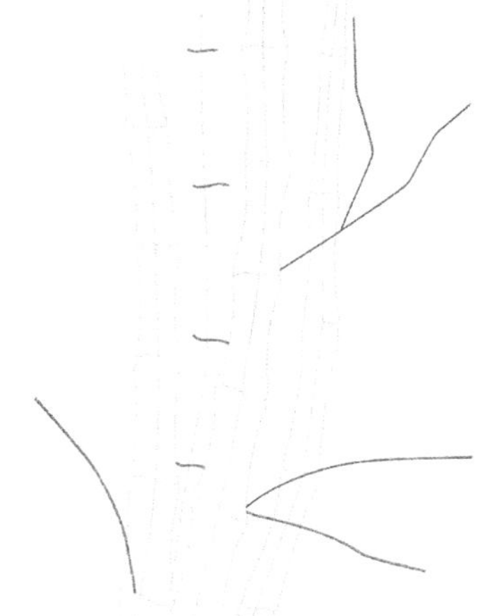

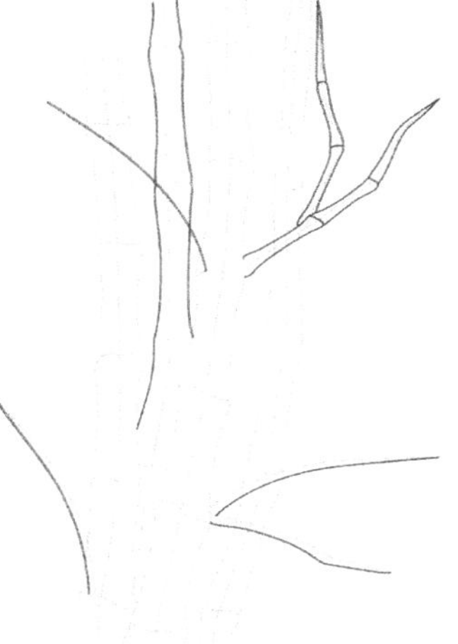

07

08

09

10

11

12

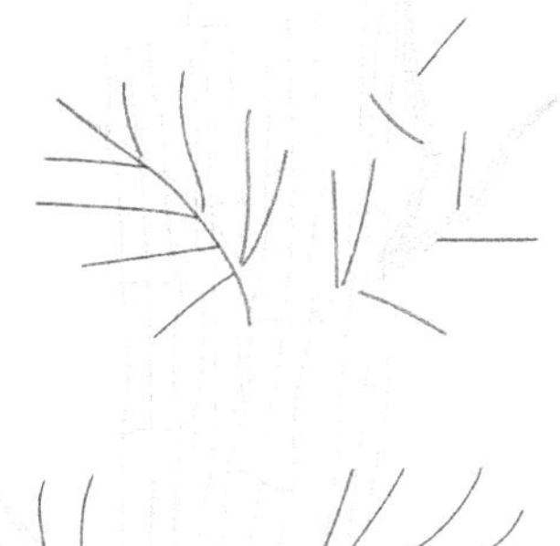

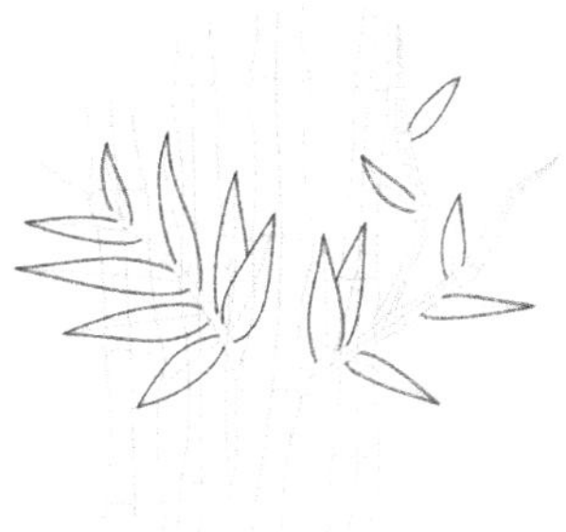

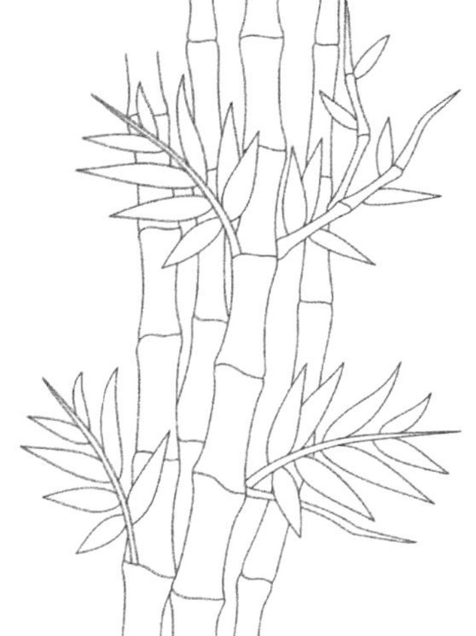

PLUM BLOSSOMS | UME

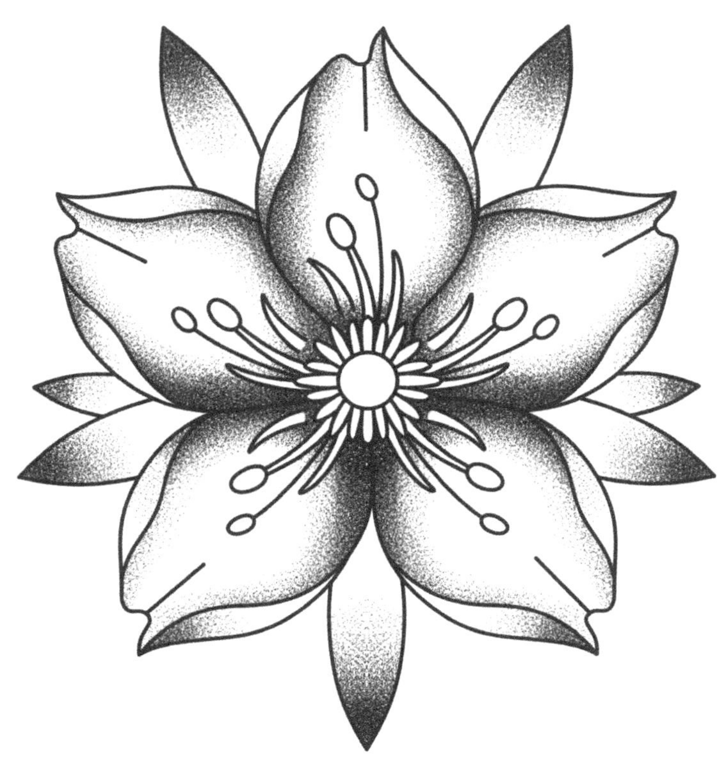

Plum blossoms symbolise elegance and purity. Blooming in late winter and early spring, they also represent resilience, hope, and beauty in the face of hardship.

01

02

03

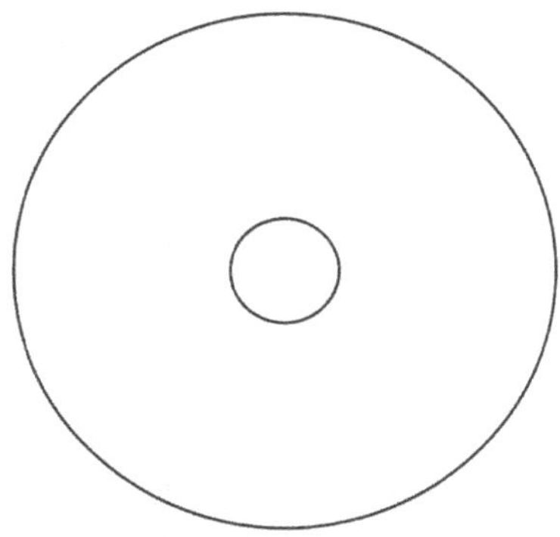

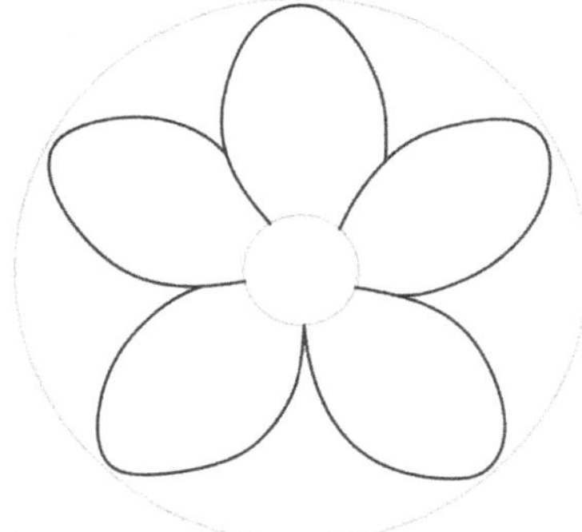

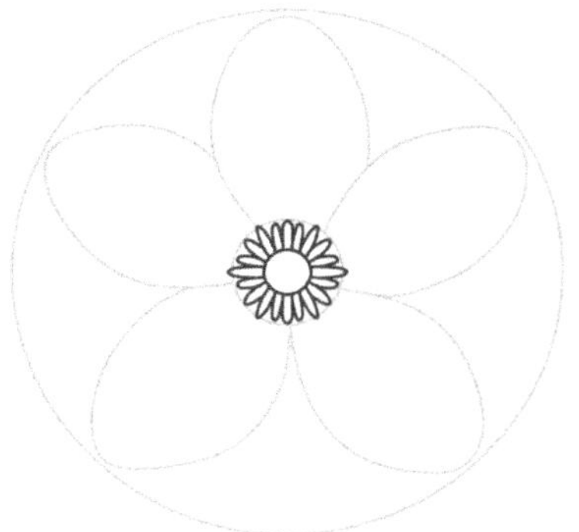

04

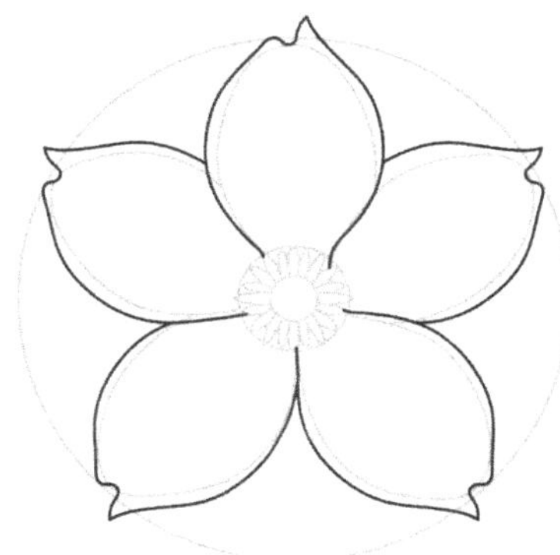

05

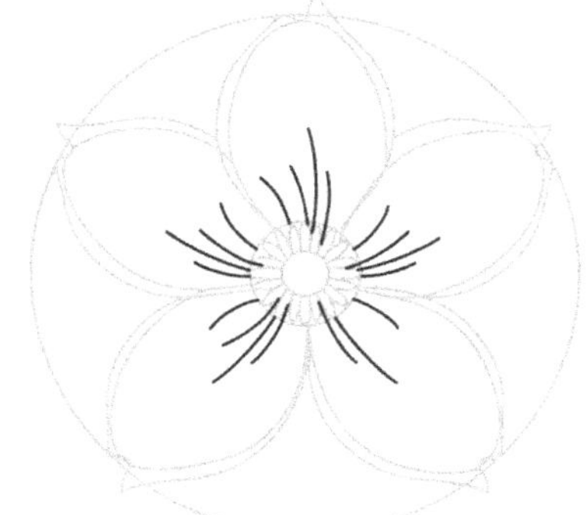

06

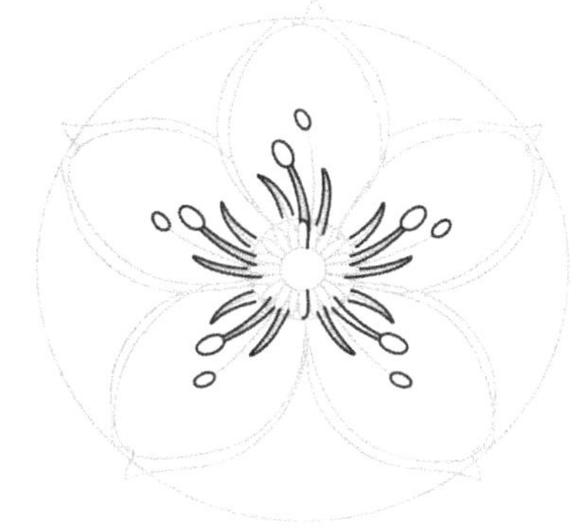

07

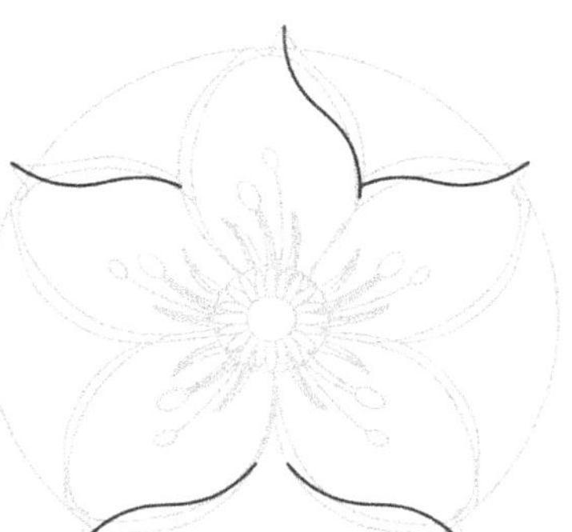

08

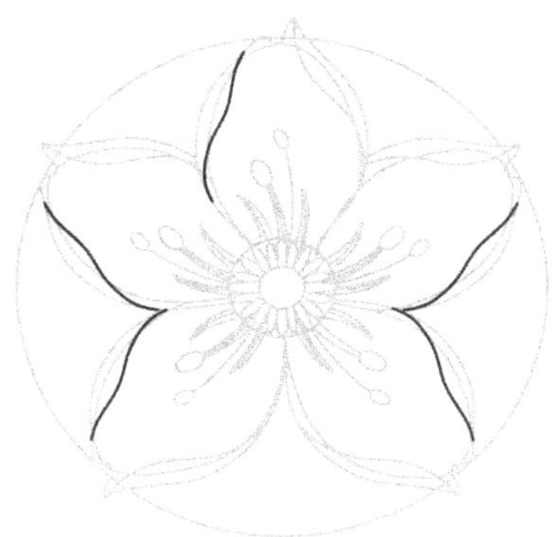

09

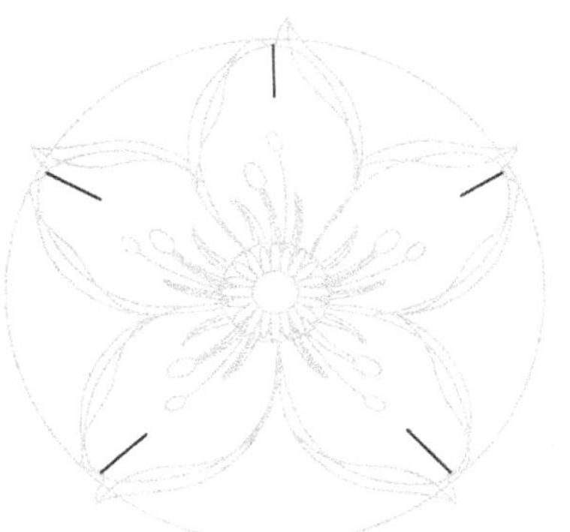

10

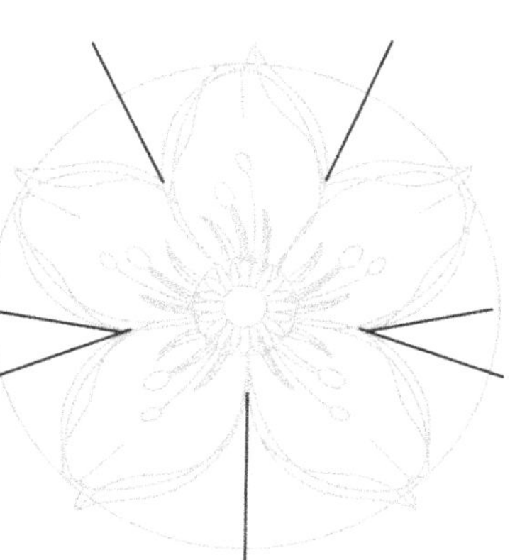

11

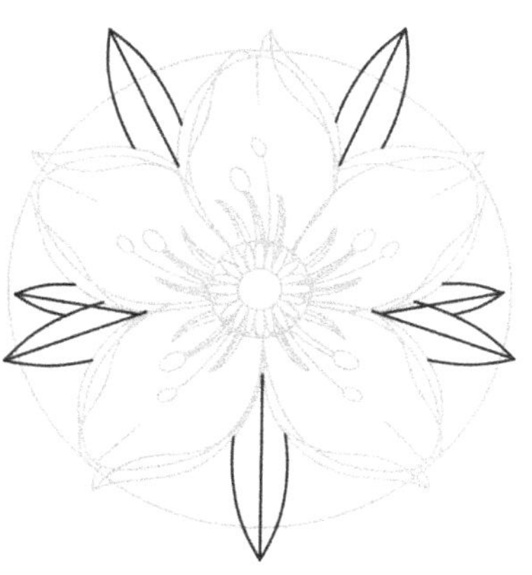

12

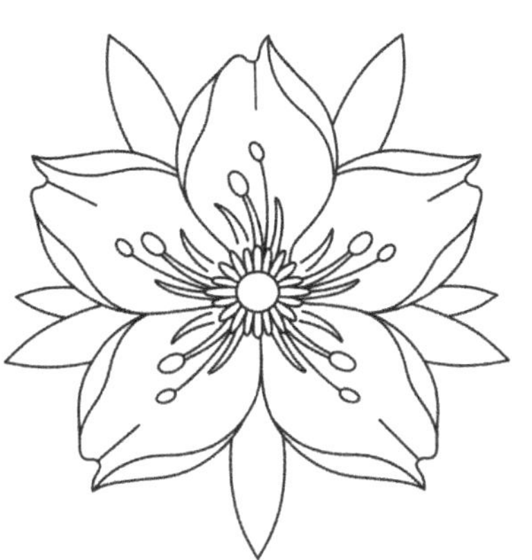

JAPANESE TATTOOS

WAVES | NAMI

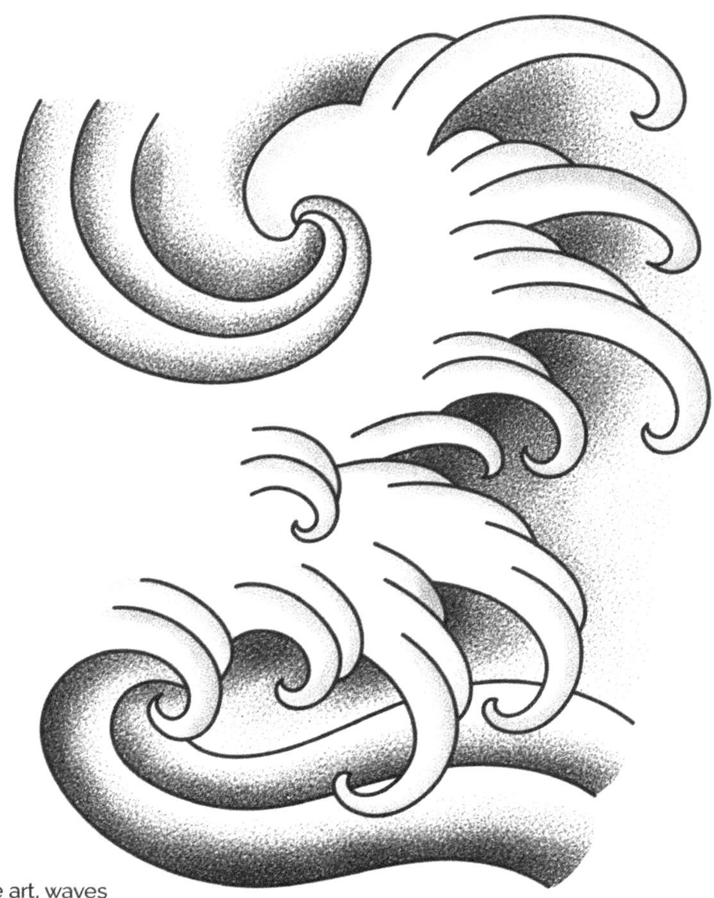

A popular theme in Japanese art, waves represent the power and unpredictability of nature, as well as strength, movement, and the ever-changing flow of life.

01

02

03

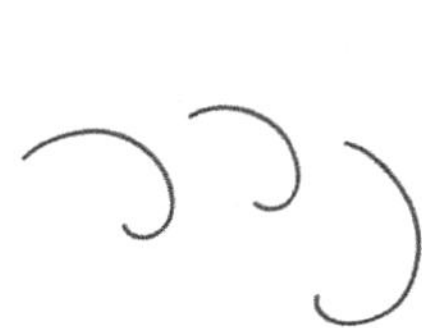

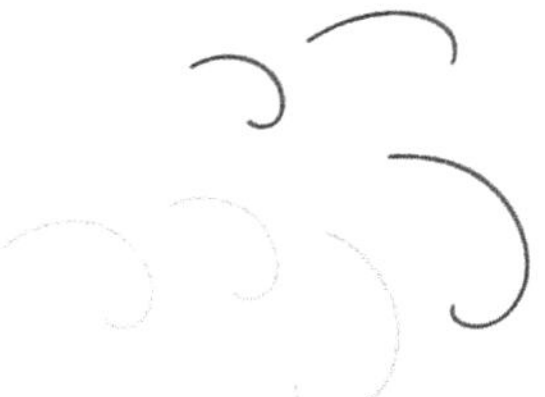

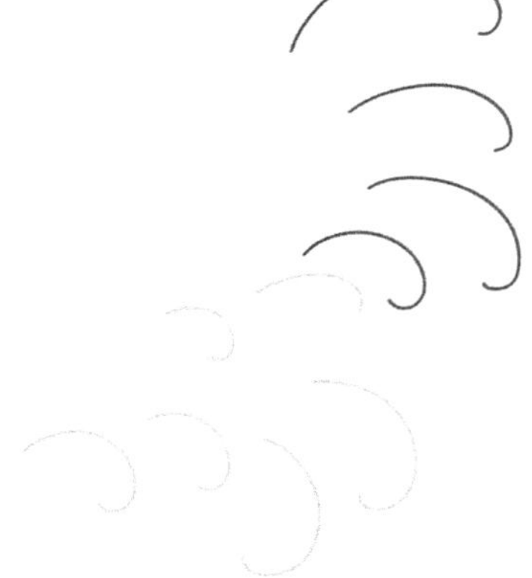

04

05

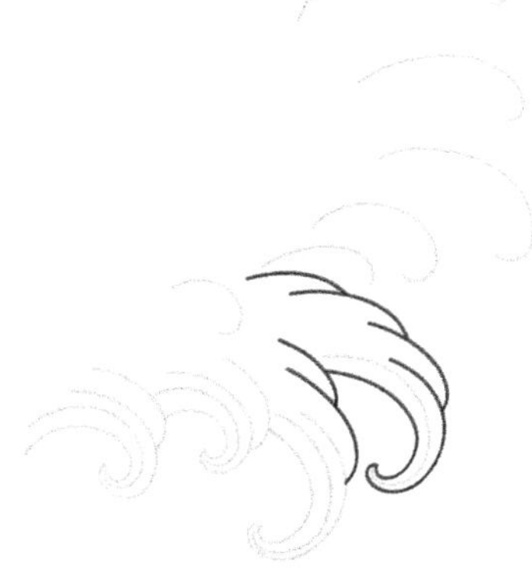

06

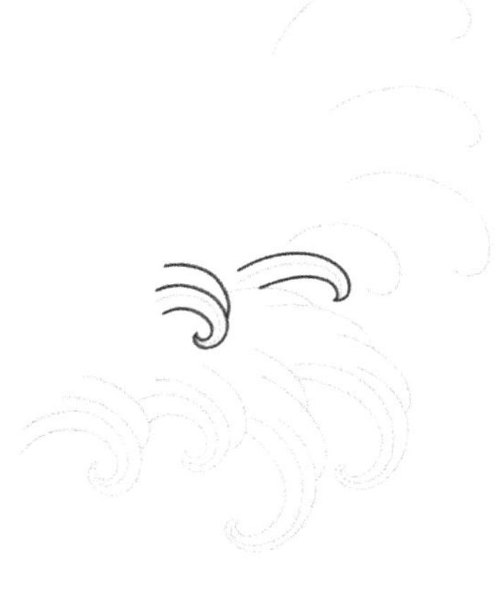

07

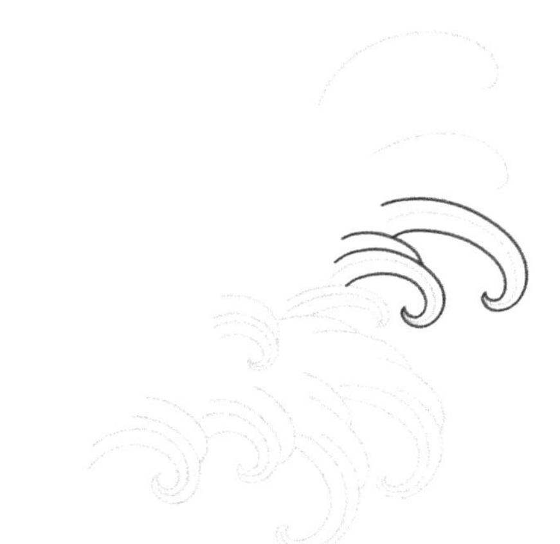

08

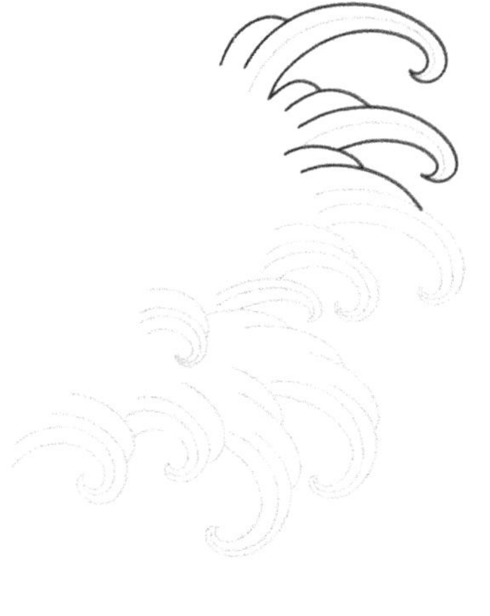

09

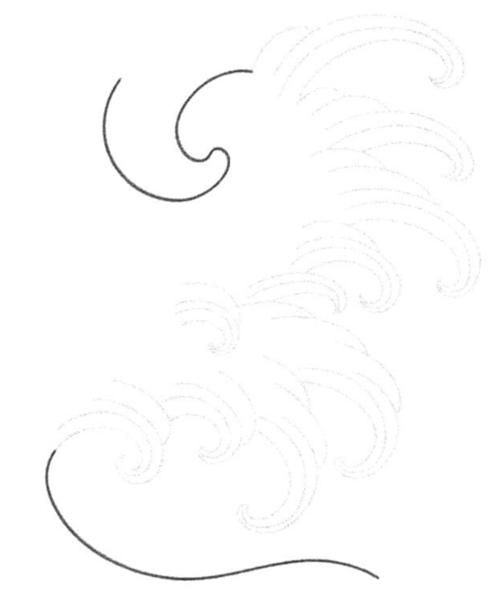

10

11

12

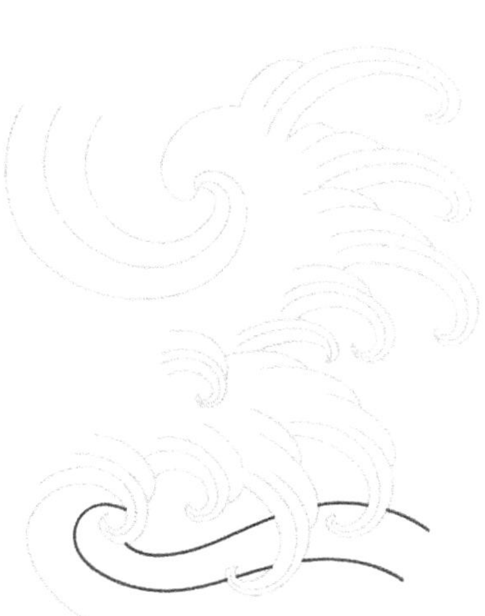

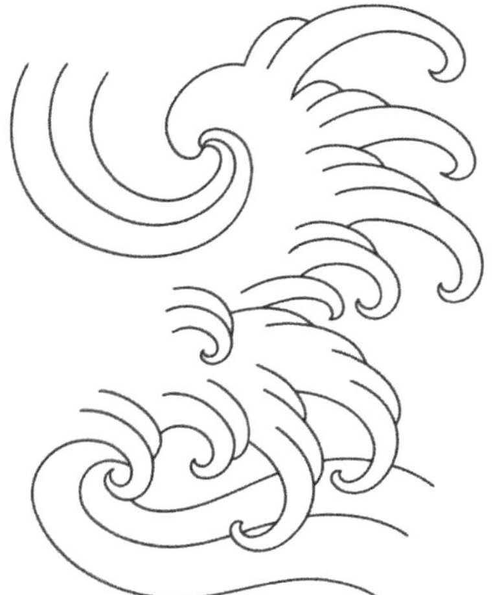

CLOUDS | KUMO

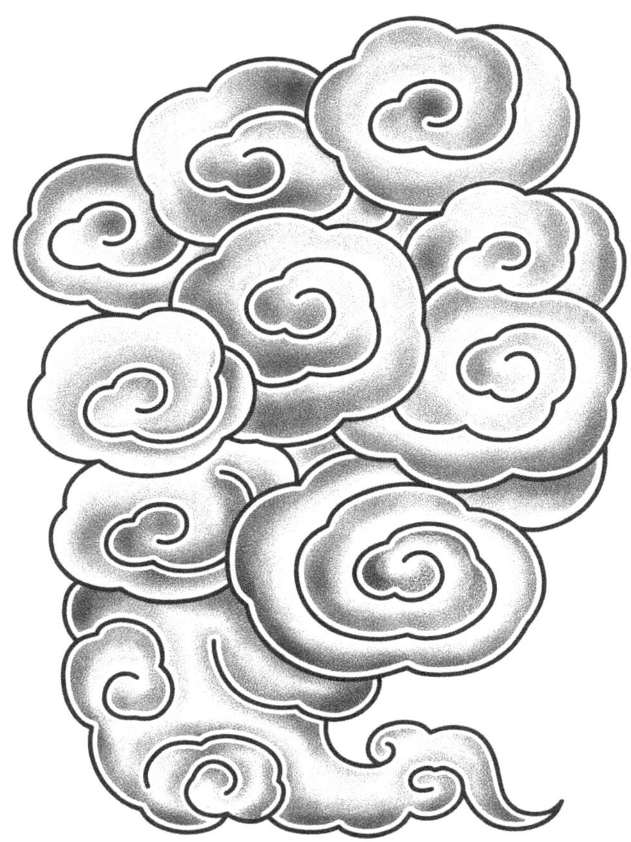

In Japanese culture, clouds symbolise
hope, change, impermanence, and
proximity to the gods. They also appear
as flowing decorative patterns in
traditional art.

01

02

03

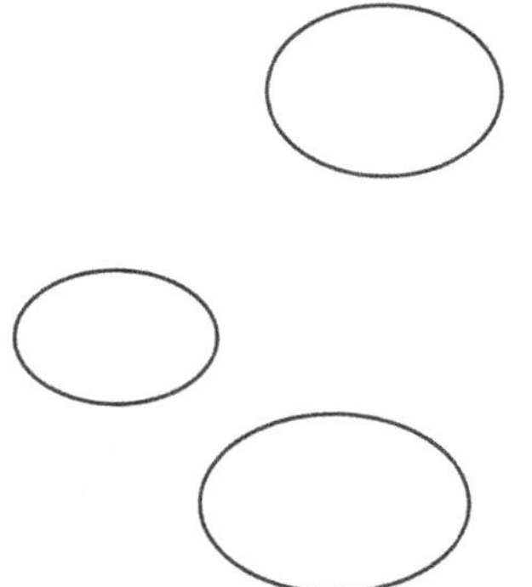

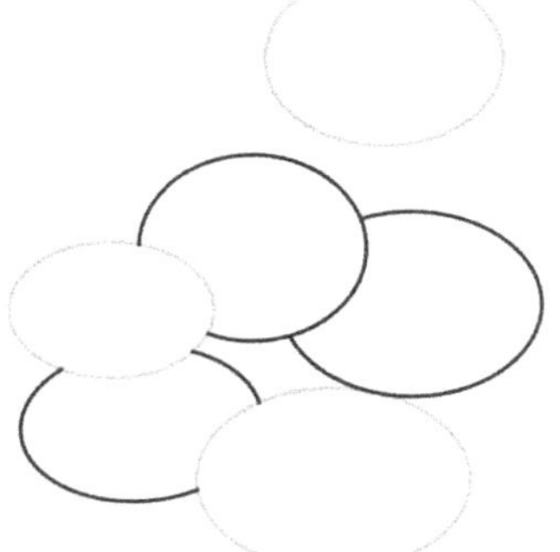

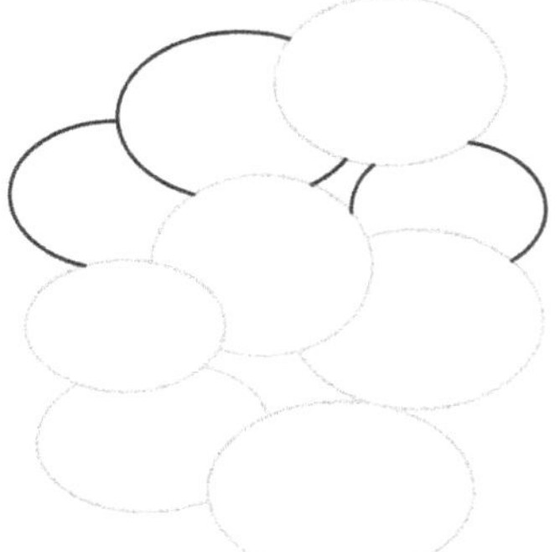

04

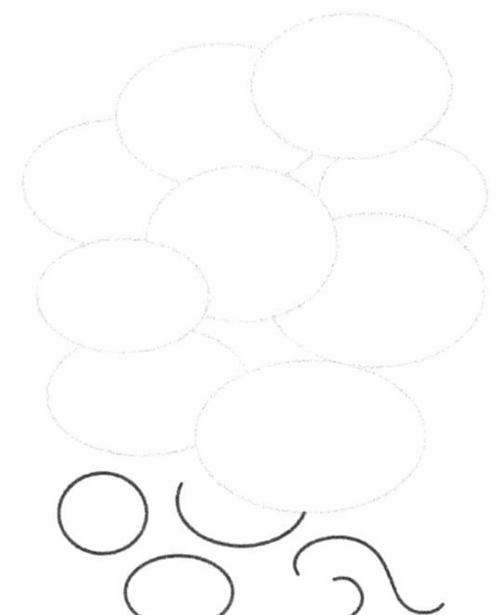

05

06

07

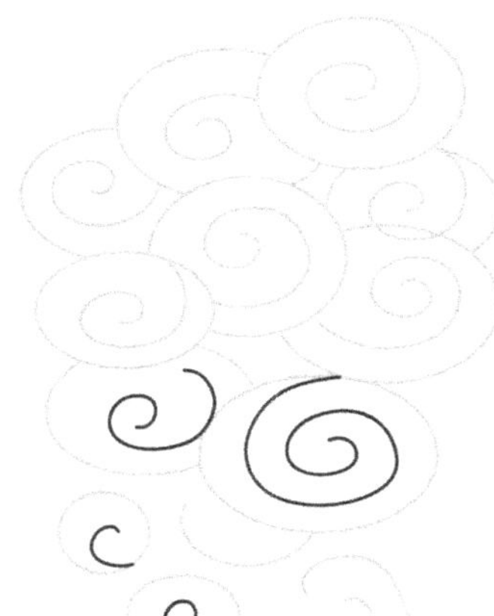

08

09

10

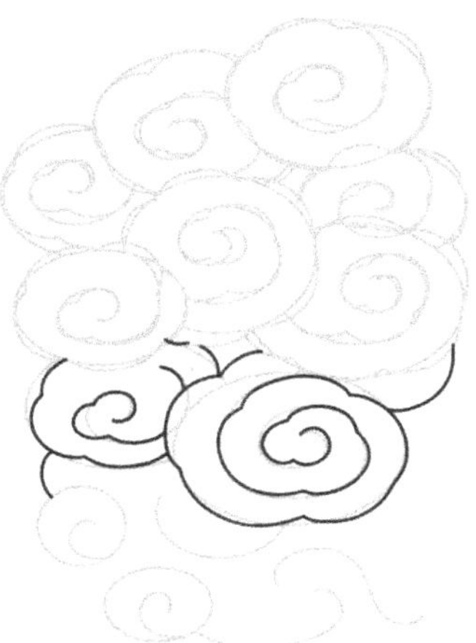

11

12

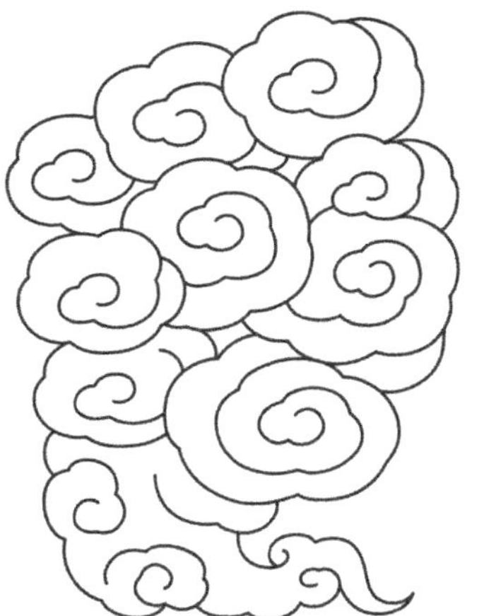

JAPANESE TATTOOS

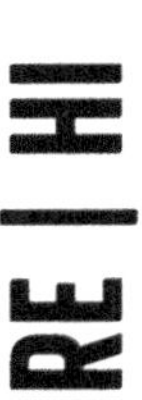

FIRE | HI

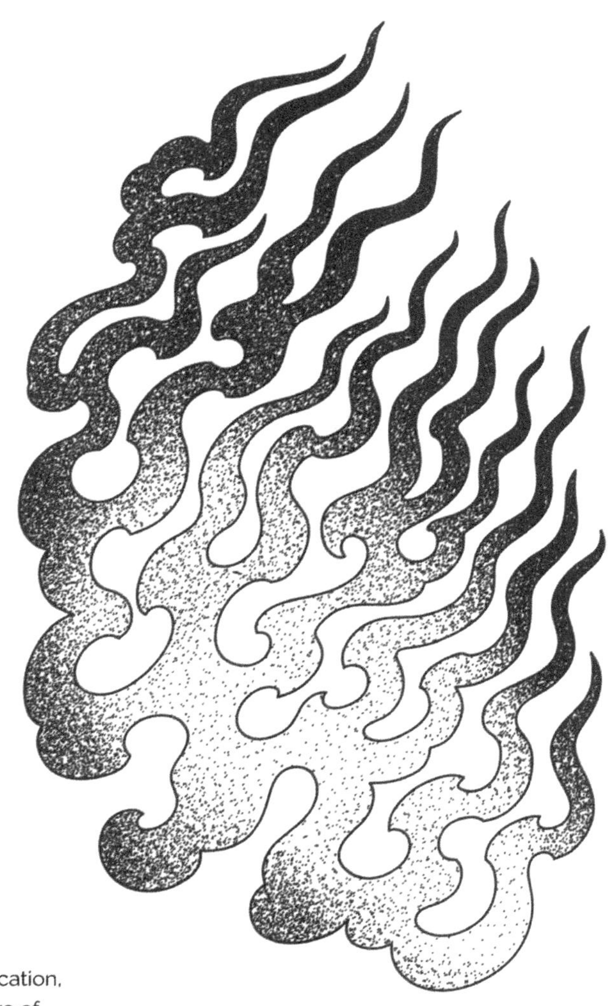

In Japanese tattoo culture, fire symbolises energy, warmth, purification, transformation, and the dual nature of life-sustaining and destructive forces.

01

02

03

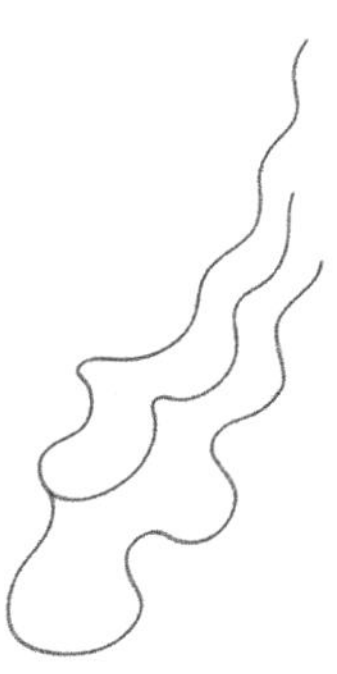

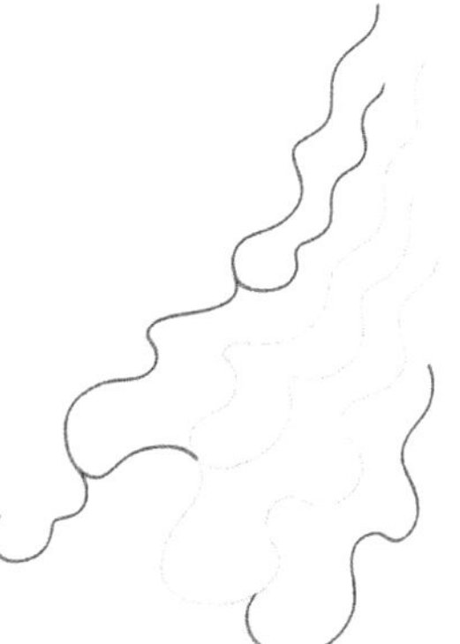

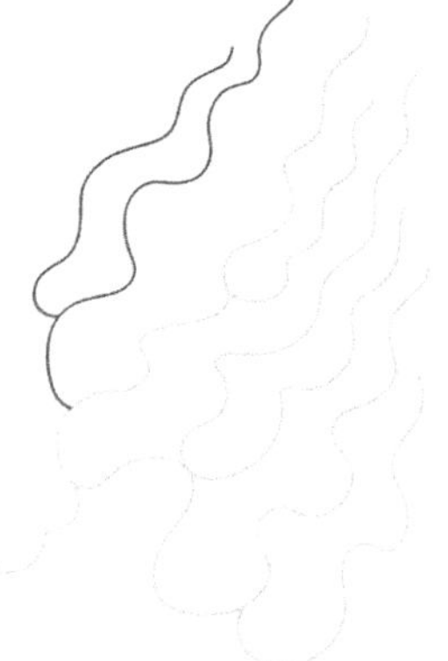

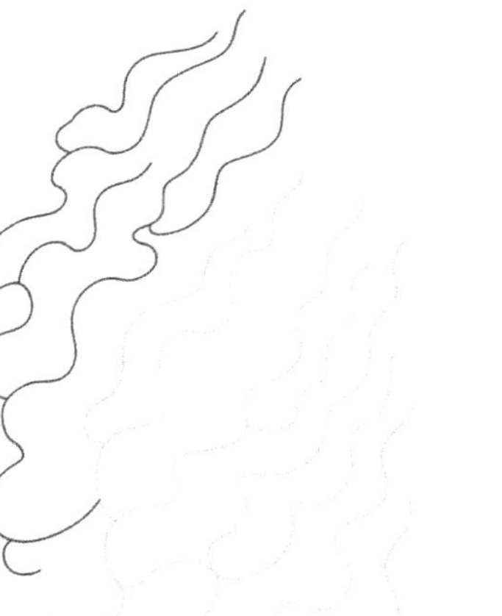

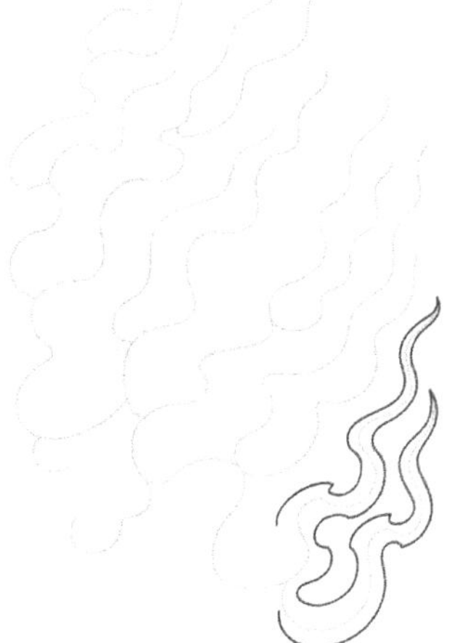

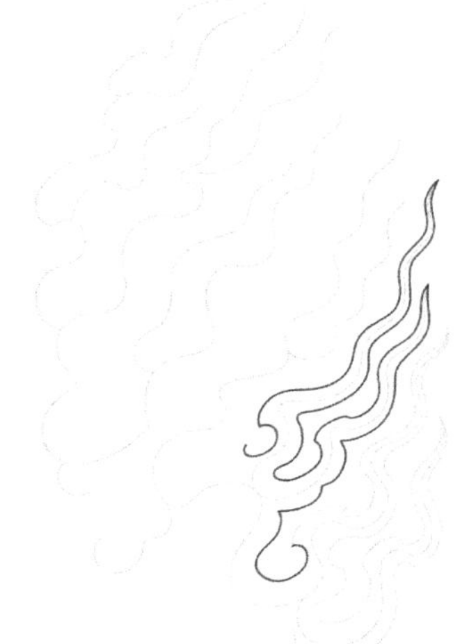

07

08

09

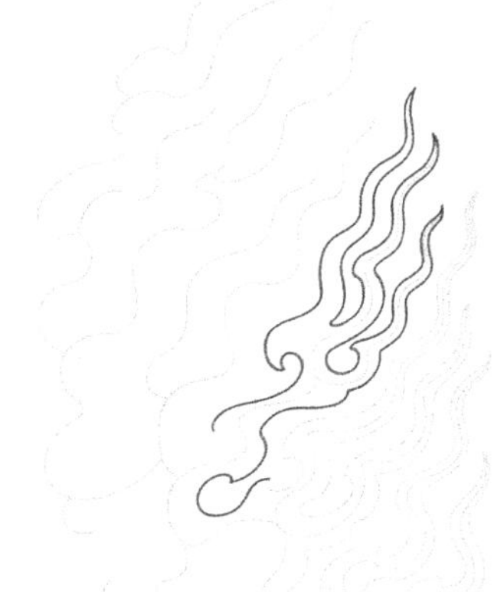

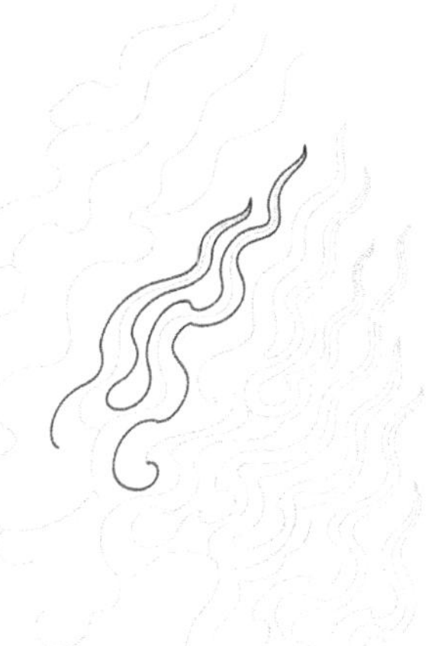

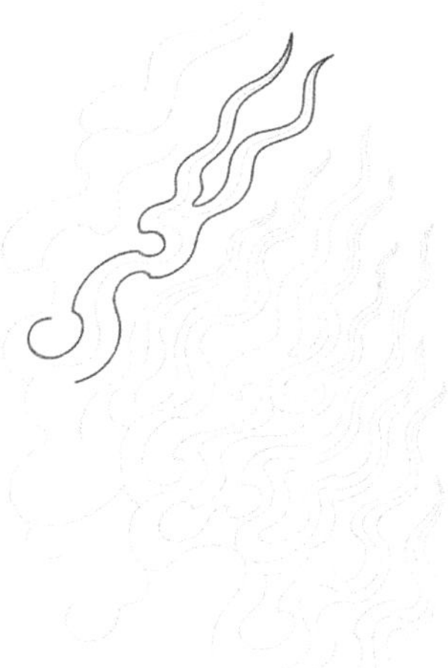

JAPANESE TATTOOS

10

11

12

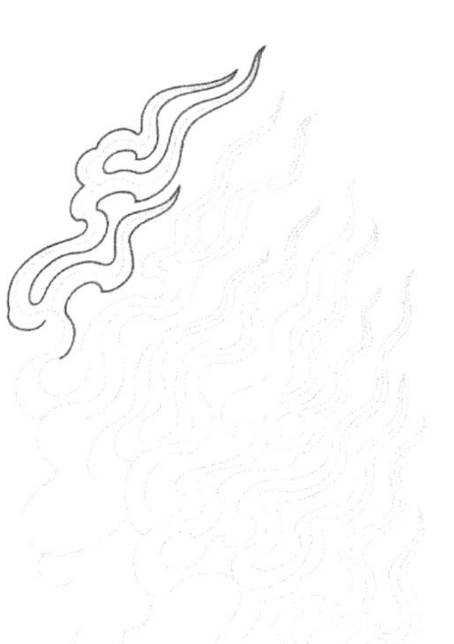

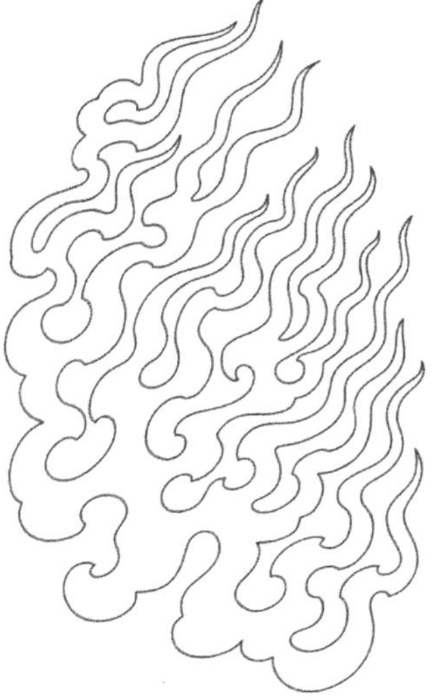

SAMURAI

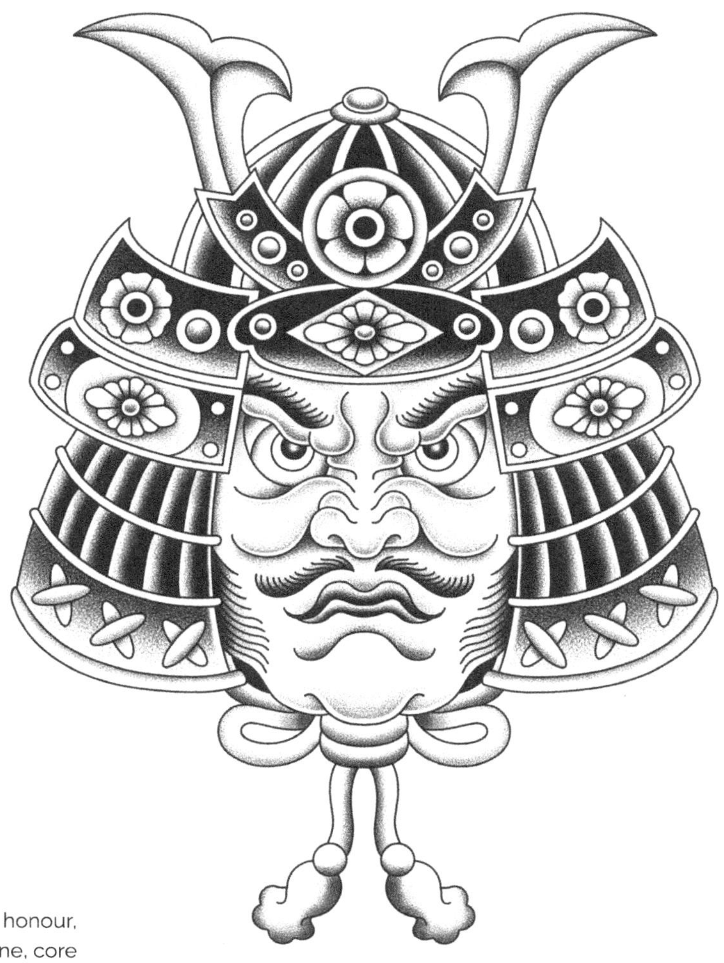

A samurai tattoo symbolises honour, courage, loyalty, and discipline, core values of Bushidō, the samurai's code of conduct, philosophy, and way of life.

01

02

03

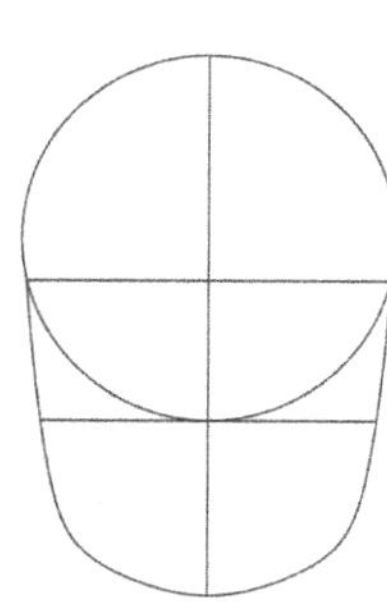

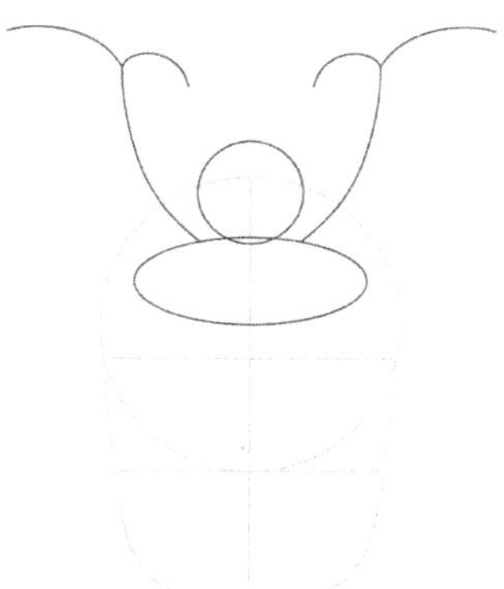

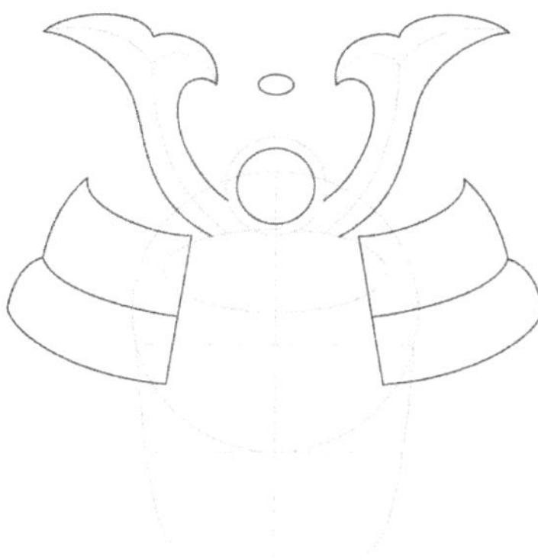

04

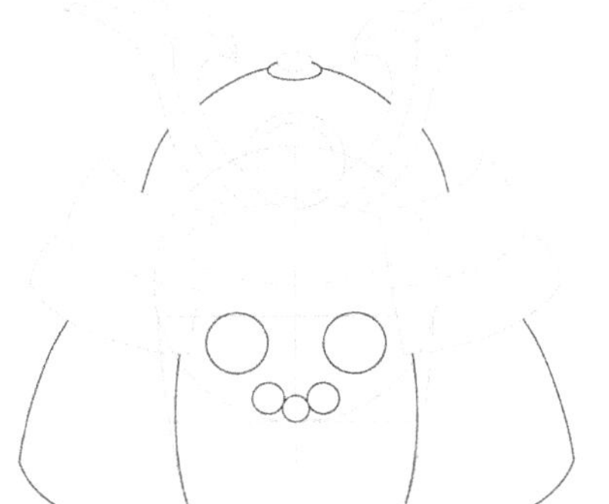

05

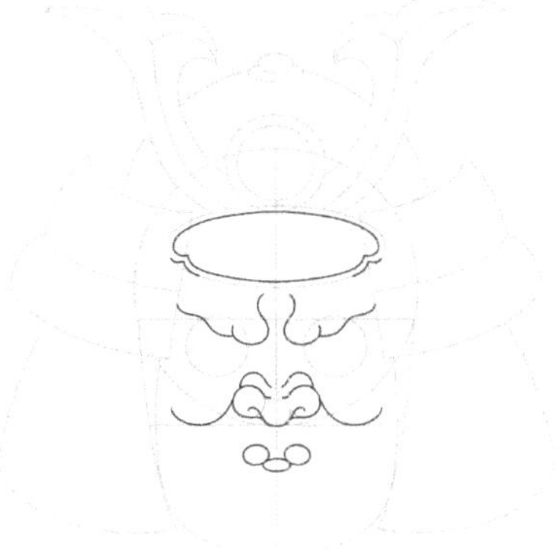

06

07

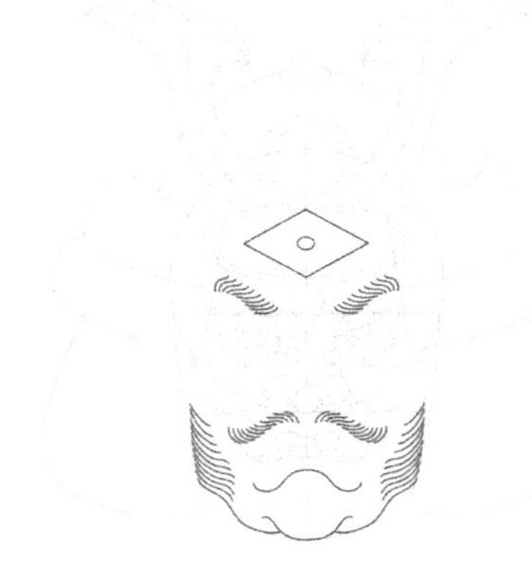

08

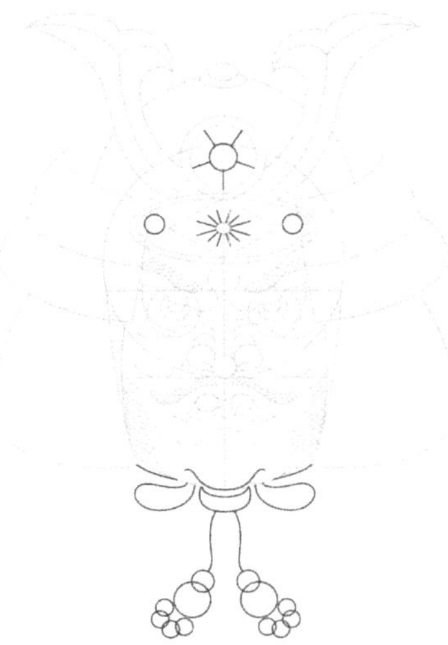

09

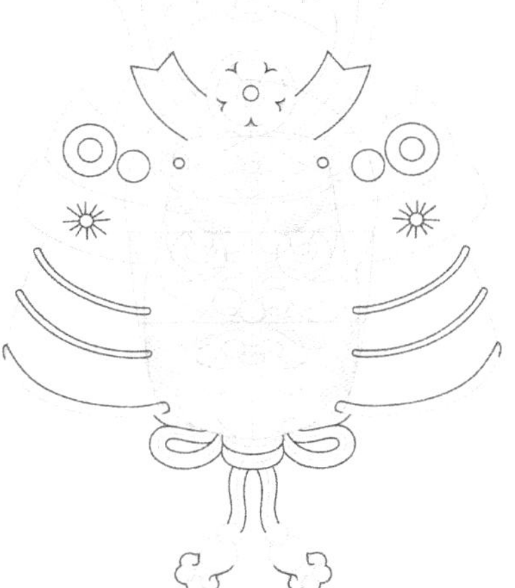

10

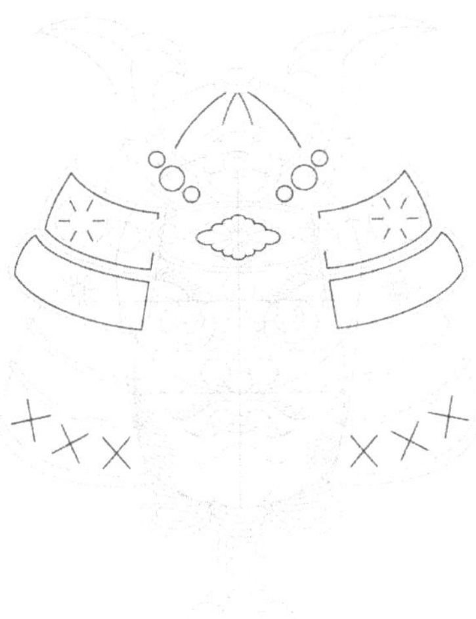

11

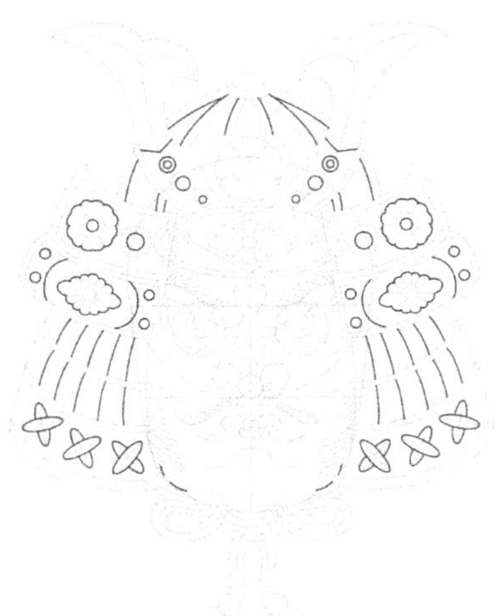

12

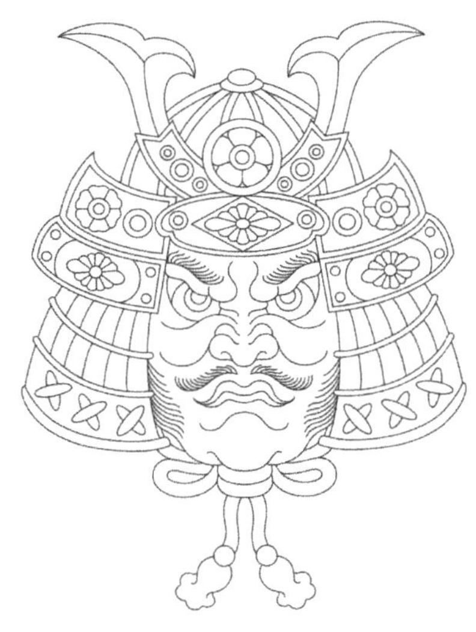

JAPANESE TATTOOS

GEISHA

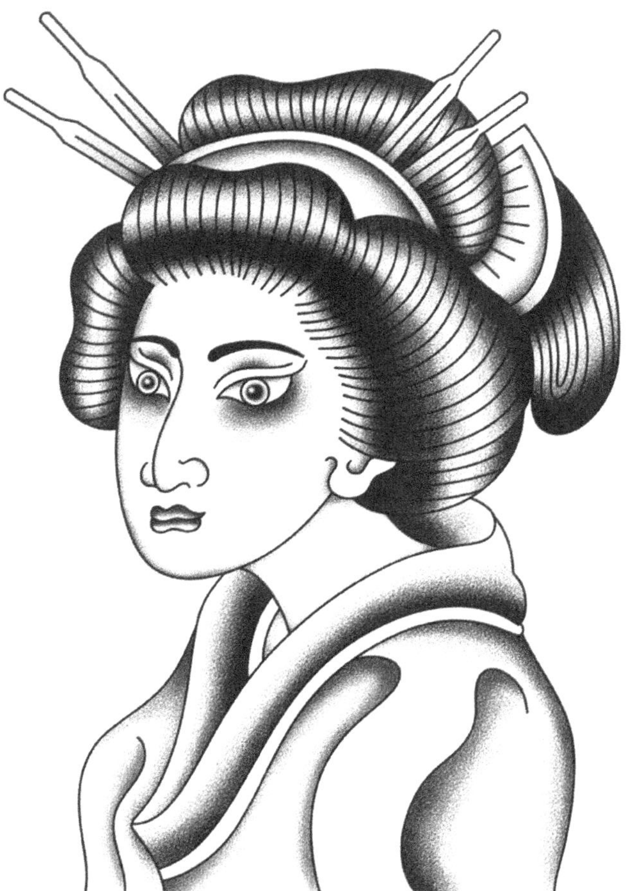

Geishas are artisans known for their proficiency in traditional Japanese arts like singing, dancing, and music. Geisha tattoos can symbolise beauty, elegance and love of the arts.

01

02

03

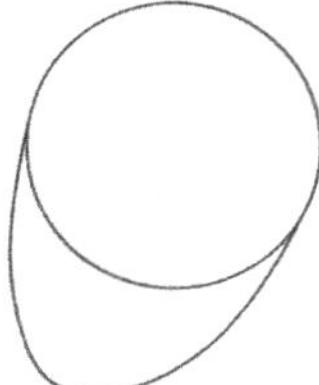

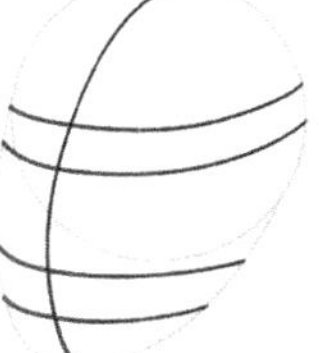

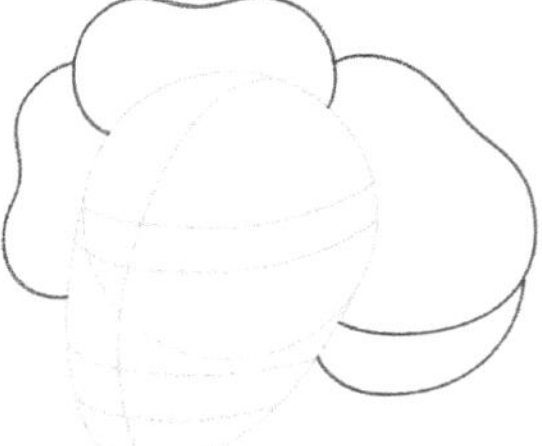

04

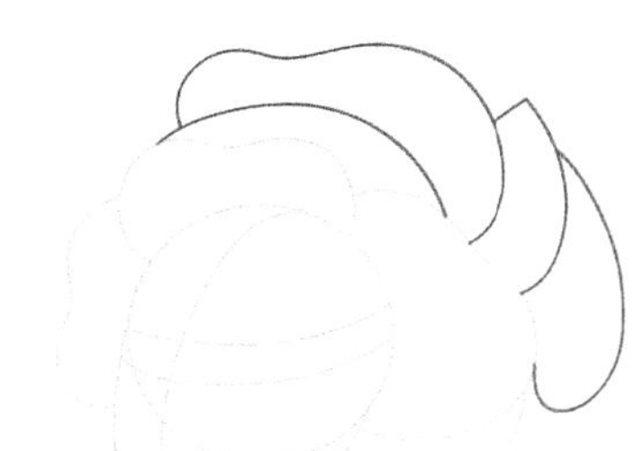

05

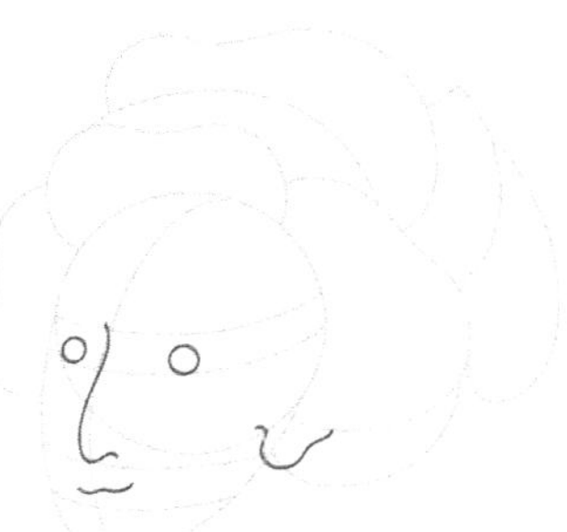

06

07

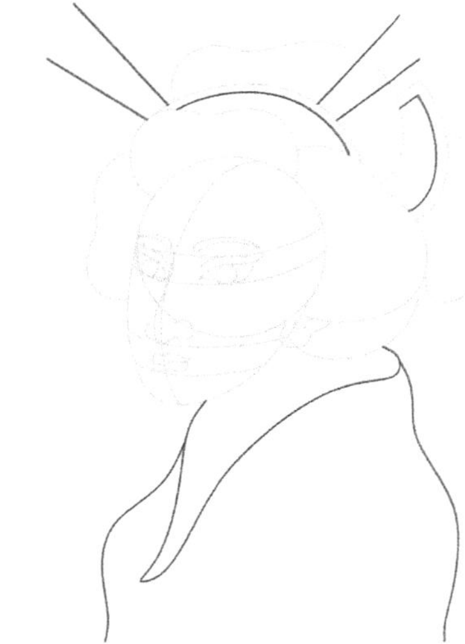

08

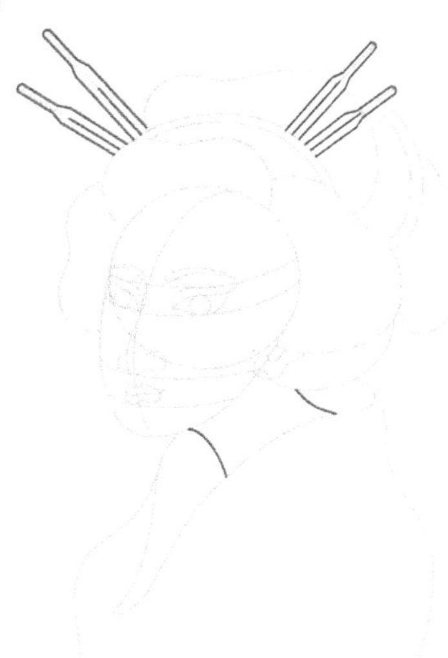

09

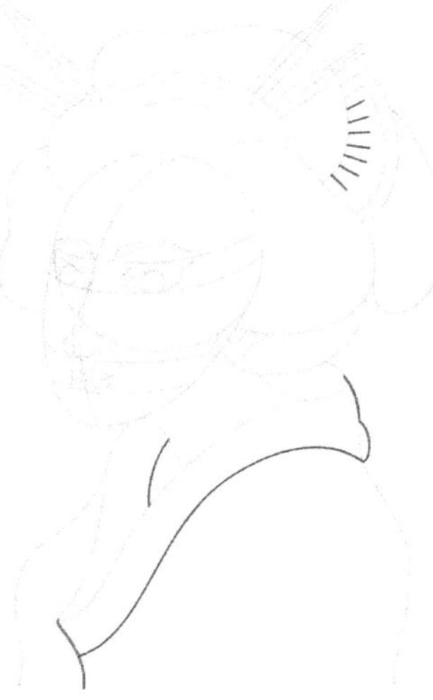

10

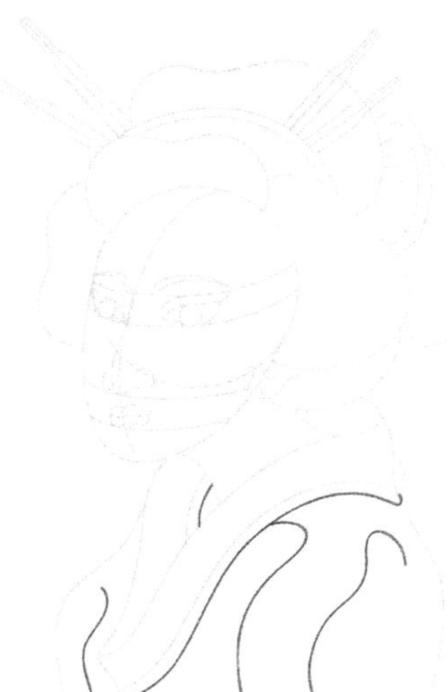

11

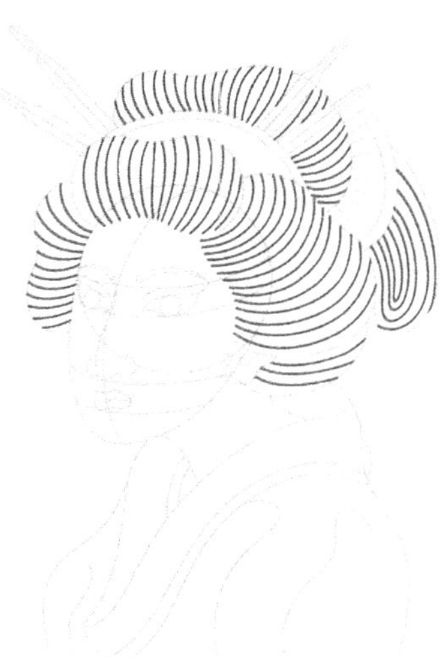

12

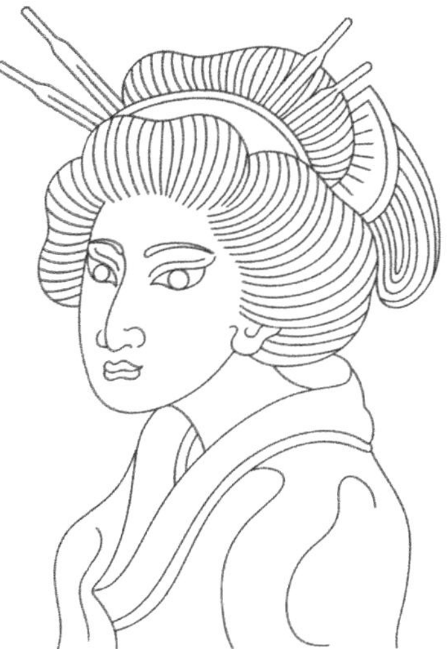

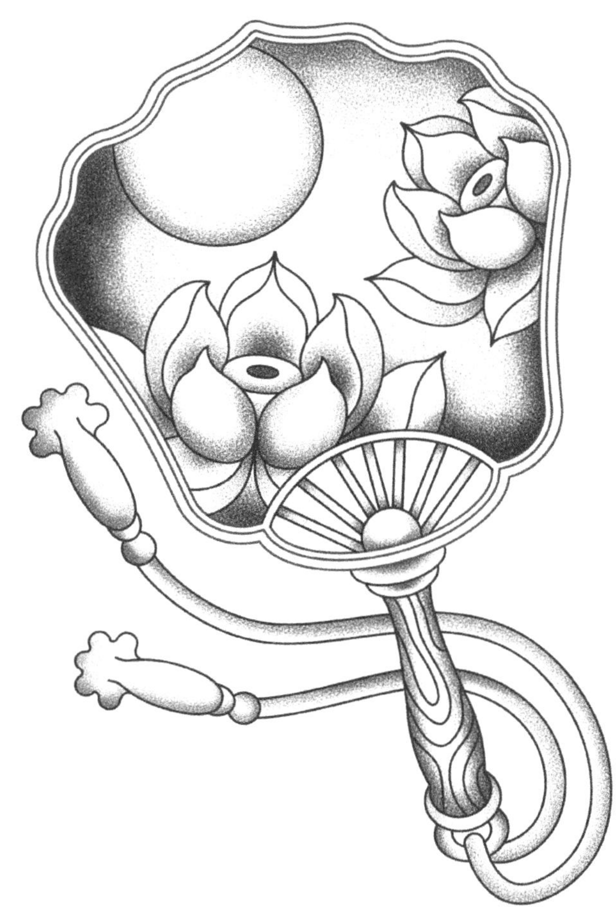

TRADITIONAL FAN UCHIWA

The uchiwa has a long history in Japan. Aside from its use as a fan, people have used uchiwa to conceal their faces to preserve their dignity and also to ward off evil spirits.

01

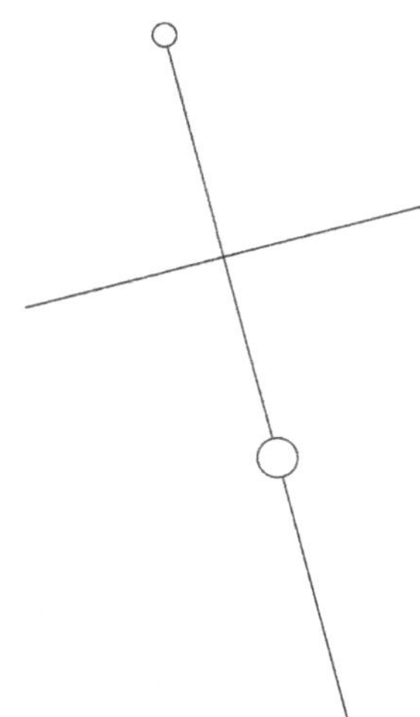

02

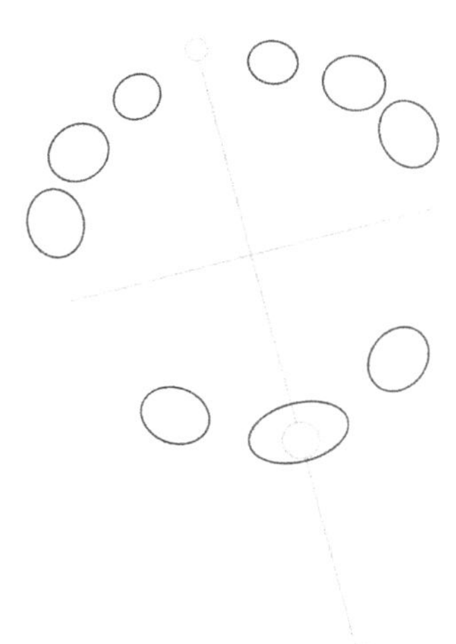

03

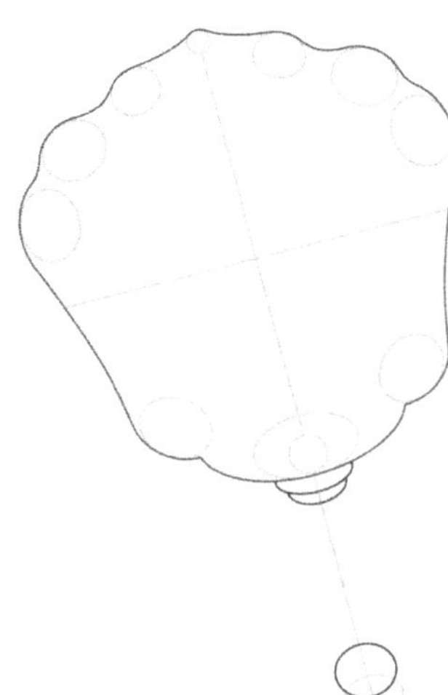

04

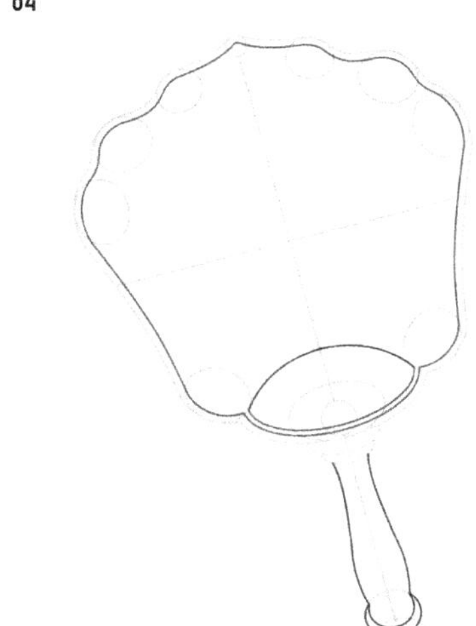

05

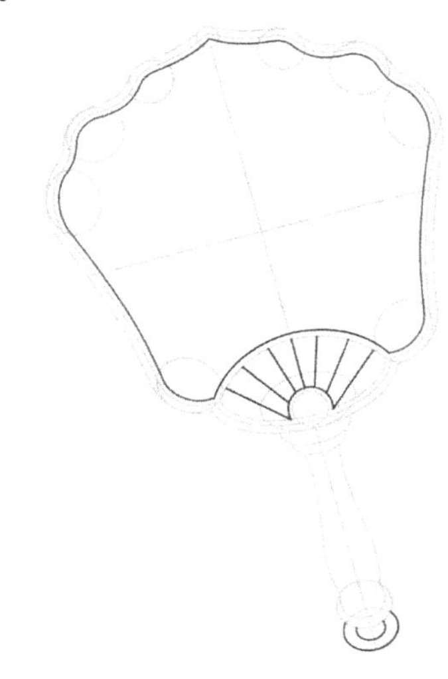

06

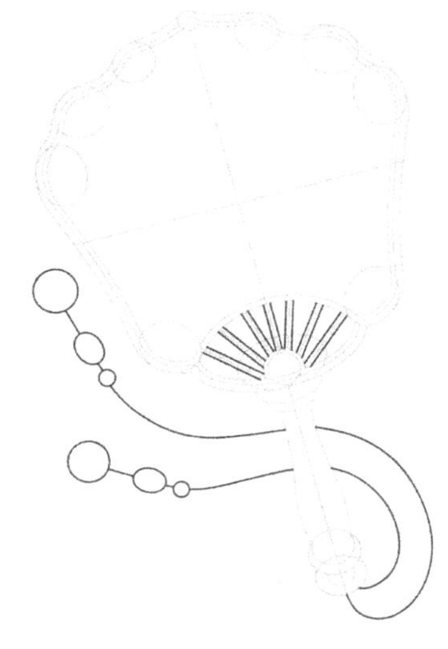

07

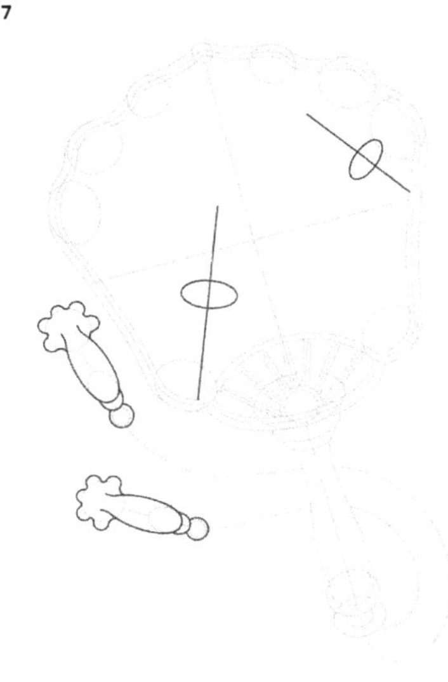

08

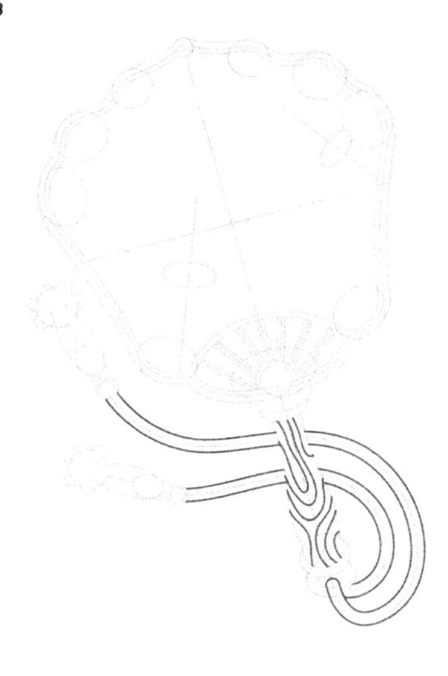

09

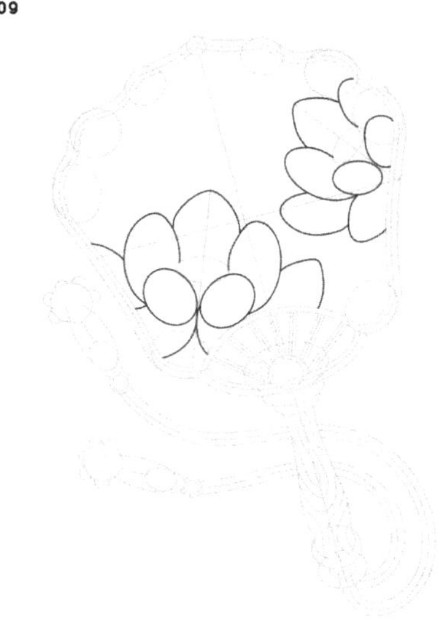

10

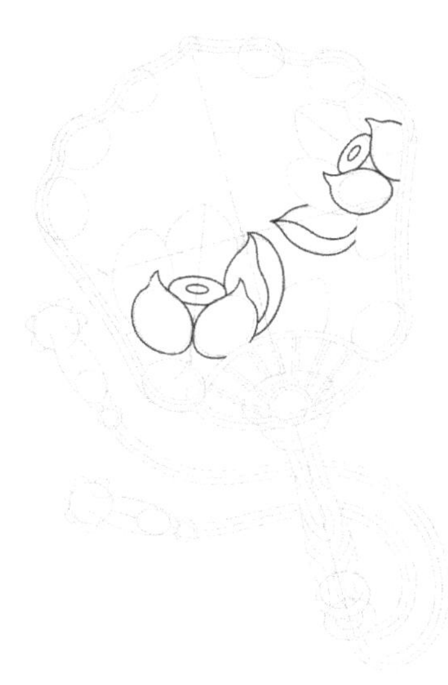

11

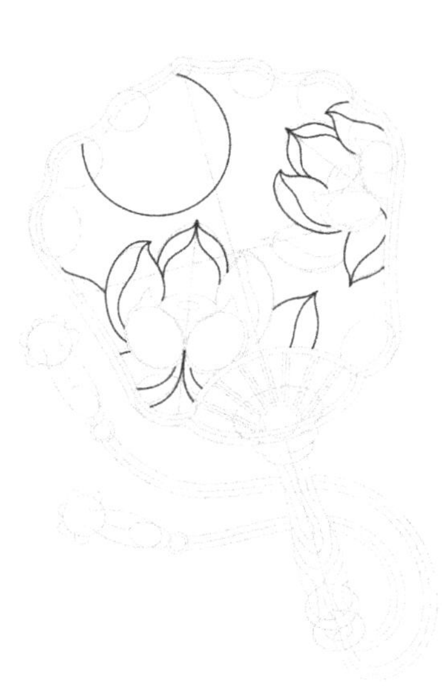

12

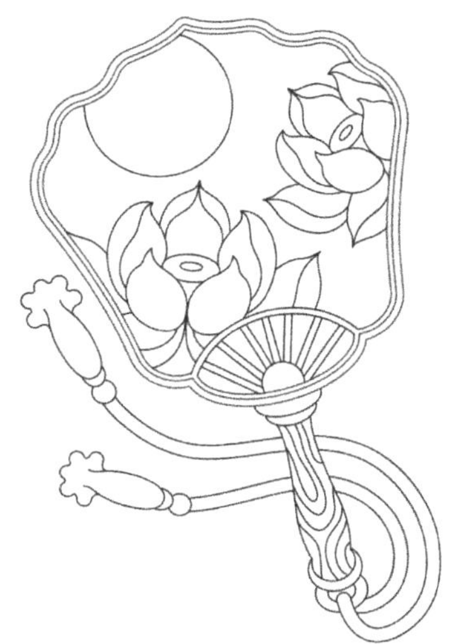

JAPANESE LANTERN
CHOCHIN

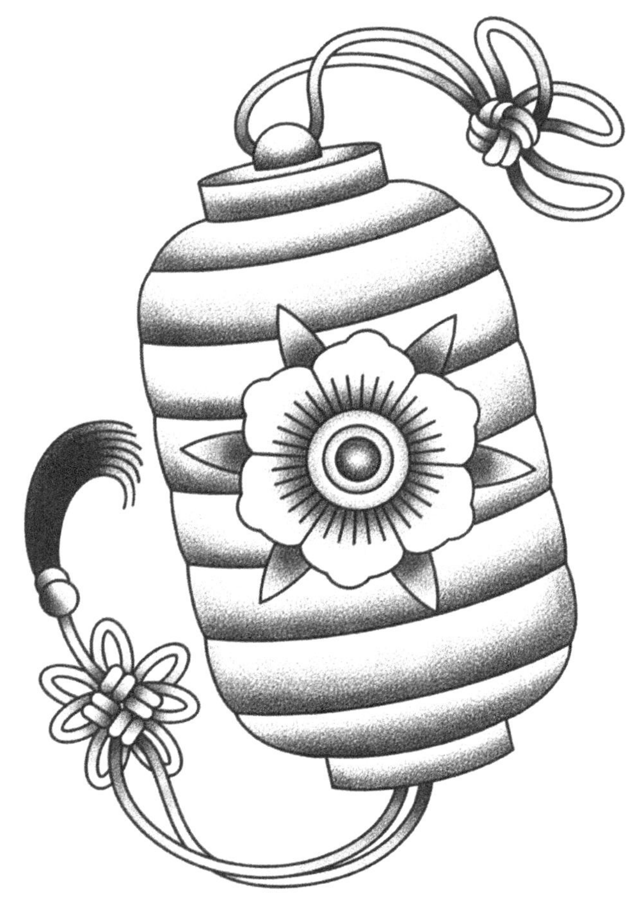

Paper lanterns are often used as decorations and to guide spirits during the Obon festival, symbolising luck, happiness, and the illumination of Buddha's teachings.

01

02

03

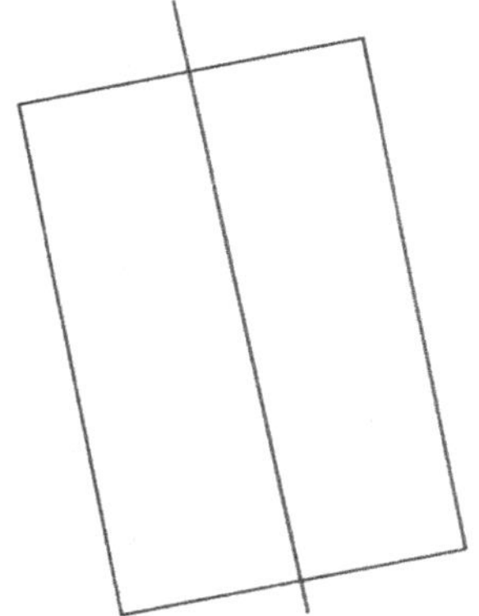

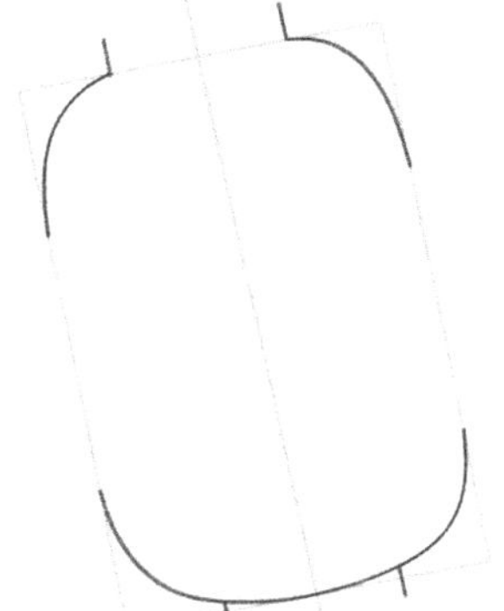

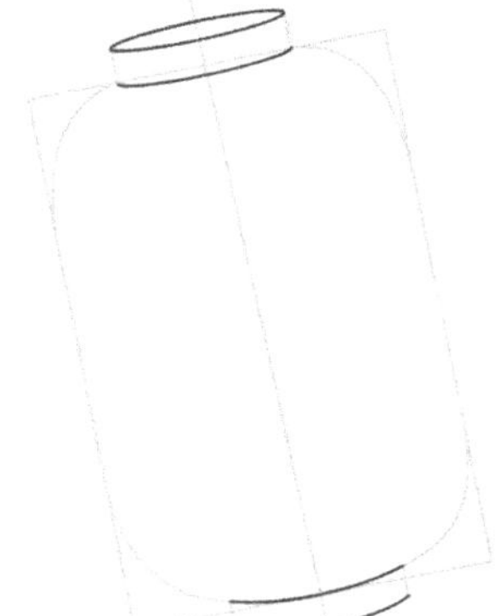

04

05

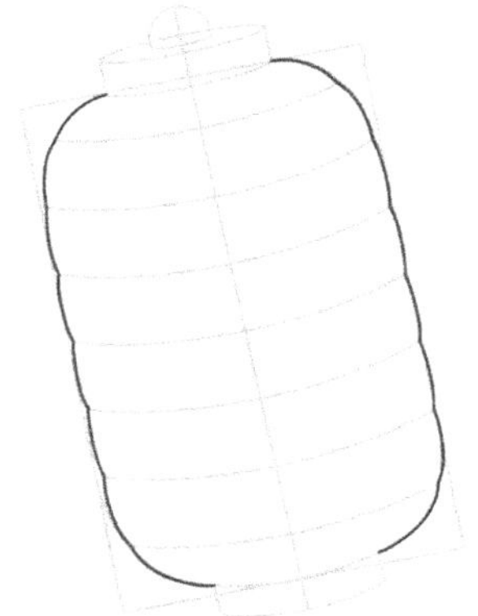

06

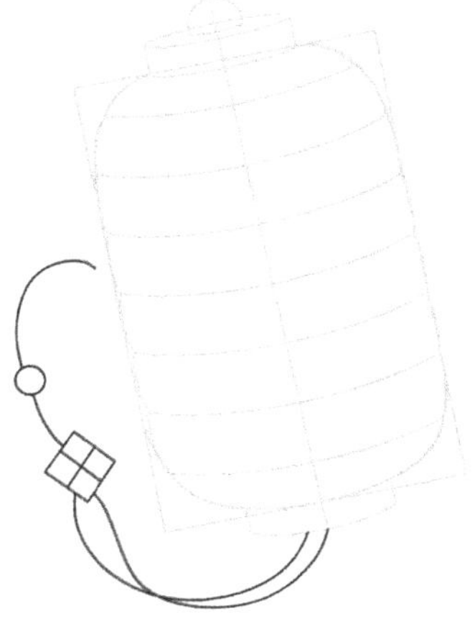

07

08

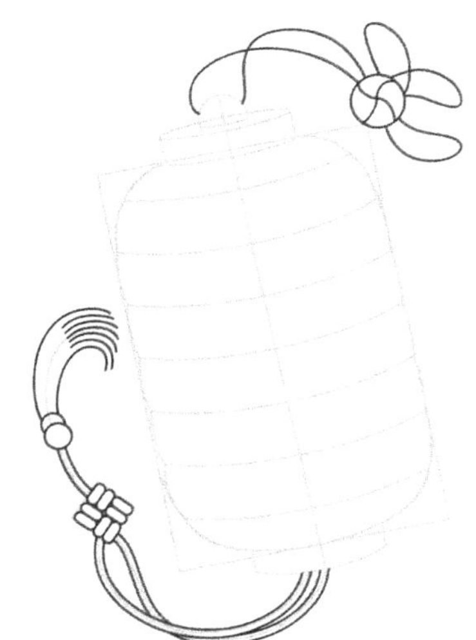

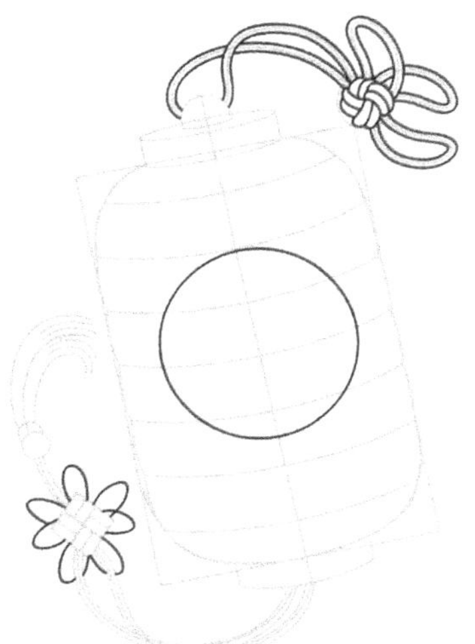

09

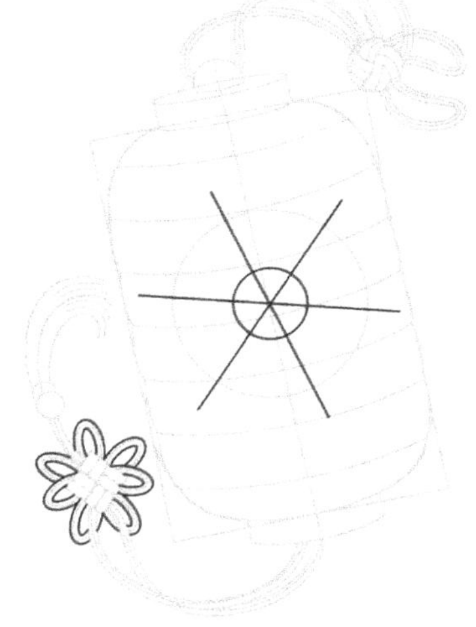

10

11

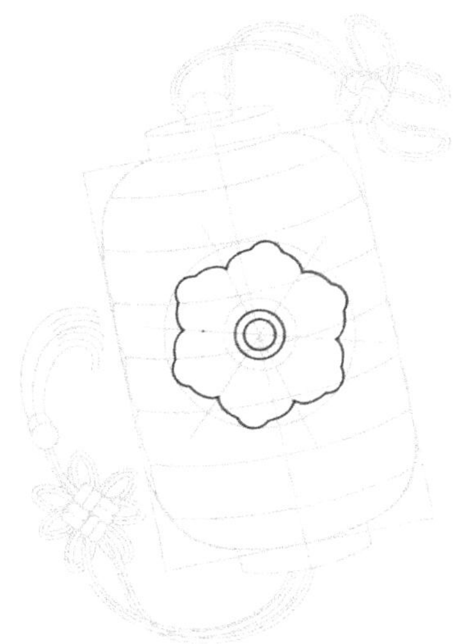

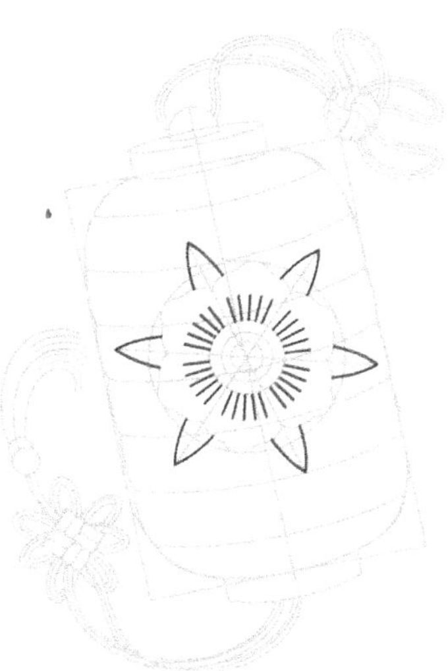

12

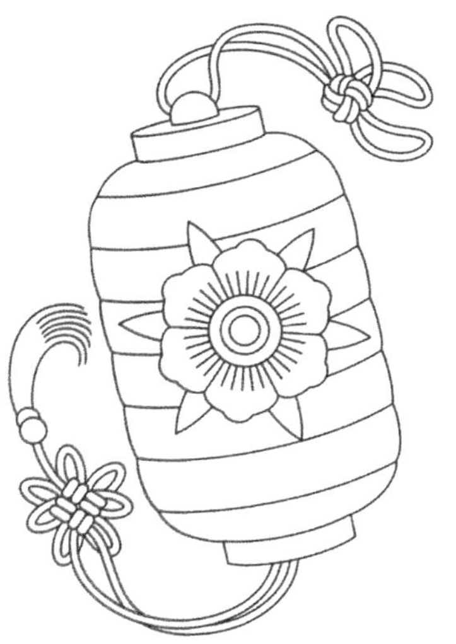

JAPANESE TATTOOS

JAPANESE TATTOOS

SWORD | KATANA

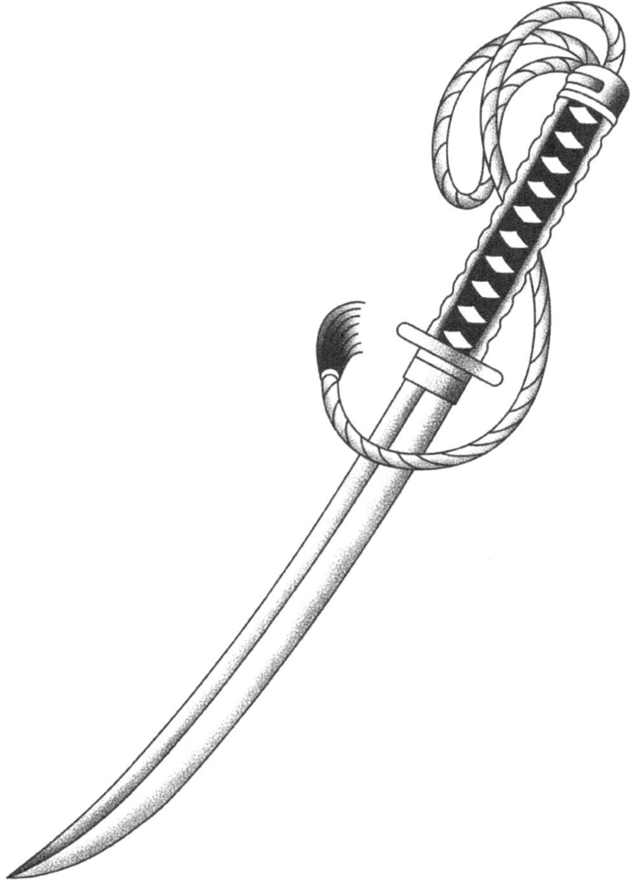

A katana symbolises strength, honour, courage, loyalty, and discipline, reflecting the values of the samurai who bears the sword and the artistry of the katana itself.

01

02

03

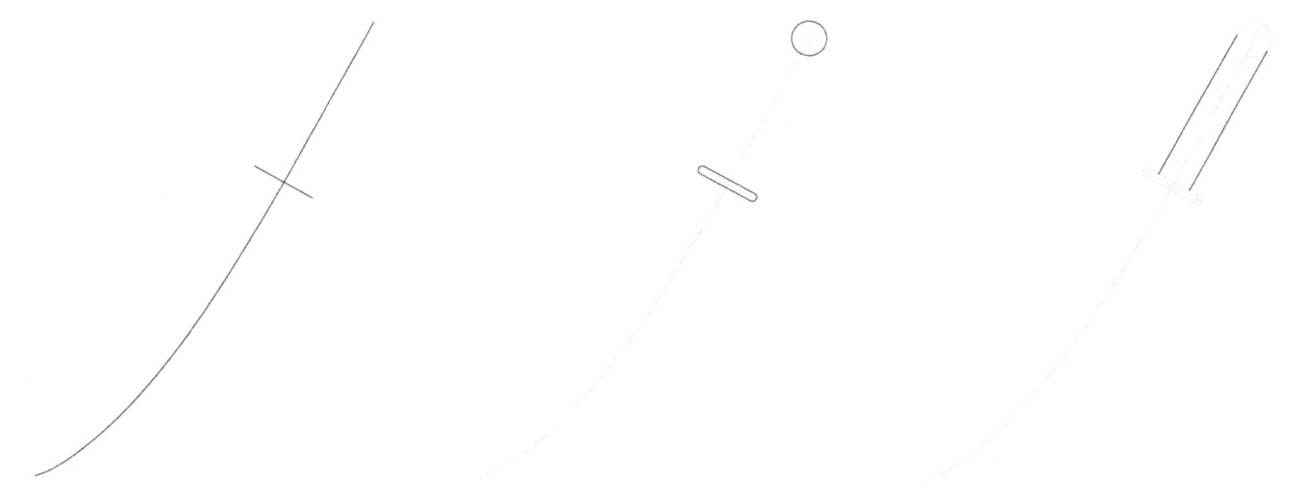

04

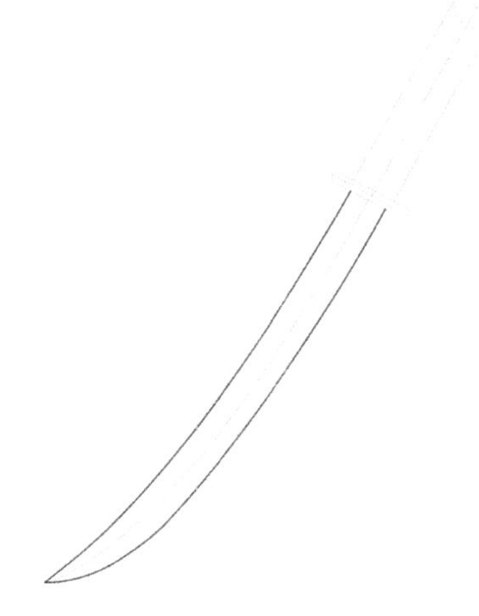

05

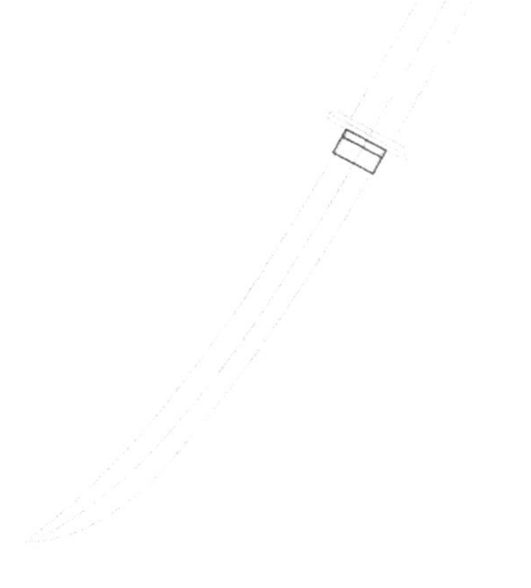

06

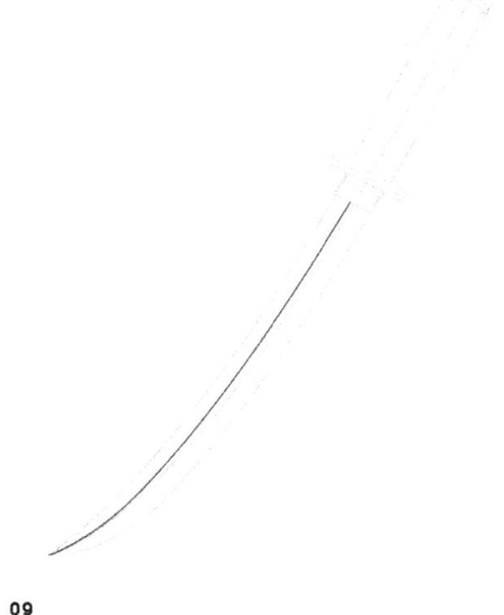

07

08

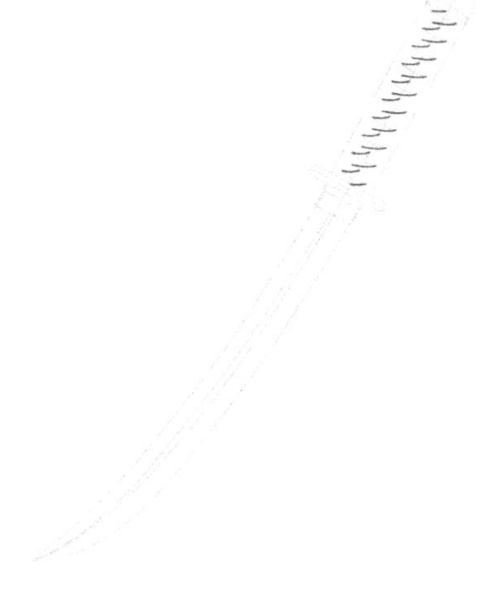

09

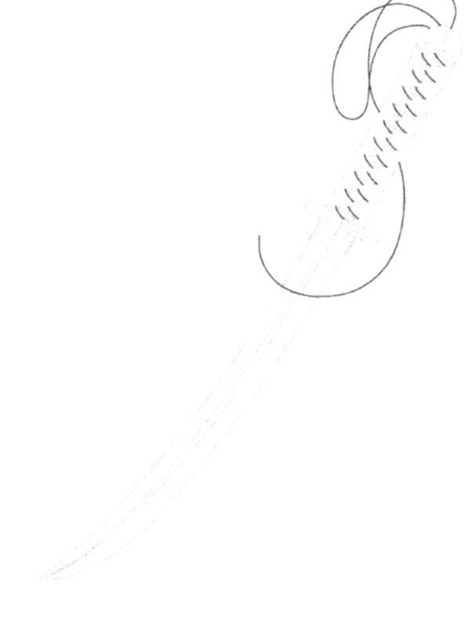

10

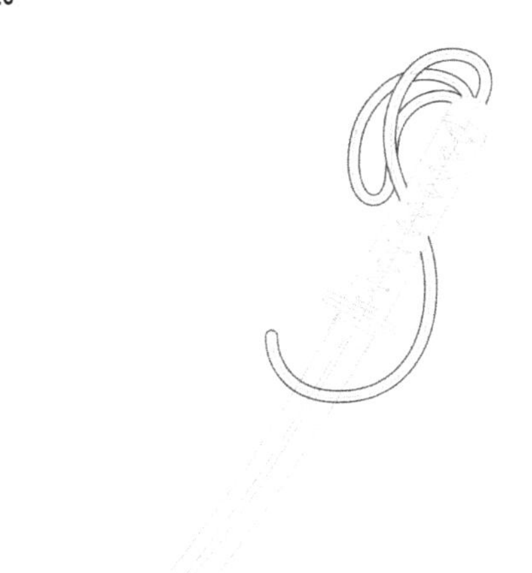

11

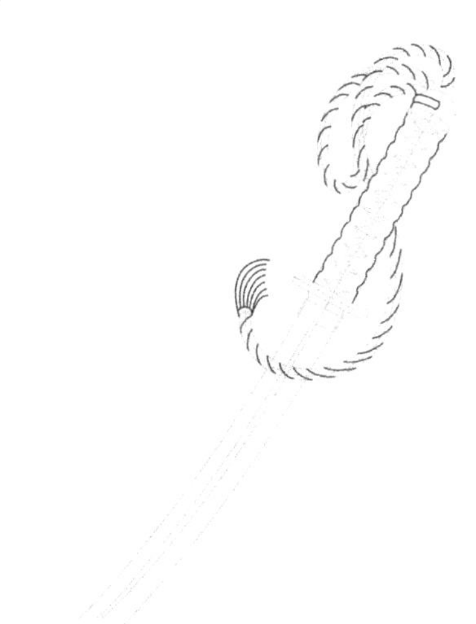

12

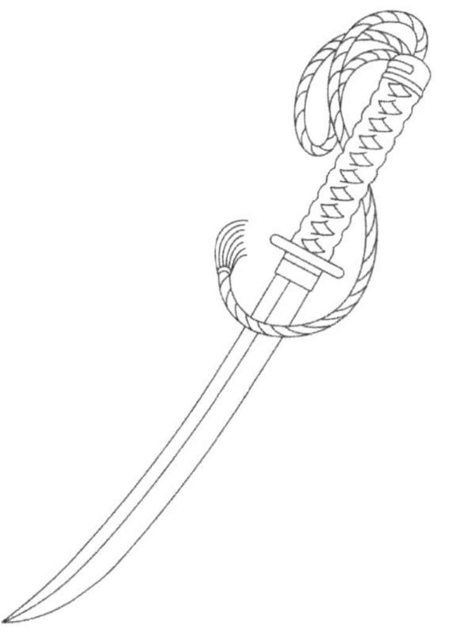

JAPANESE TATTOOS

SEVERED HEAD | NAMAKUBI

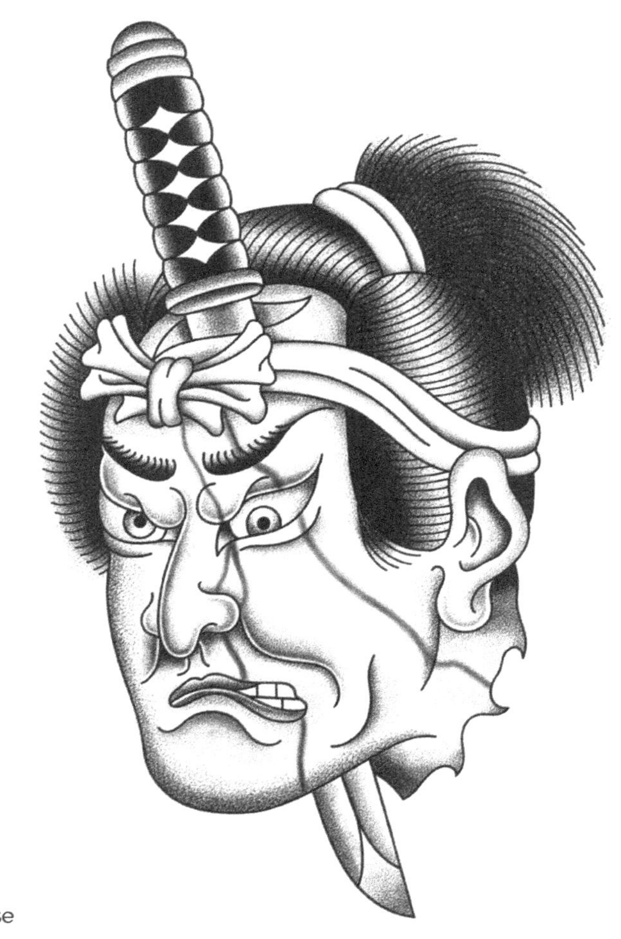

A namakubi tattoo can symbolise bravery, respect for the enemy, acceptance of fate, and the warrior's courage to face death and overcome extreme trials.

01

02

03

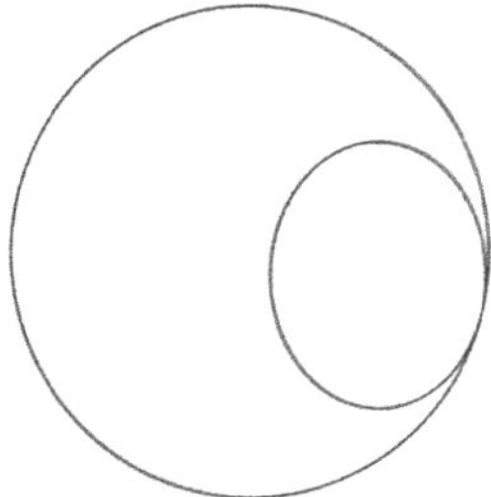

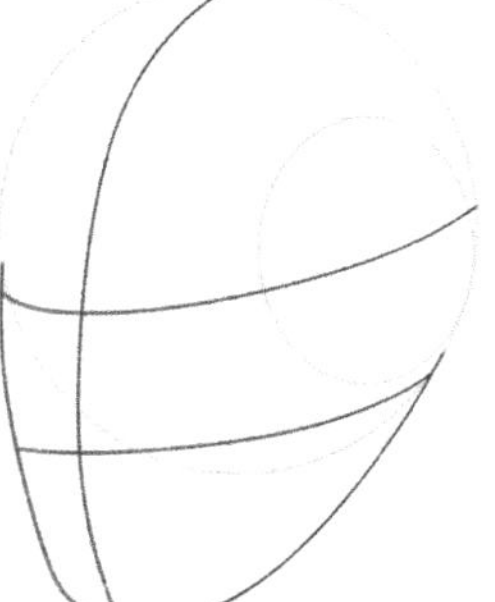

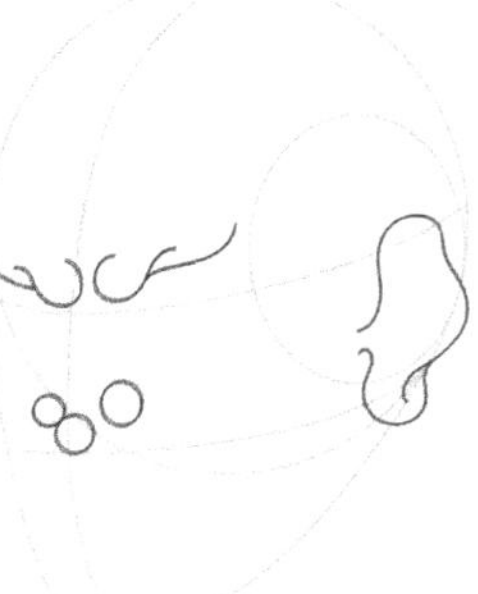

04

05

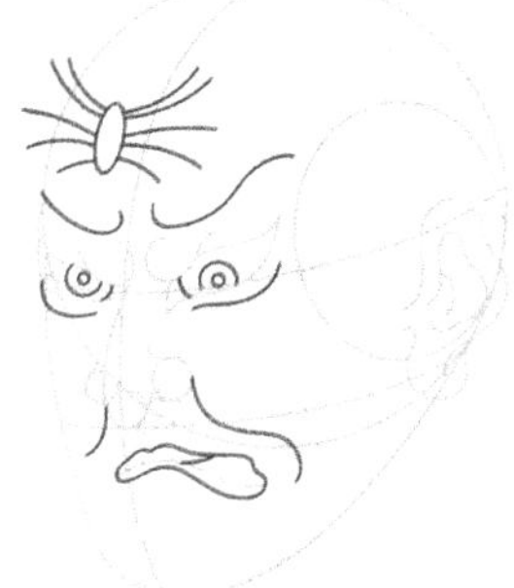

06

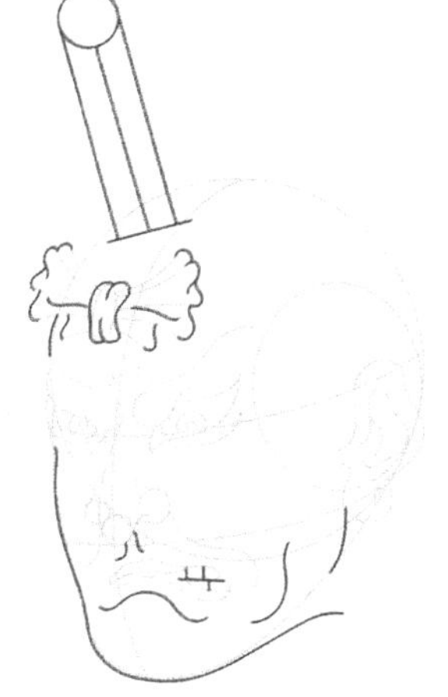

07

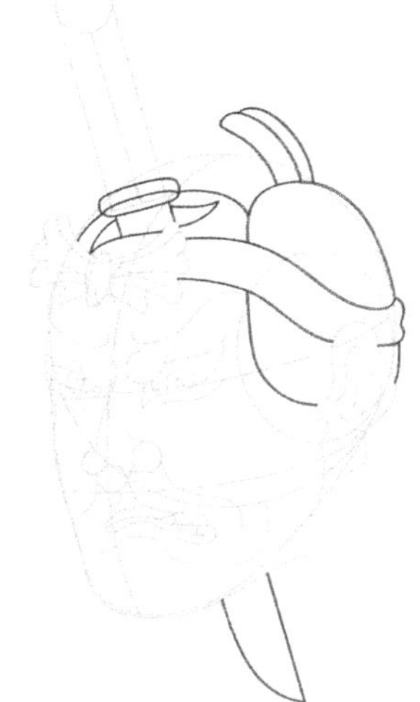

08

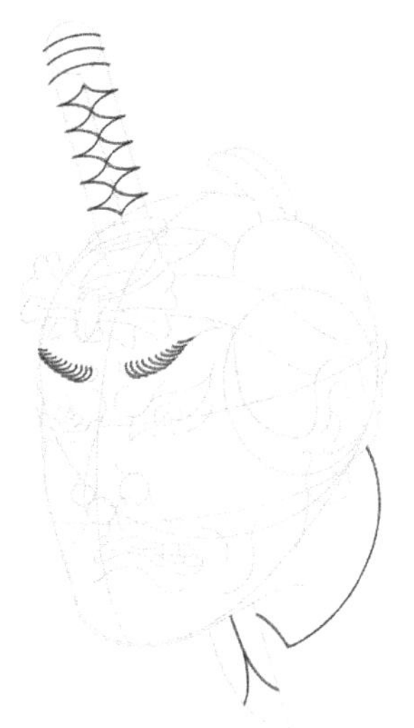

09

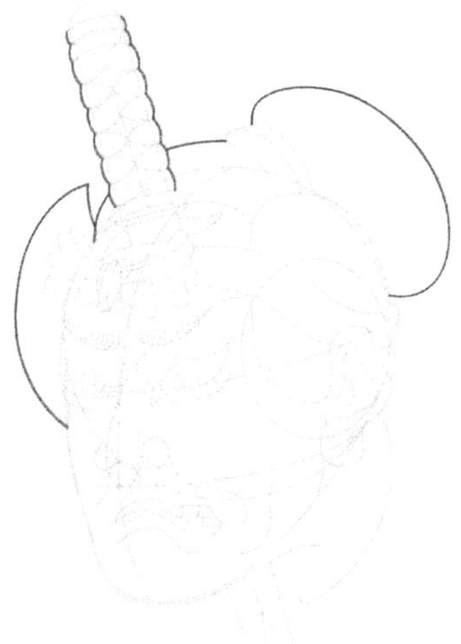

10

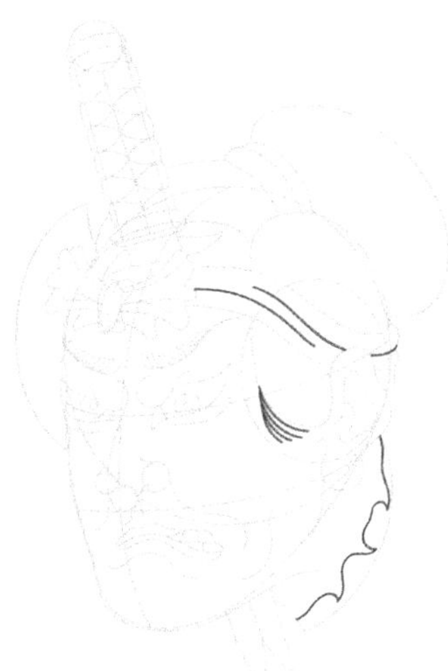

11

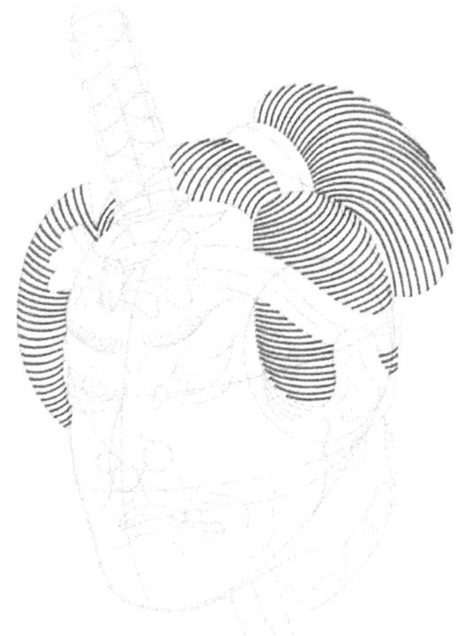

12

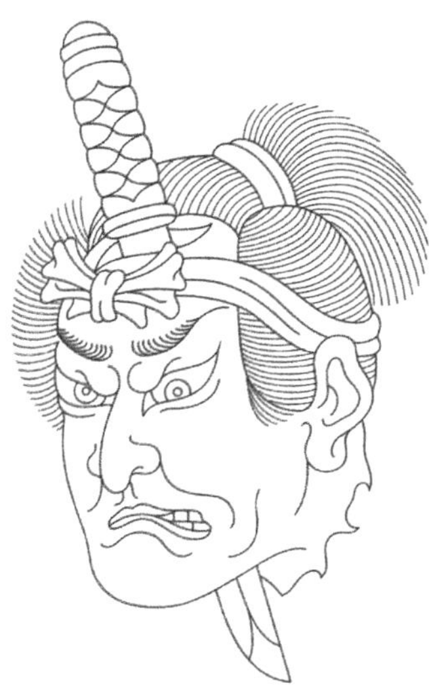

WOMAN-SPIDER JOROGUMO

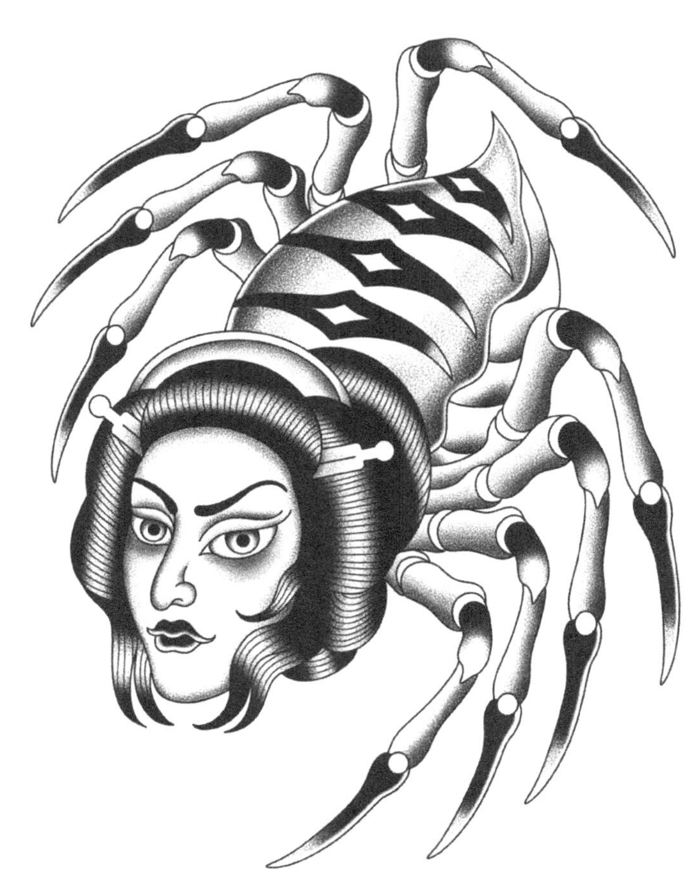

A Jorogumo is a dangerous spider-like spirit that can shapeshift into a beautiful woman. A tattoo could represent deception, seduction and the risks of love at first sight.

01

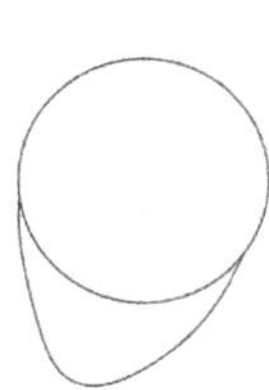

02

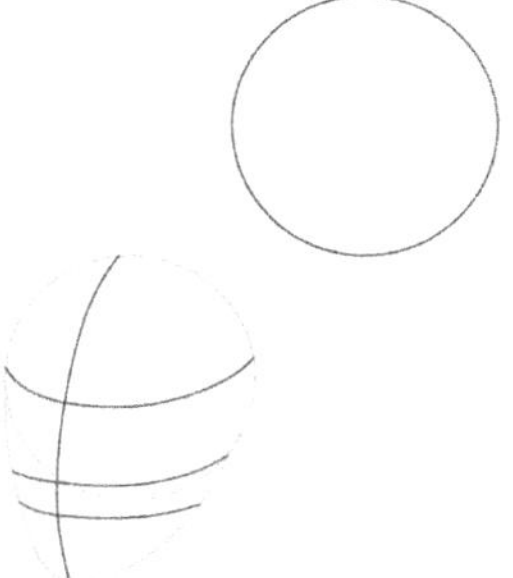

03

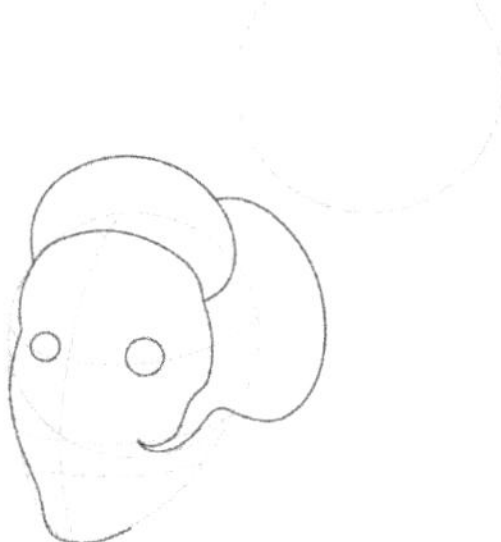

04

05

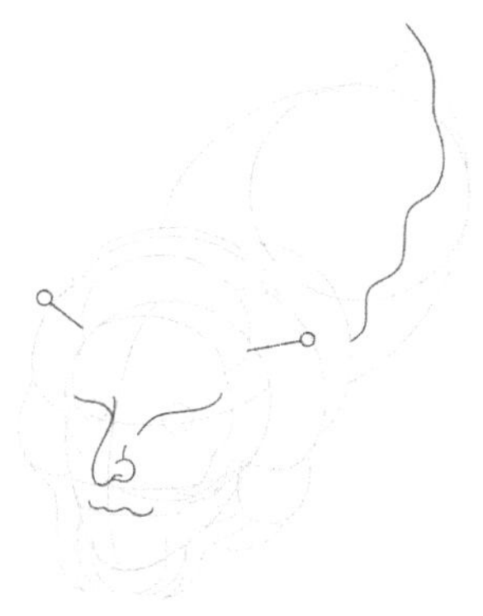

06

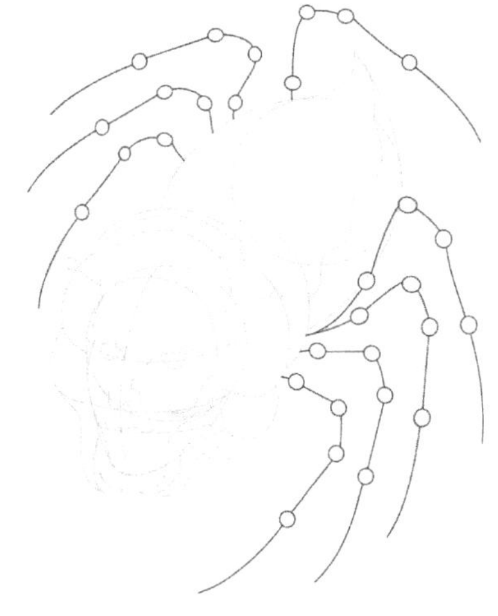

07

08

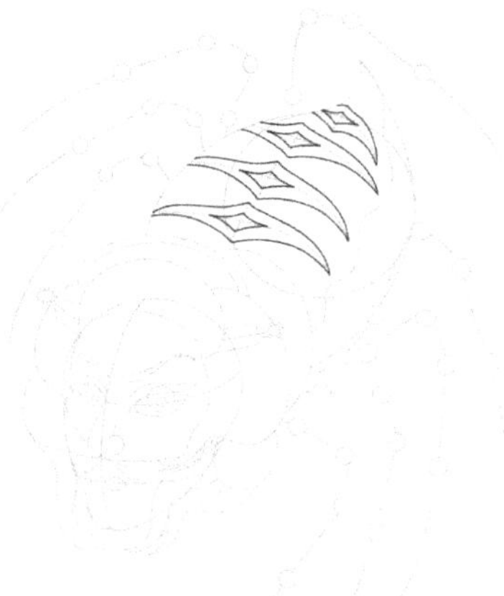

09

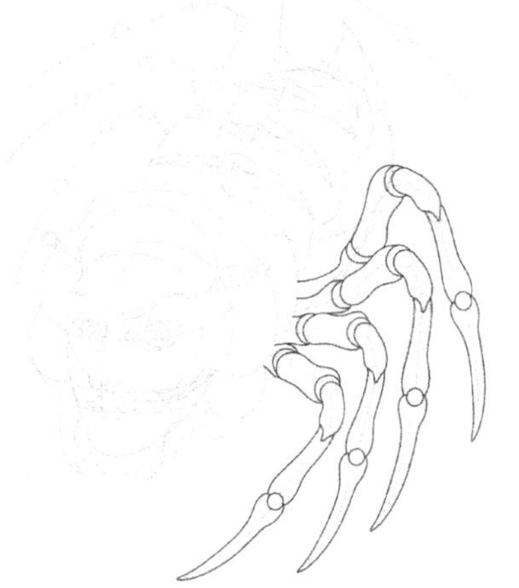

10

11

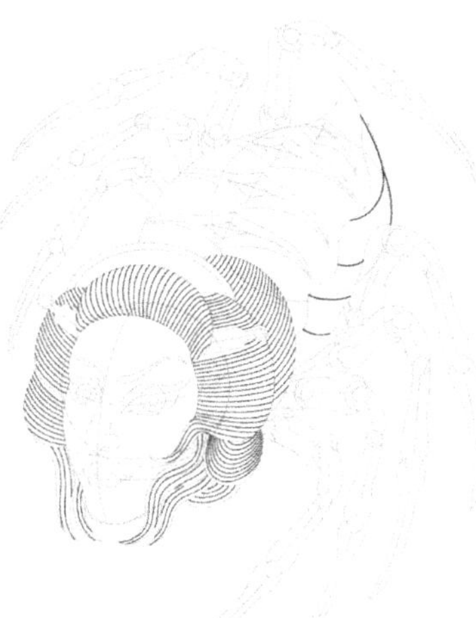

12

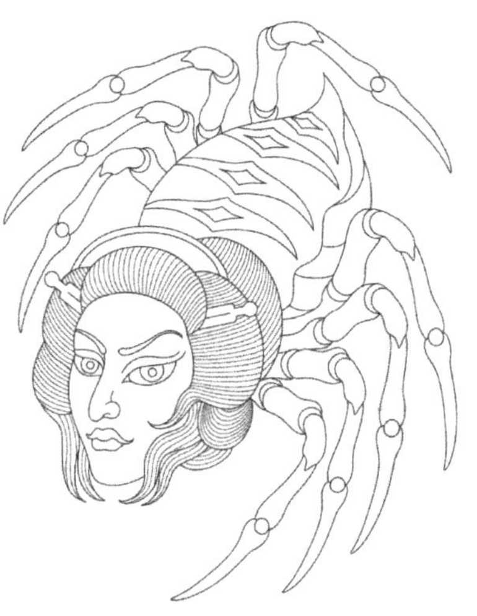

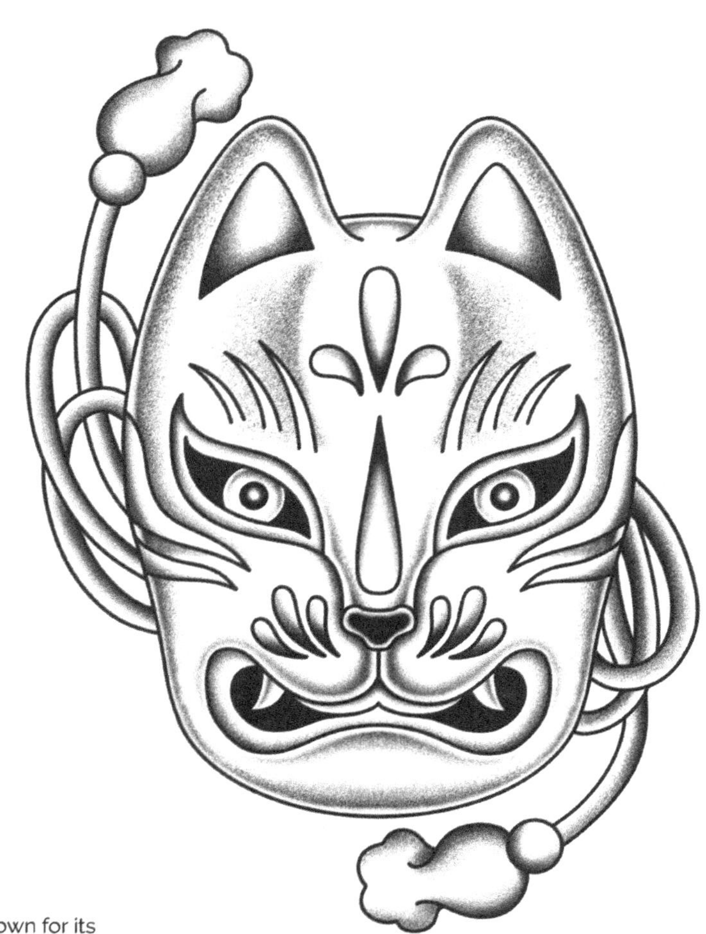

FOX SPIRIT
KITSUNE KABUKI MASK

The kitsune is a fox spirit known for its ability to shapeshift, mischievous nature, and other powers such as strength, flight, and pyrokinesis.

01

02

03

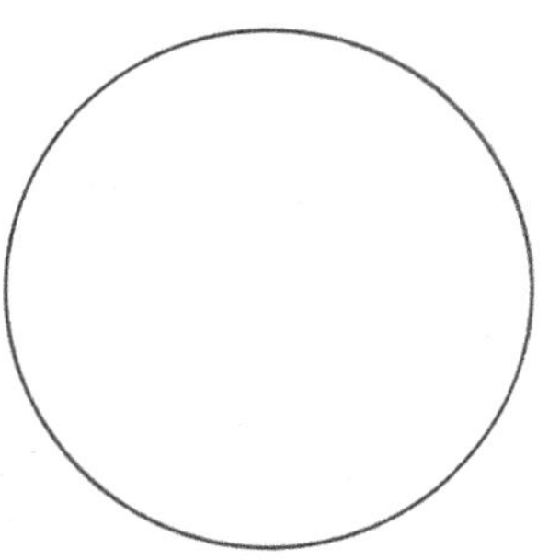

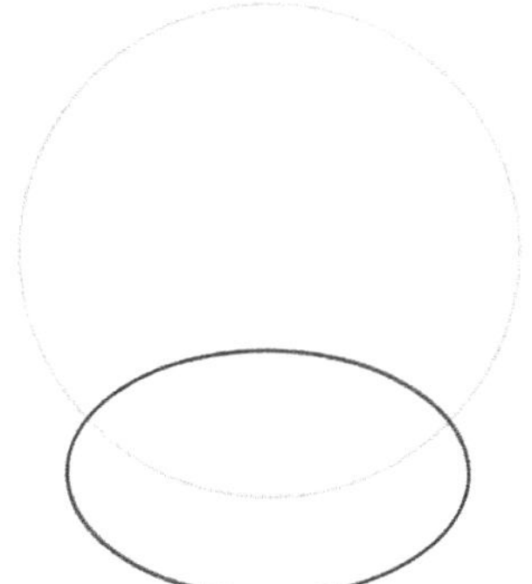

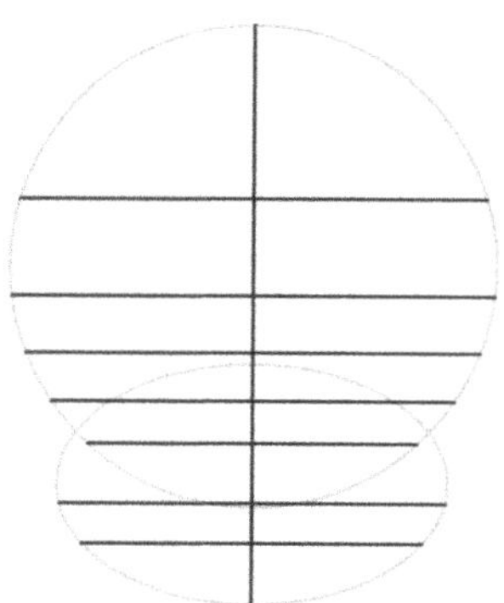

04

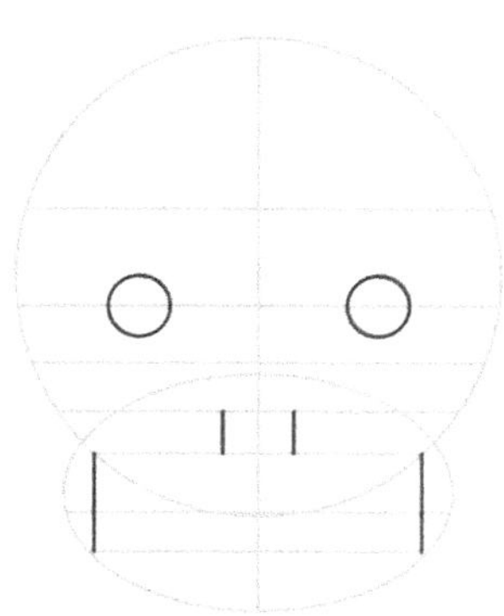

05

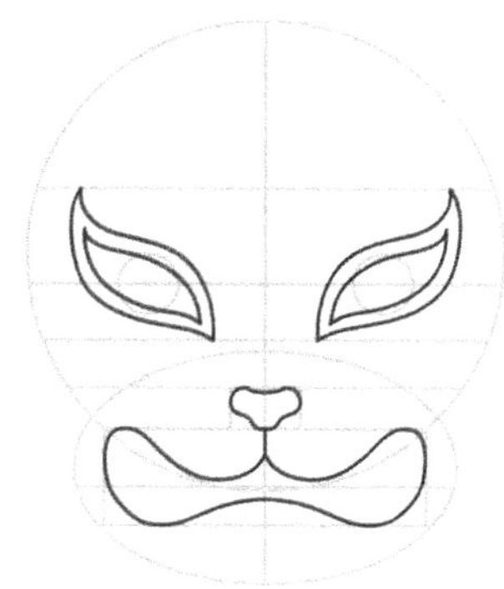

06

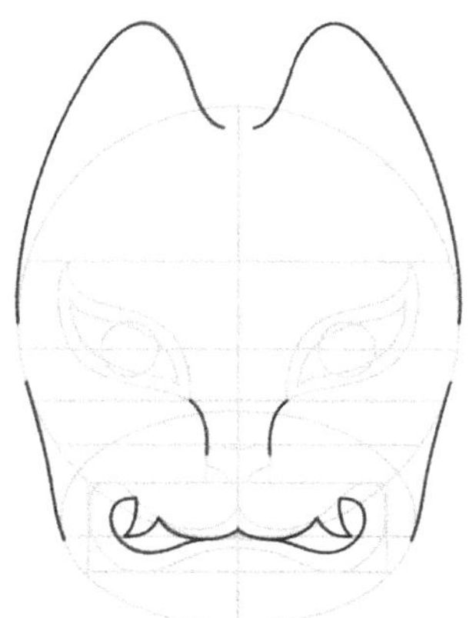

07

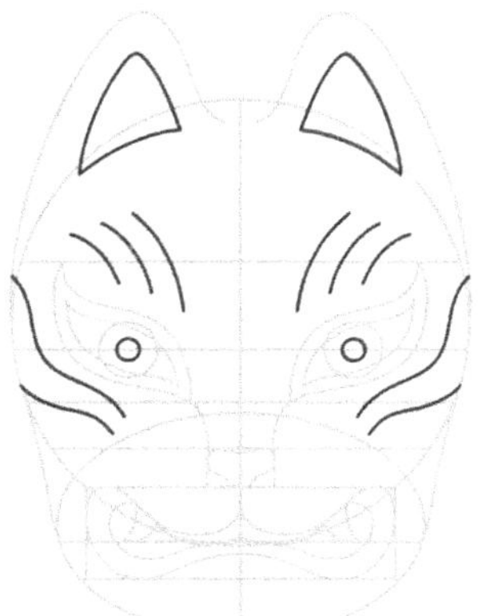

08

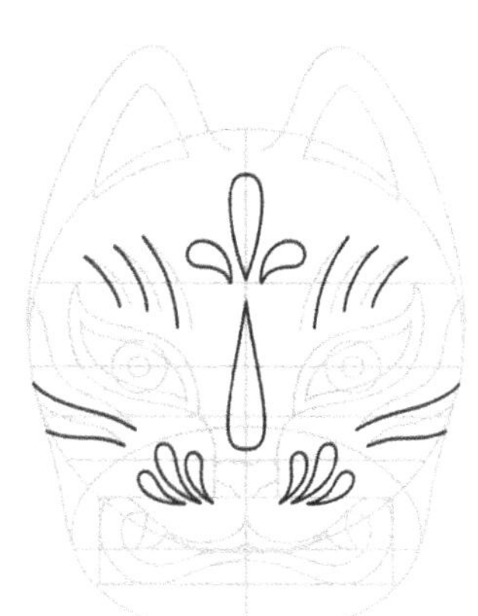

09

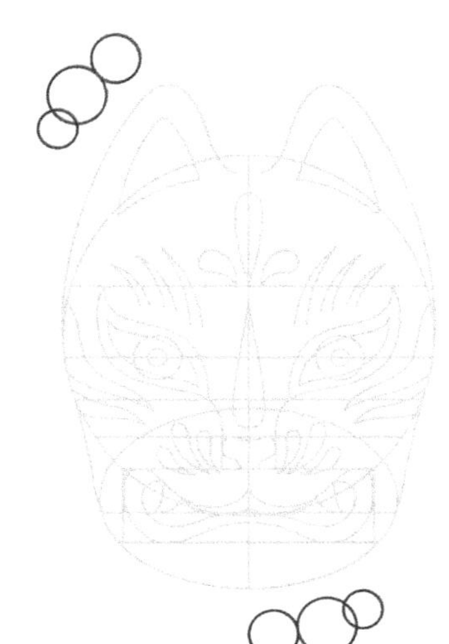

10

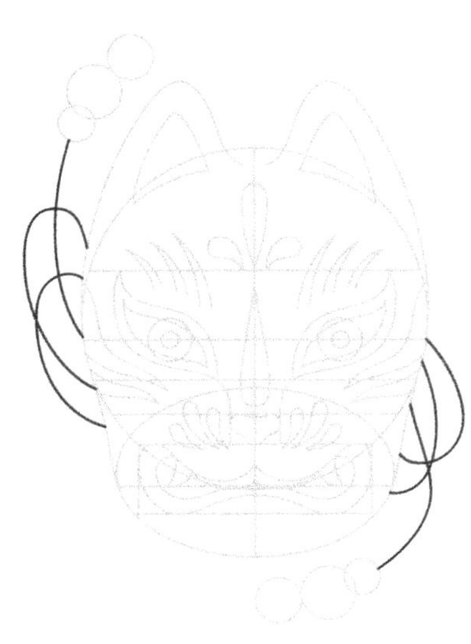

11

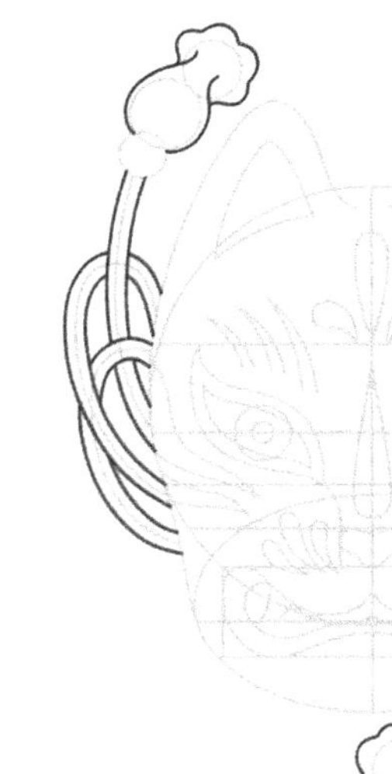

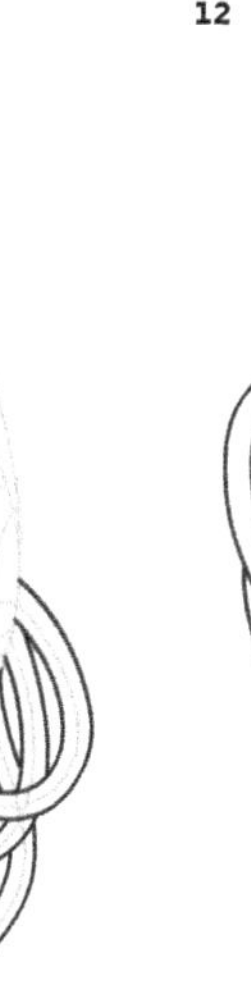

12

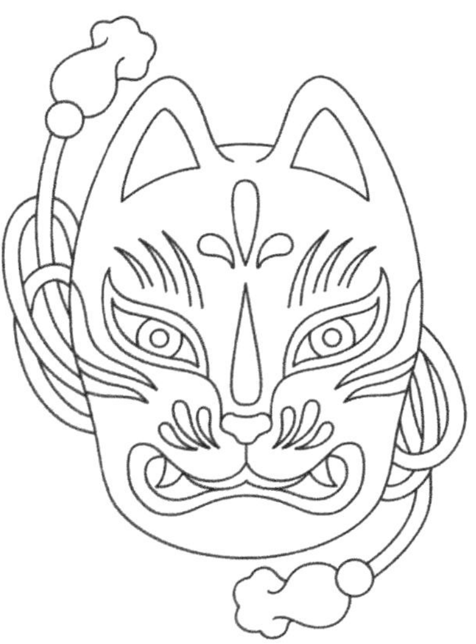

FOX | KITSUNE

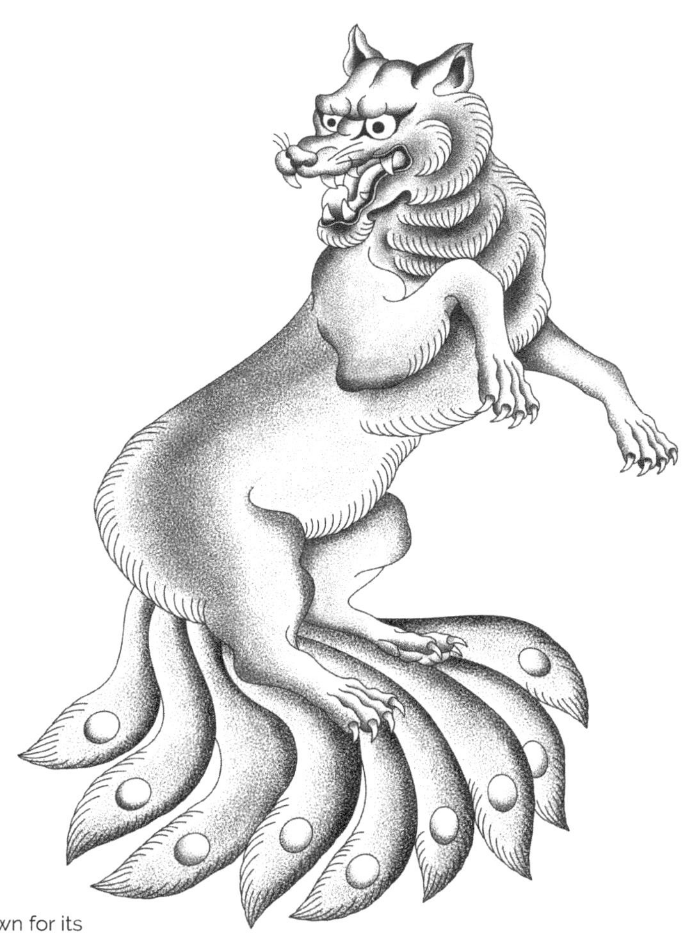

The kitsune is a fox spirit known for its shapeshifting abilities, mischievous nature, and supernatural powers such as strength, flight, and control over fire.

01

02

03

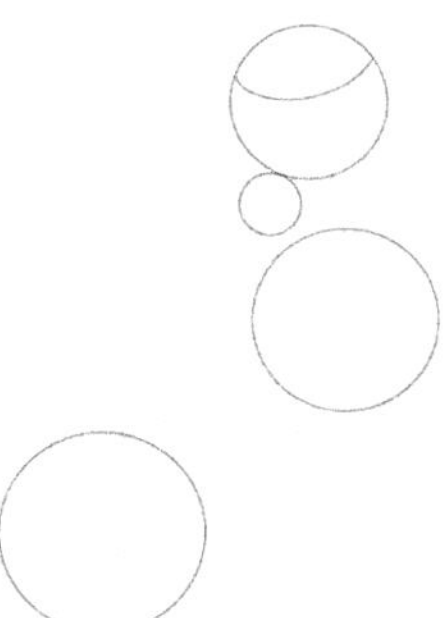

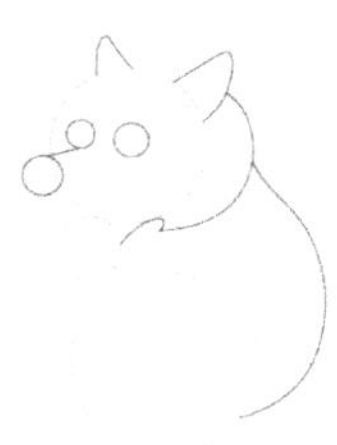

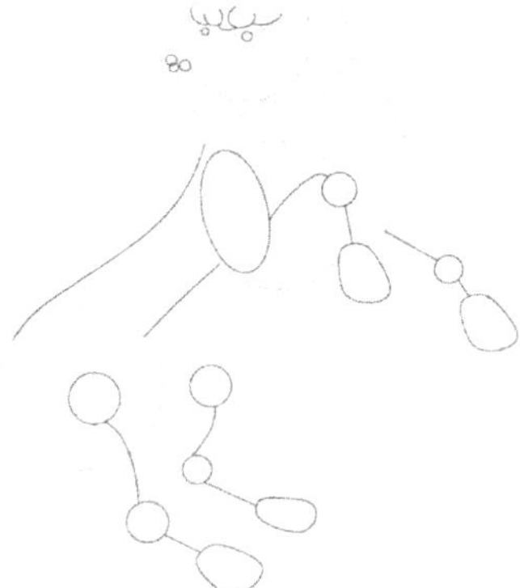

04

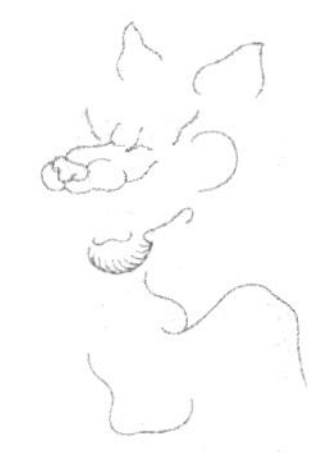

05

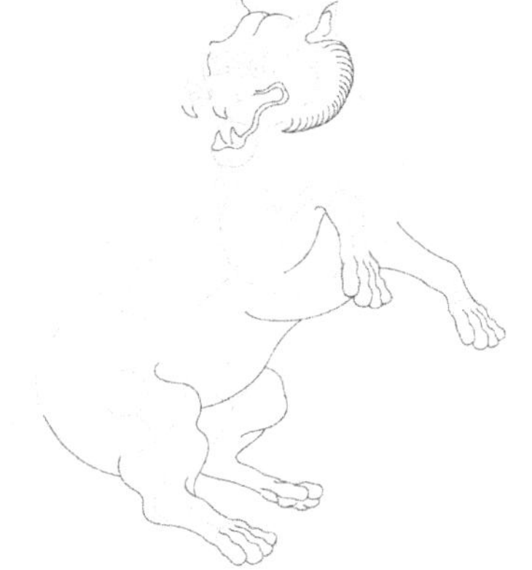

06

07

08

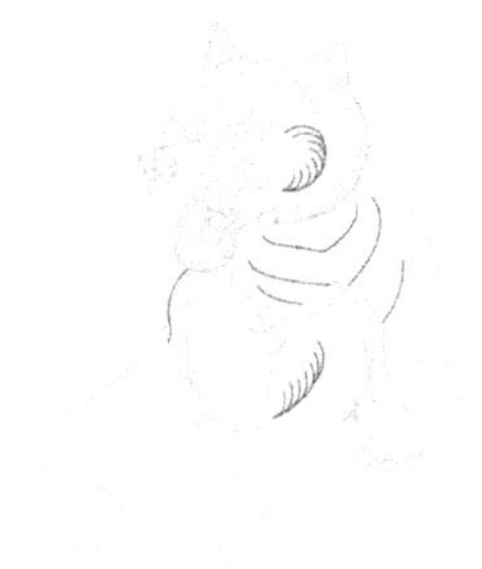

09

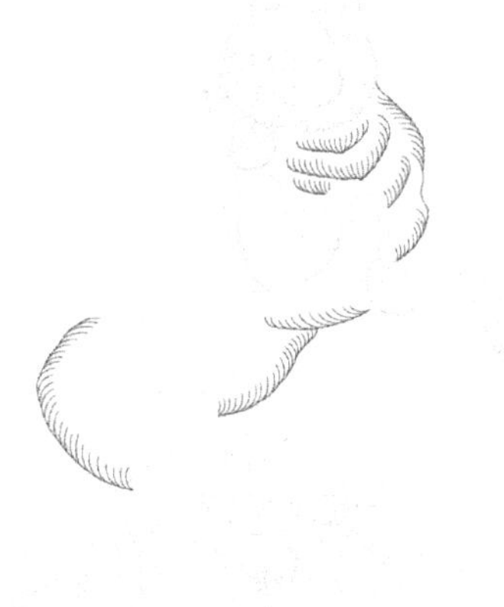

10

11

12

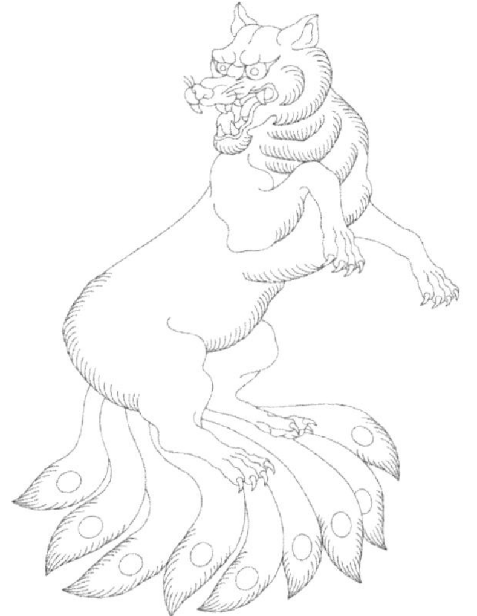

DARUMA DOLL

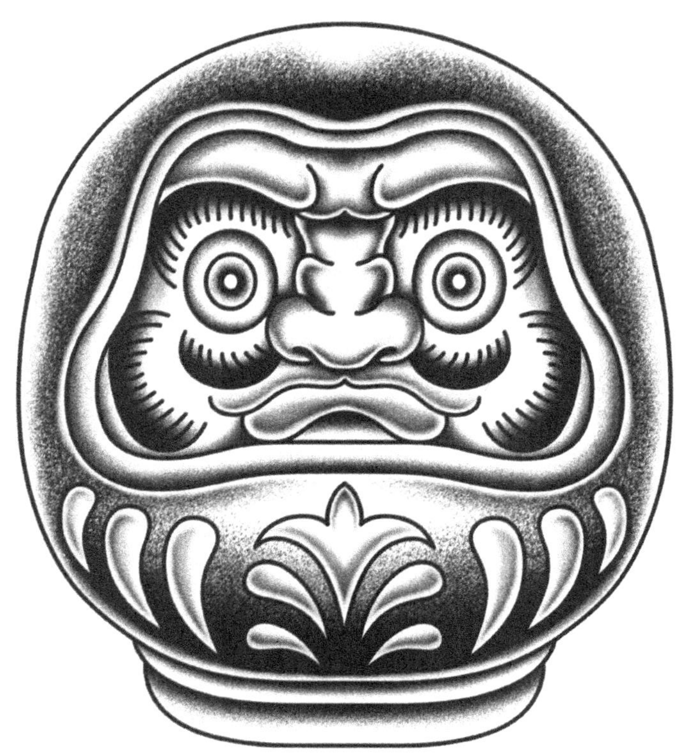

The Daruma doll, inspired by the Japanese good-luck charm, often symbolises perseverance, resilience, and pursuing goals. It is inspired by the Buddhist monk Bodhidharma.

01   02   03

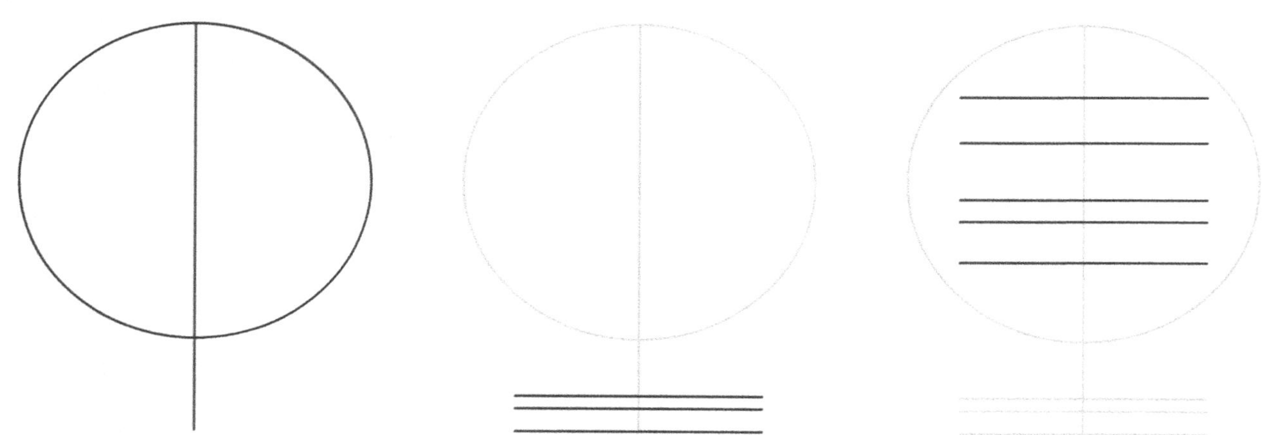

04

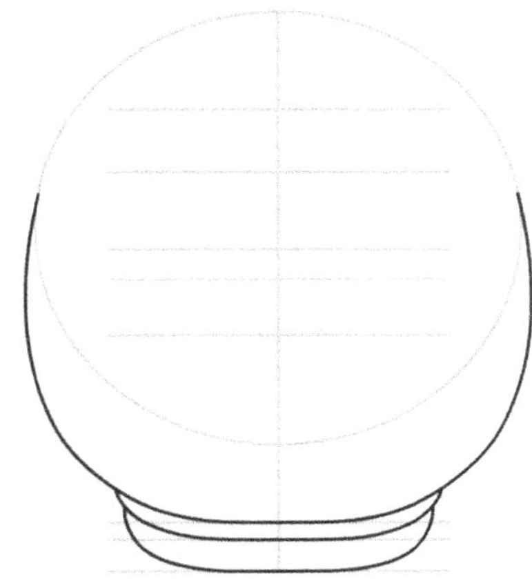

05

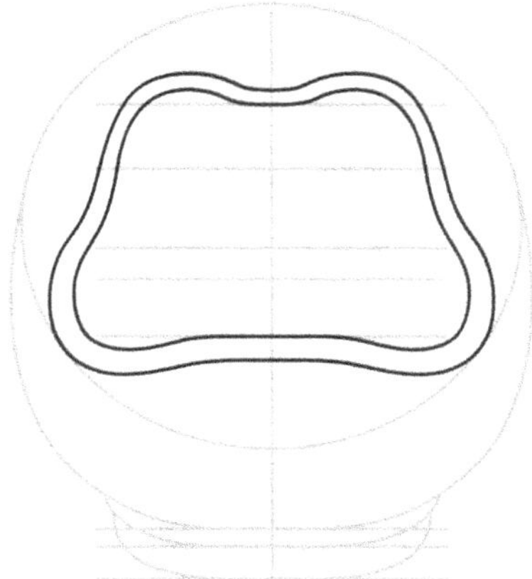

06

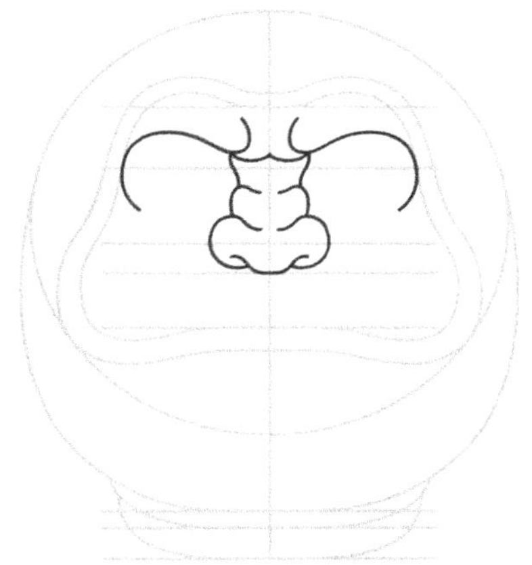

07

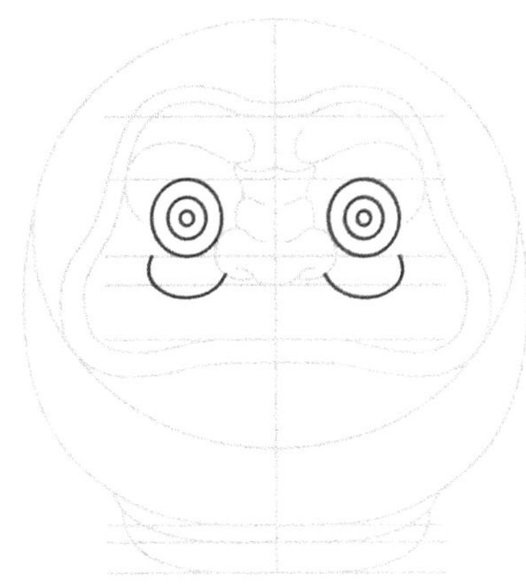

08

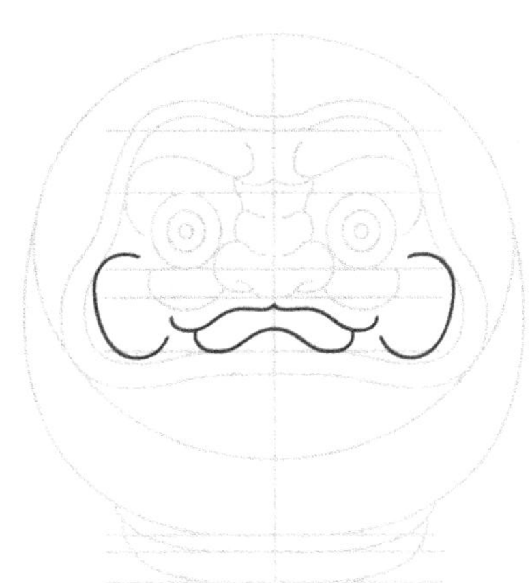

09

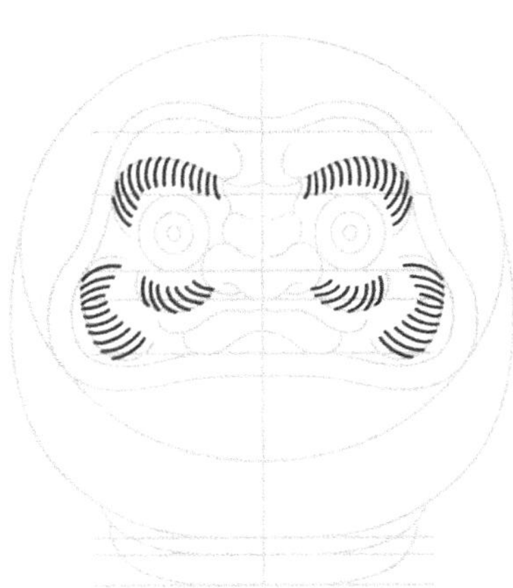

10

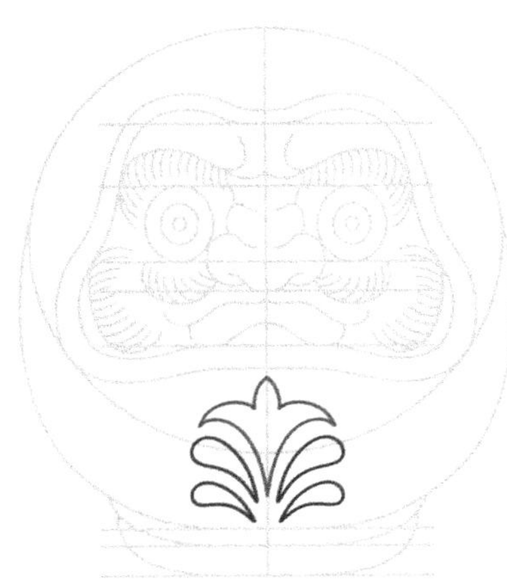

11

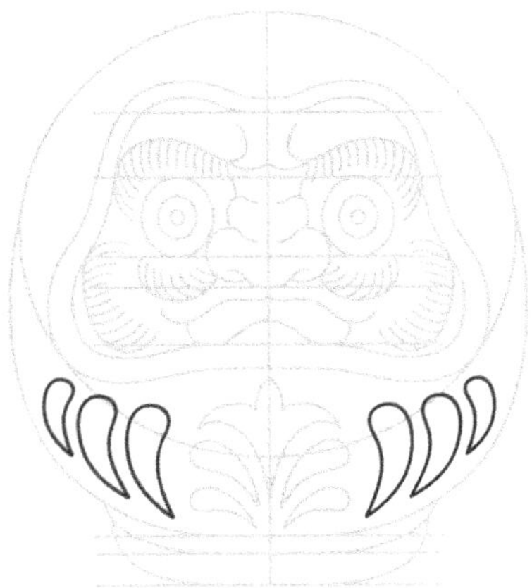

12

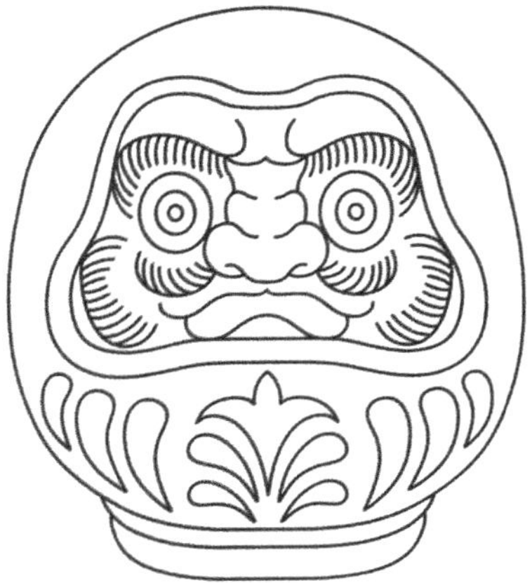

BECKONING CAT MANEKI-NEKO

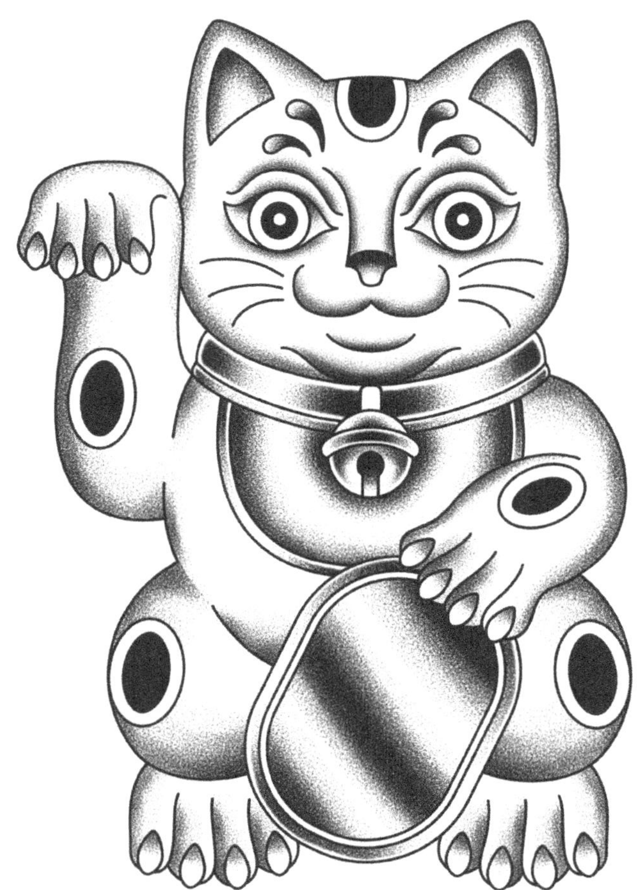

A Maneki-neko tattoo represents good luck, fortune, and prosperity.

01

02

03

04
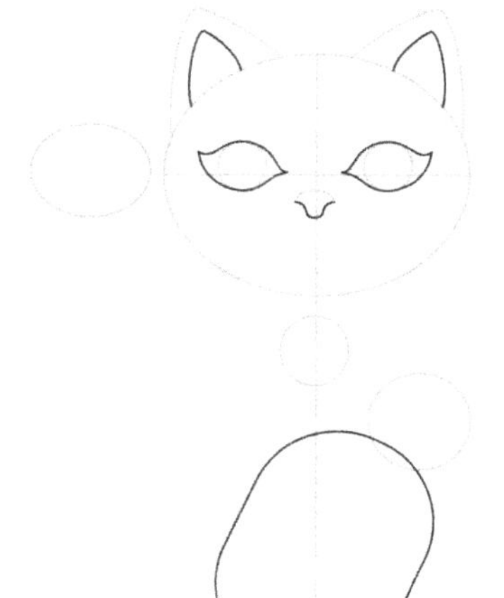

05
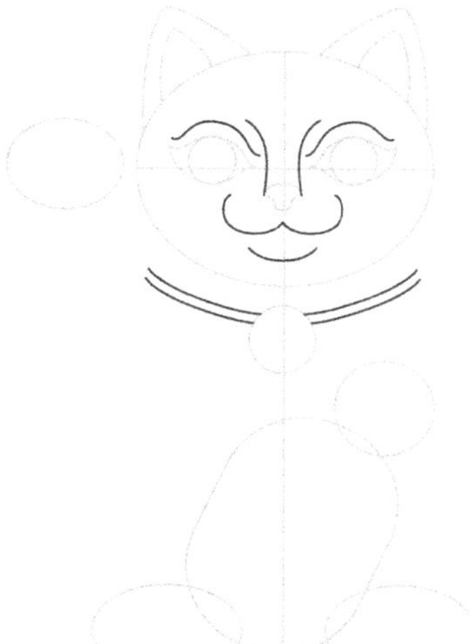

06
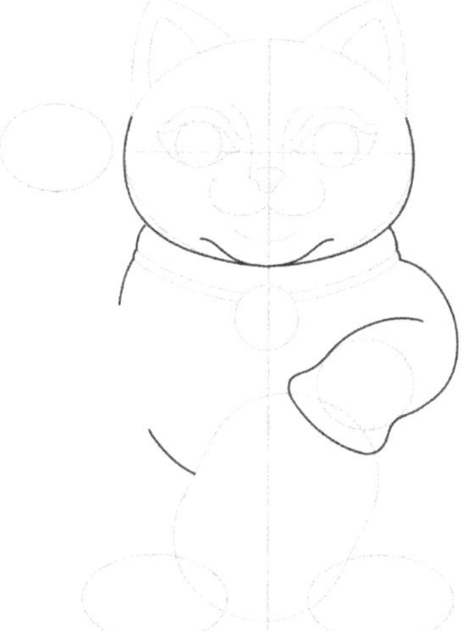

07
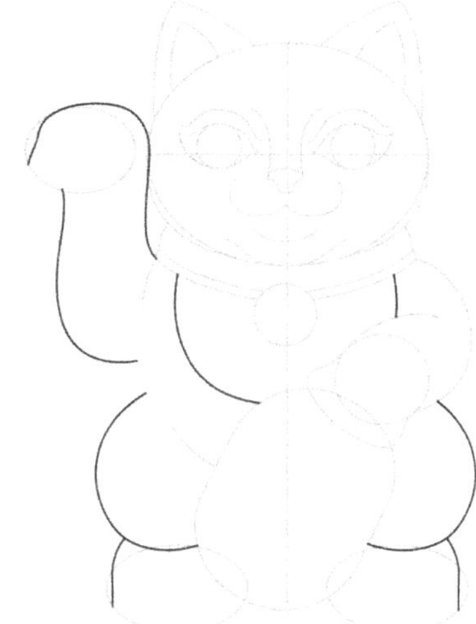

08
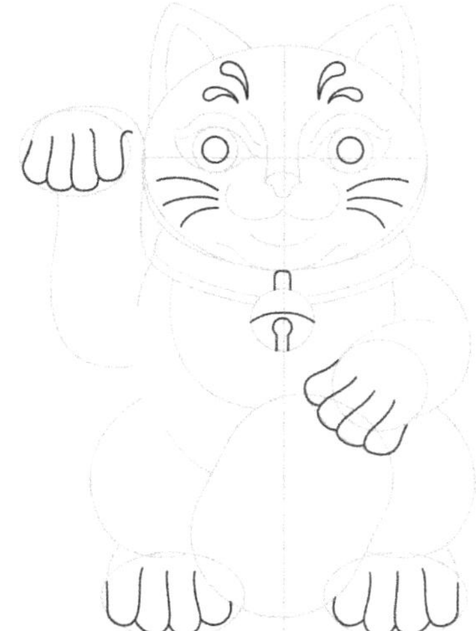

09
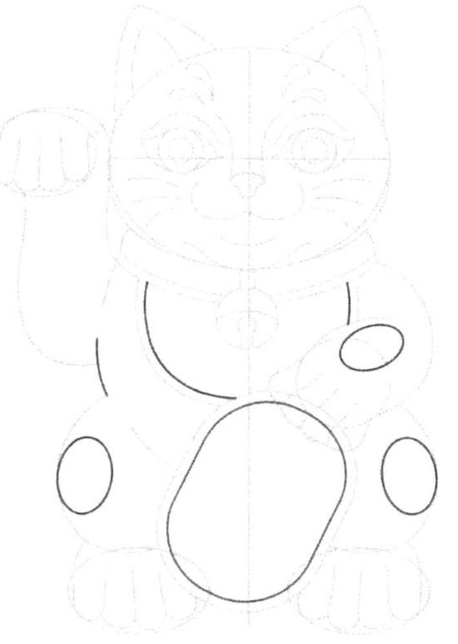

10
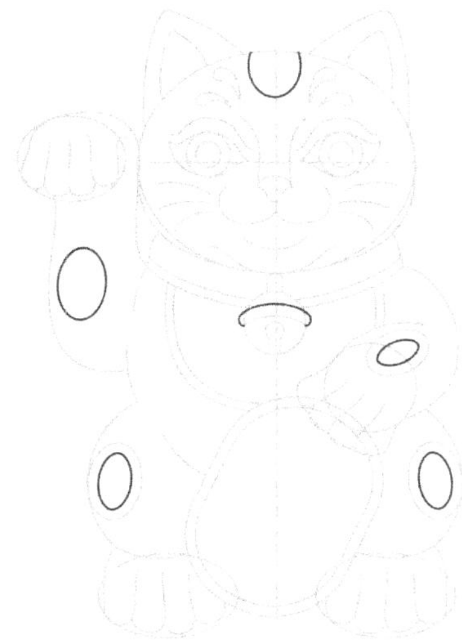

11
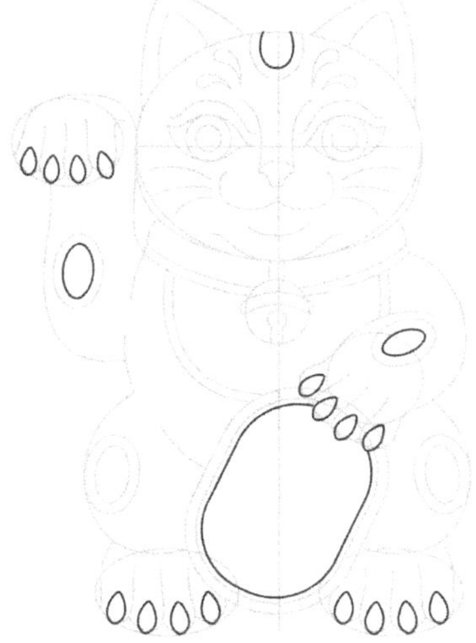

12
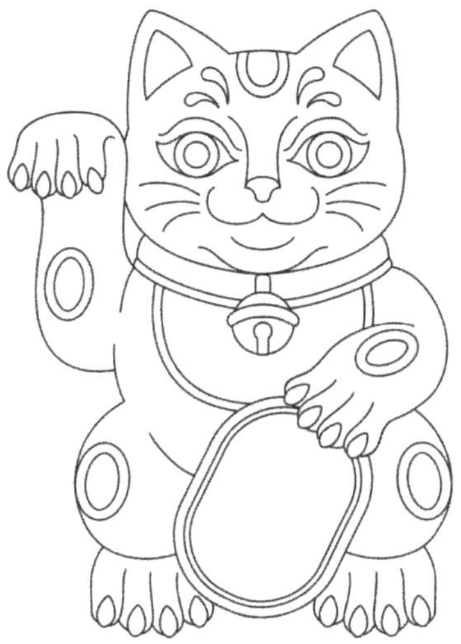

JAPANESE TATTOOS

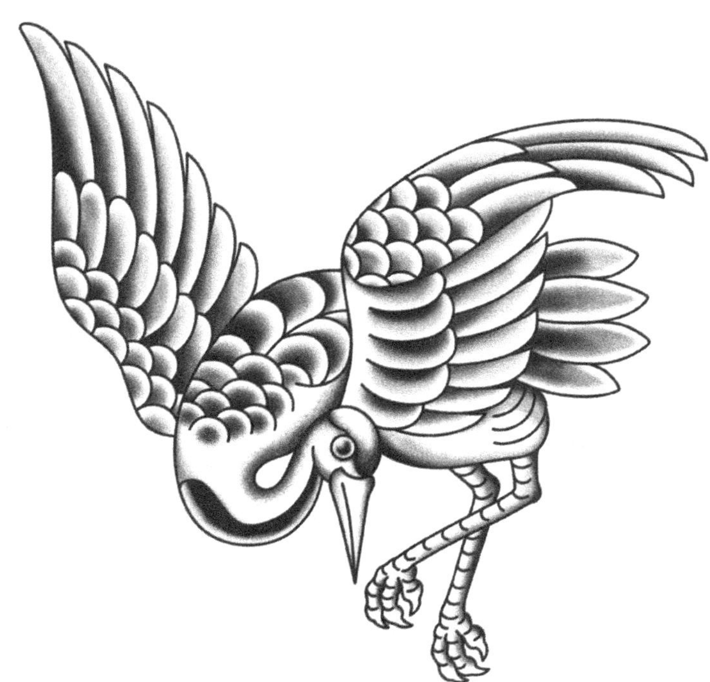

CRANE | TSURU

A Japanese crane tattoo symbolises good fortune, longevity, fidelity, and peace. Often called the 'bird of happiness', the crane holds a deep cultural significance.

01

02

03

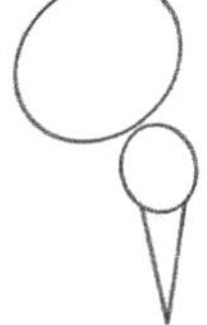

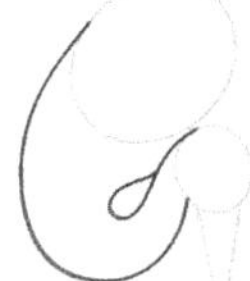

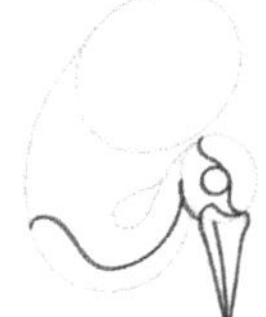

04

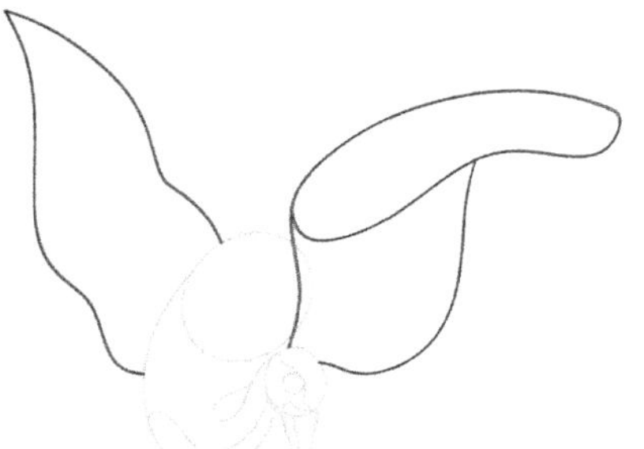

05

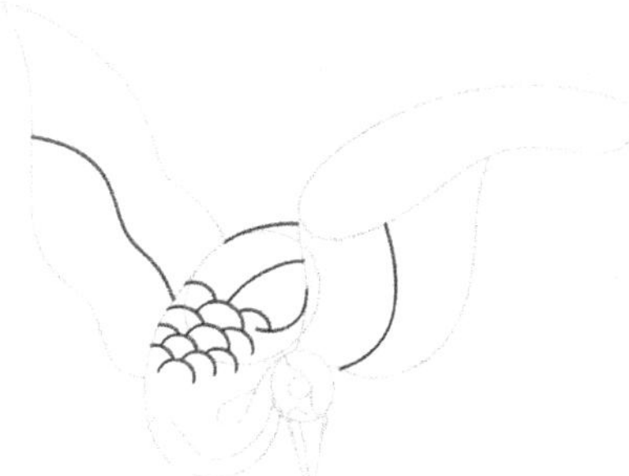

06

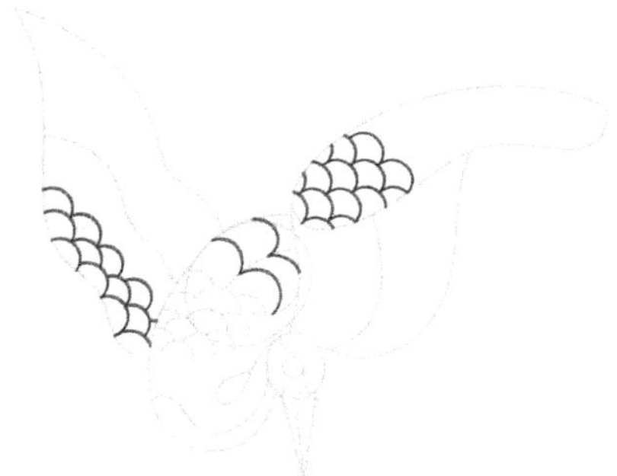

07

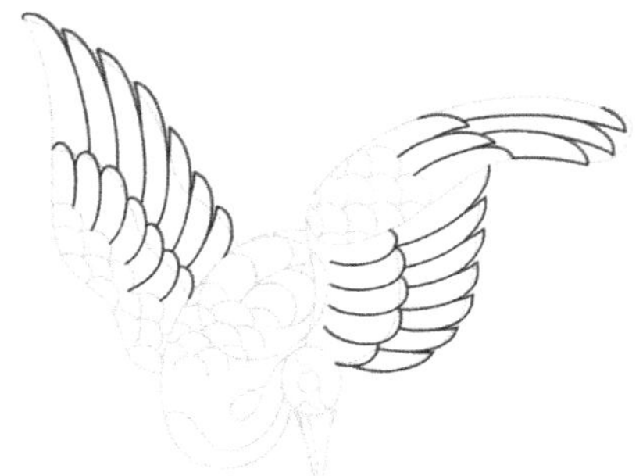

08

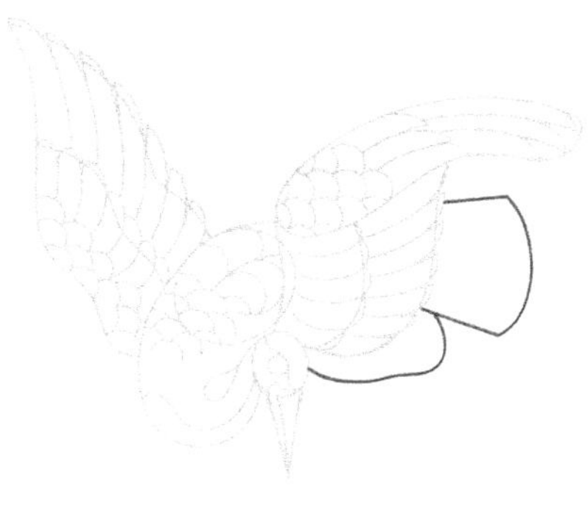

09

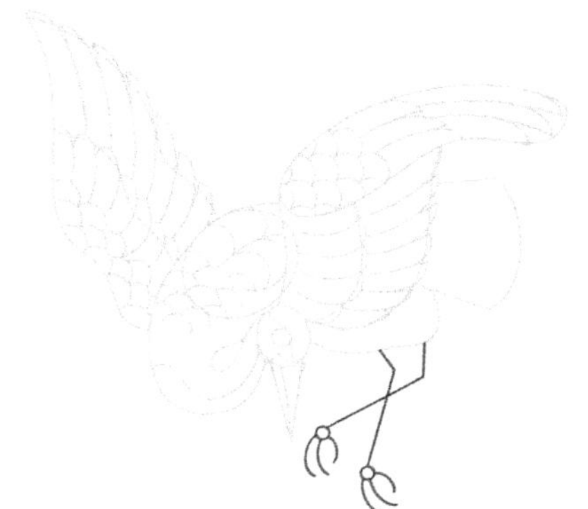

10

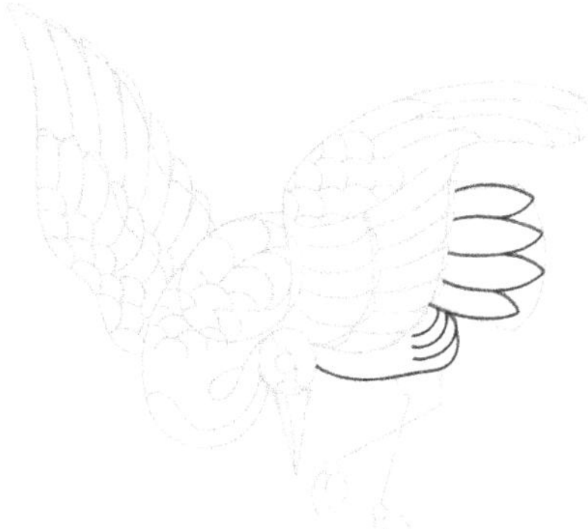

11

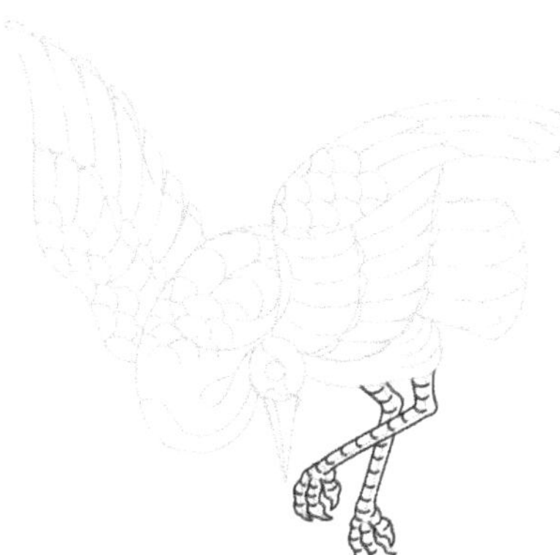

12

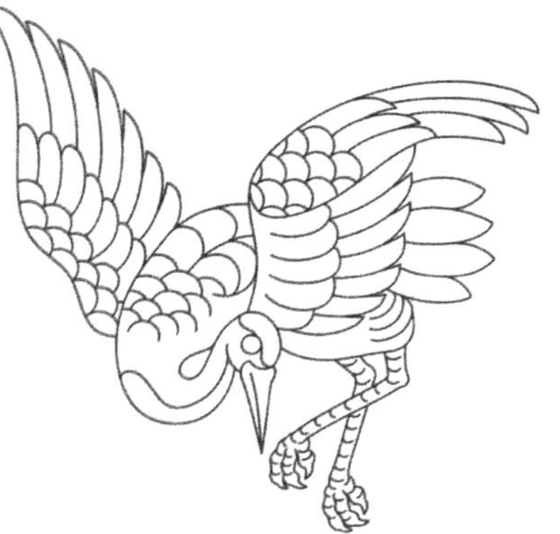

ROOSTER | ONDORI

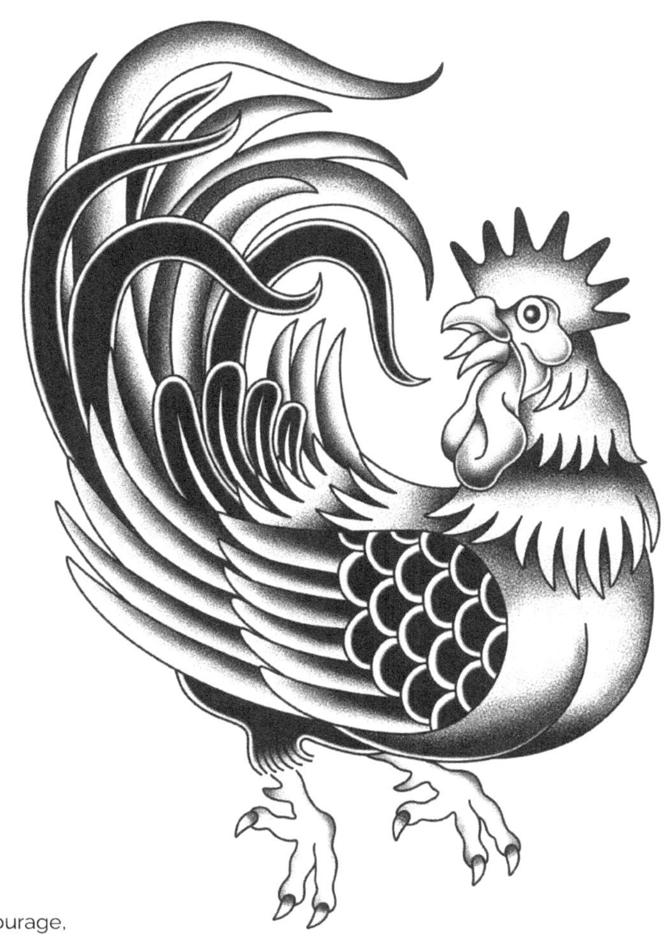

A rooster tattoo symbolises courage, strength, a fighting spirit, and beauty, representing the rooster's bold, spirited nature and its readiness to face danger.

01

02

03

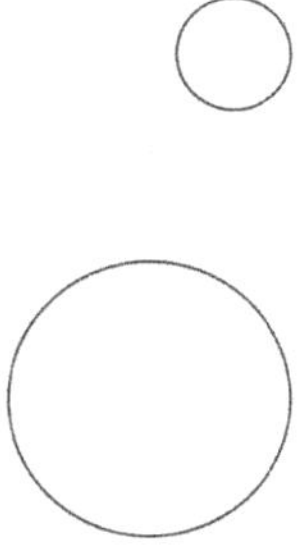

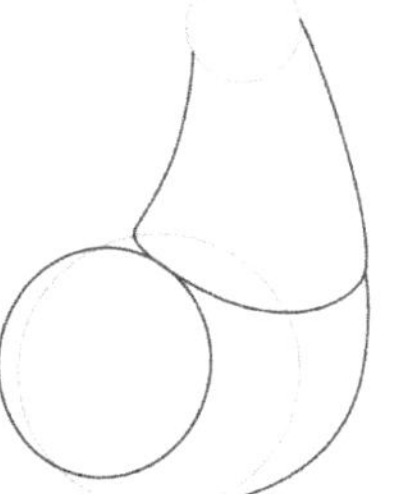

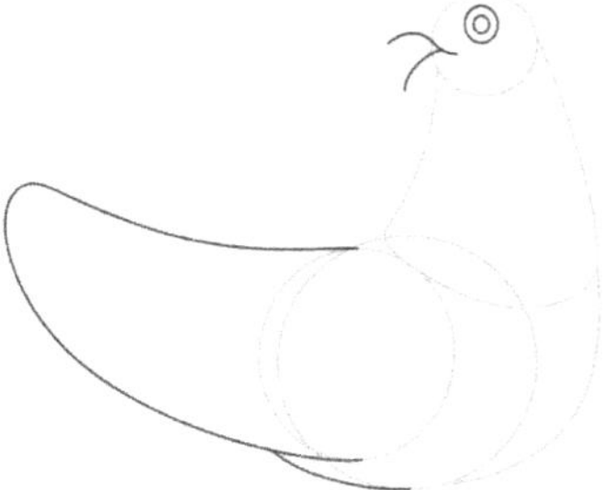

04

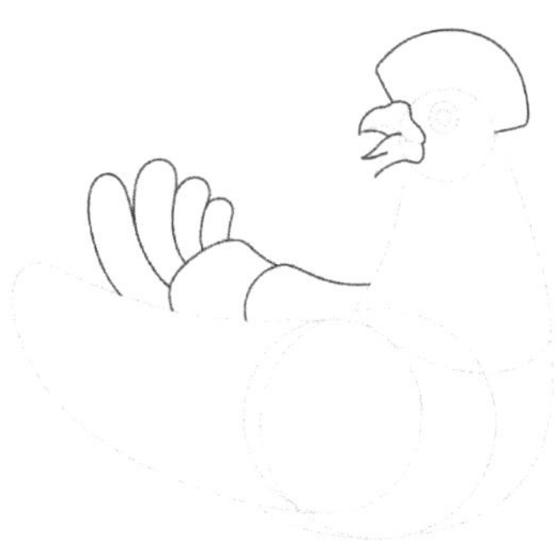

05

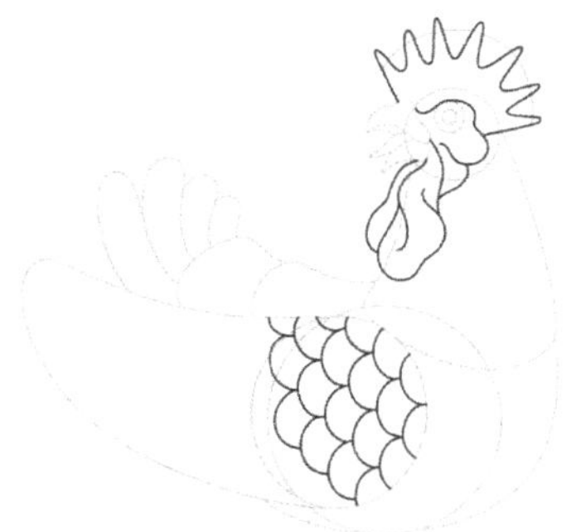

06

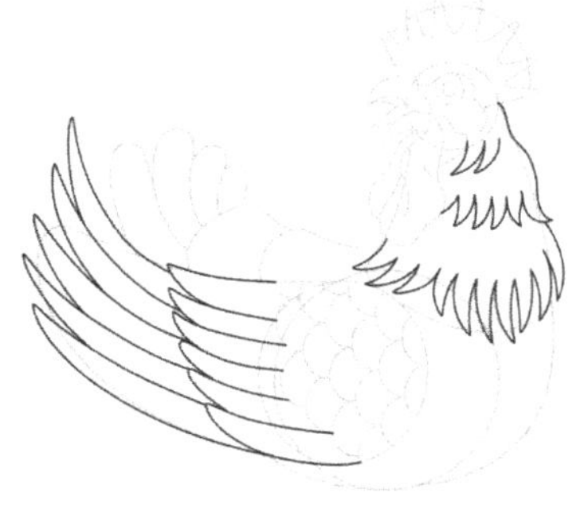

07

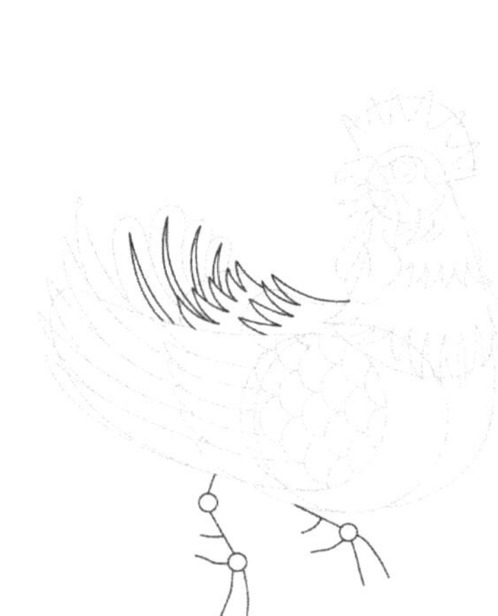

08

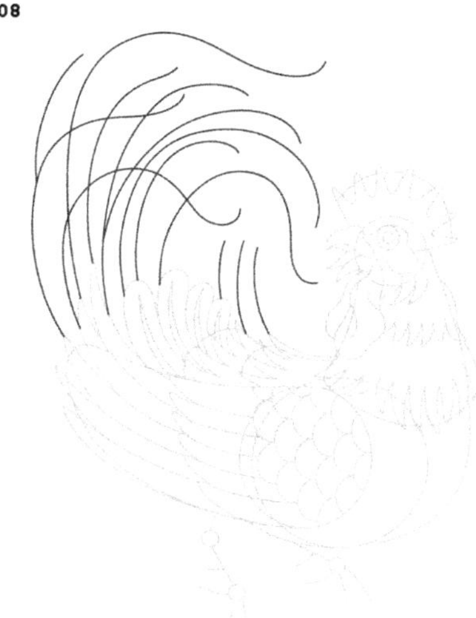

09

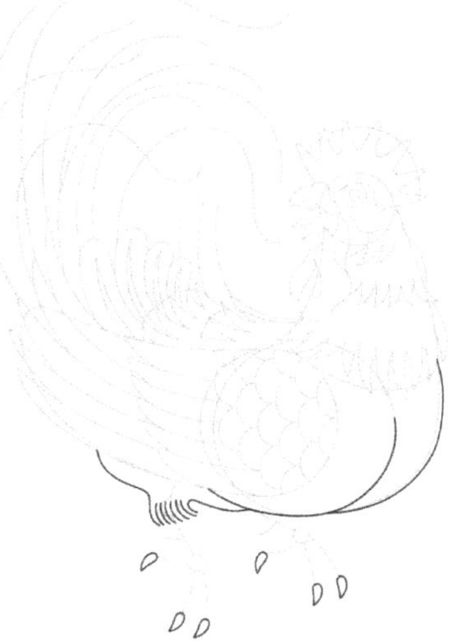

10

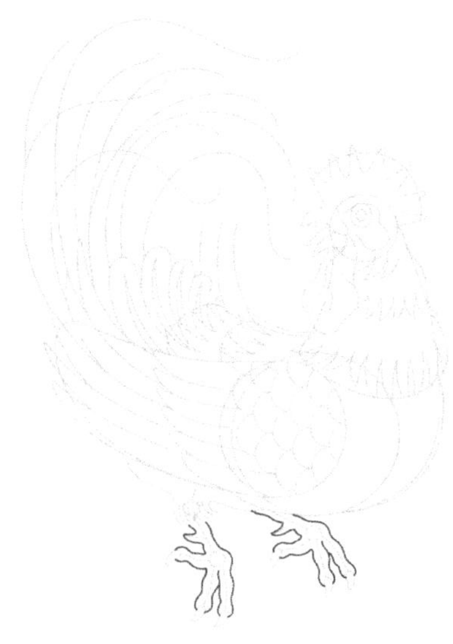

11

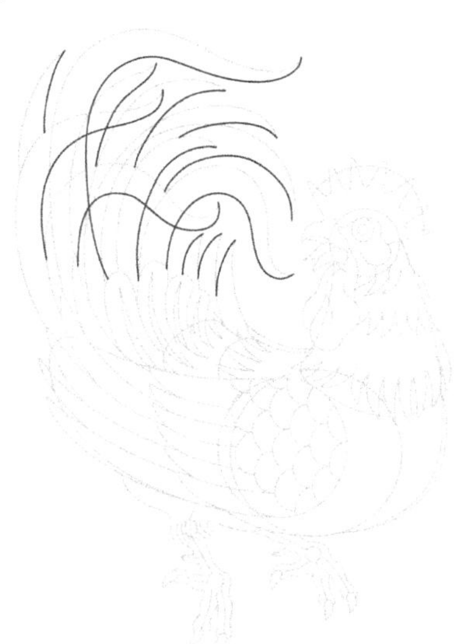

12

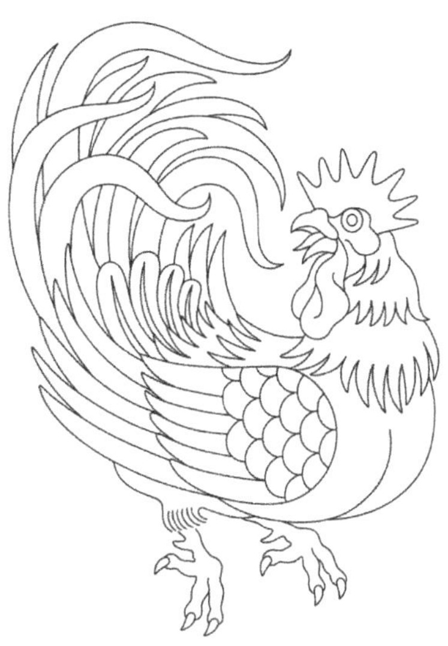

JAPANESE TATTOOS

SAMURAI CRAB HEIKEGAN

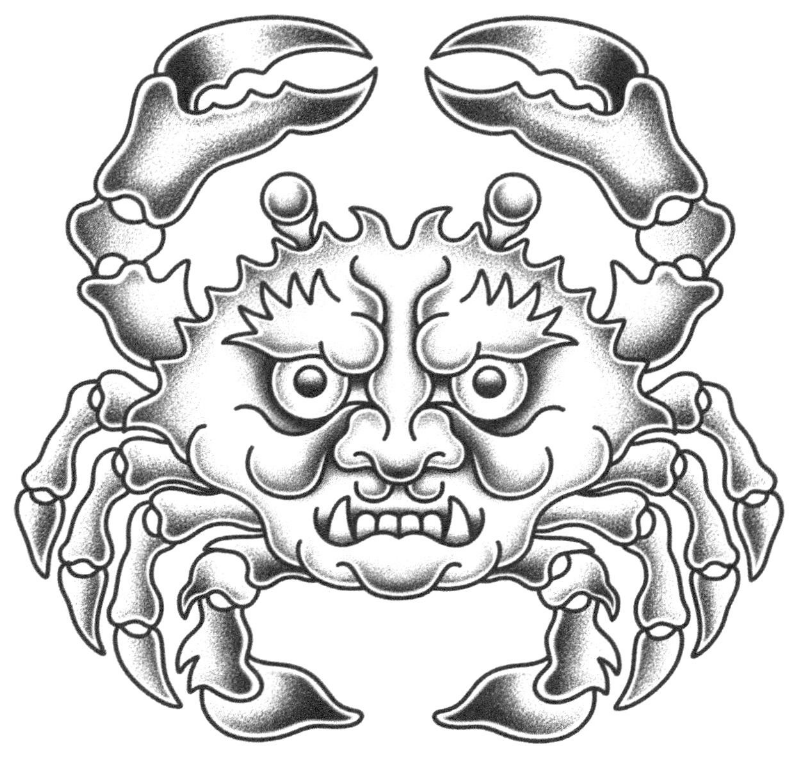

A samurai crab's shell looks like a warrior's face. Said to be fallen samurai, they symbolise courage, longevity, and perseverance. If caught, fishermen return them out of respect.

01

02

03

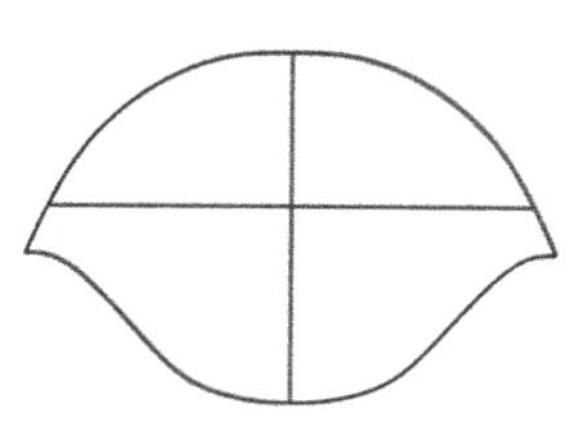

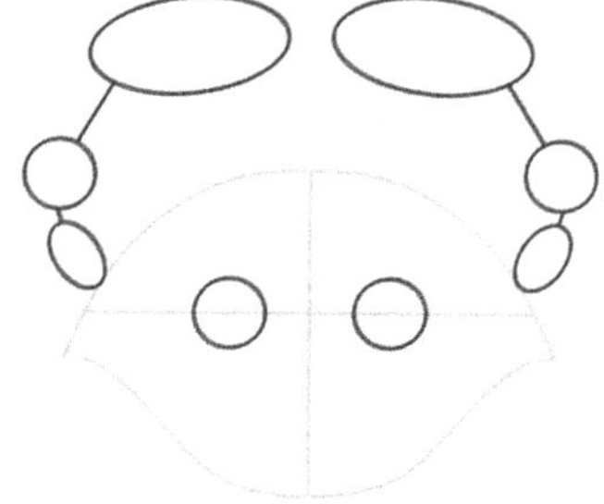

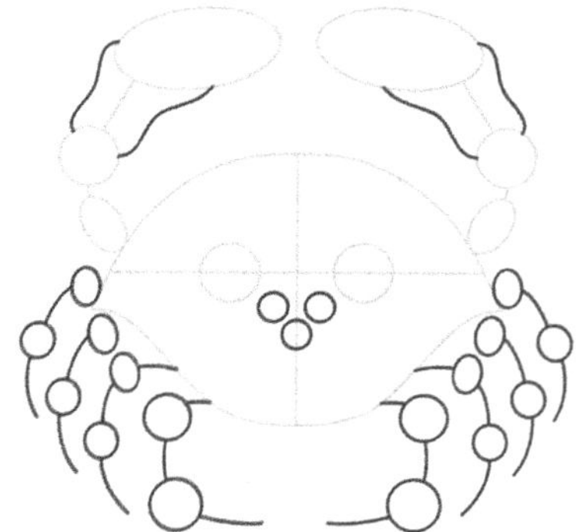

04

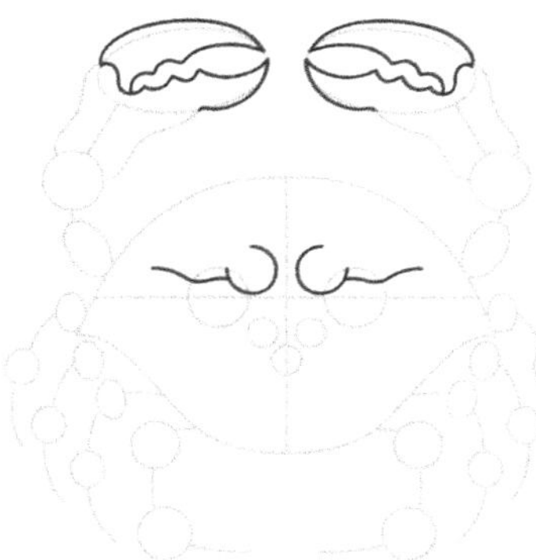

05

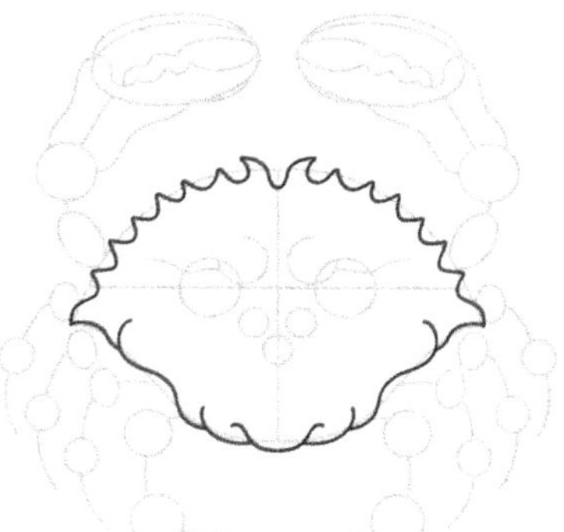

06

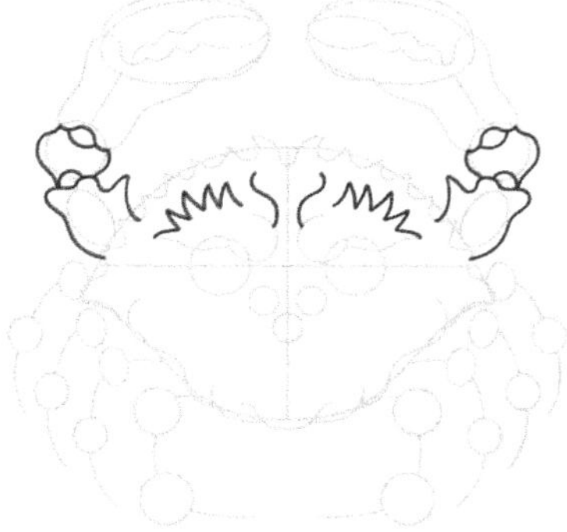

07

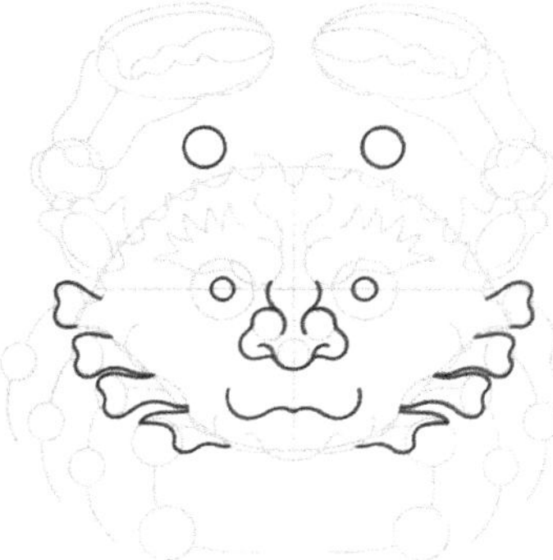

08

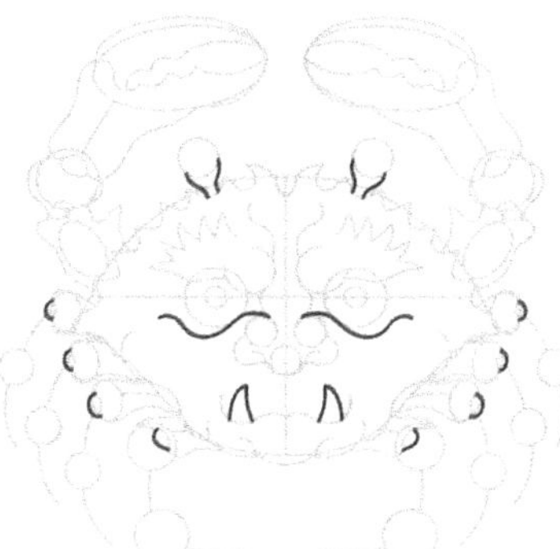

09

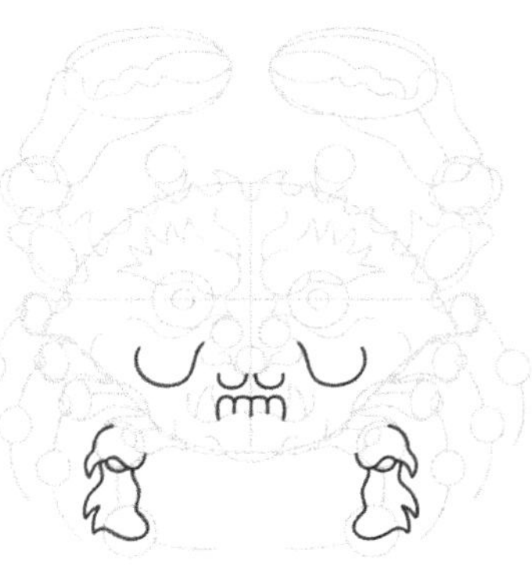

10

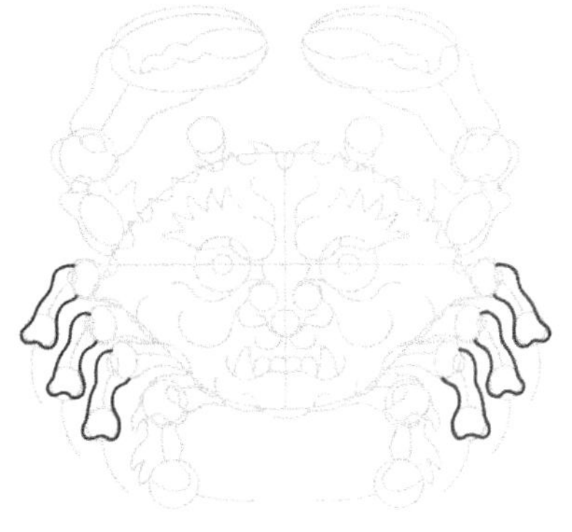

11

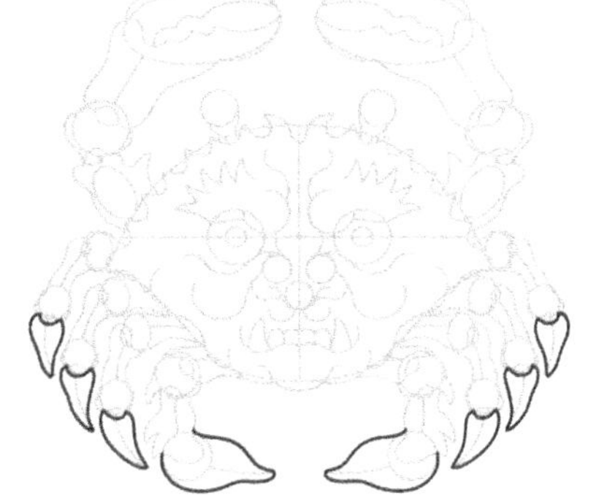

12

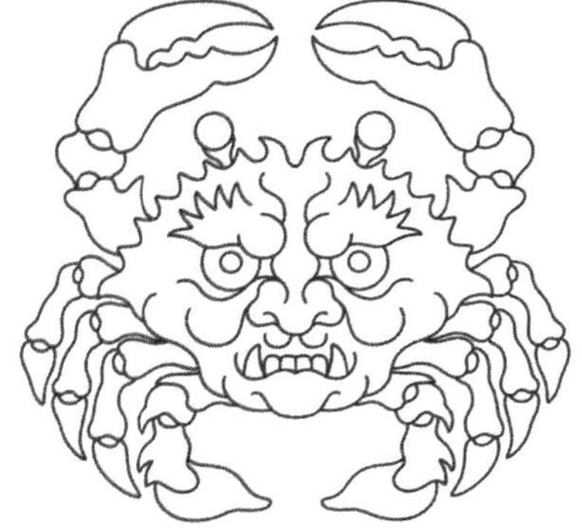

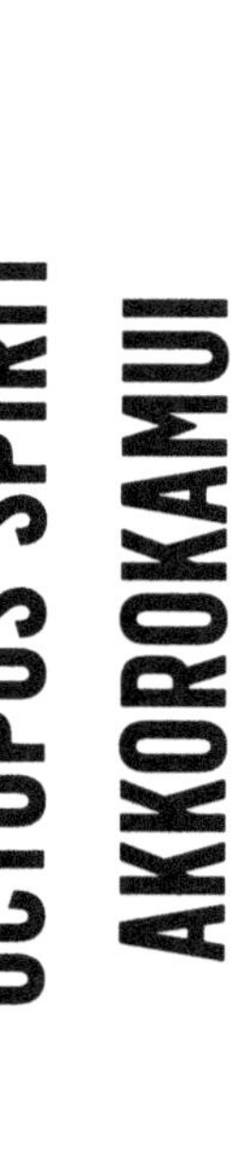

OCTOPUS SPIRIT AKKOROKAMUI

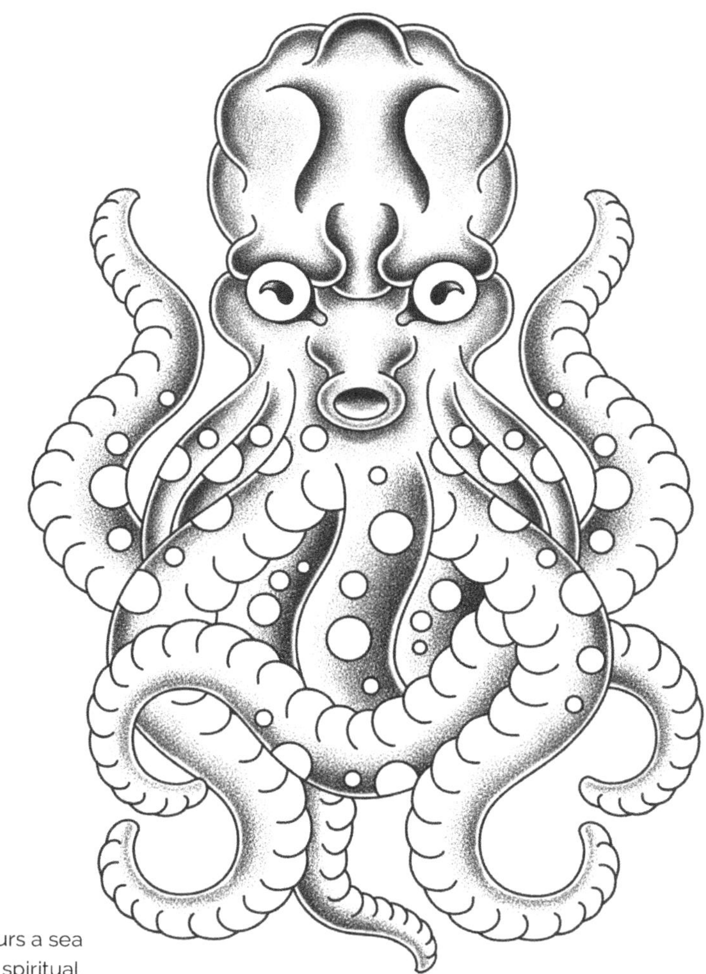

An Akkorokamui tattoo honours a sea deity of physical, mental and spiritual healing and wisdom. Fickle by nature, its grasp is unbreakable without permission.

01

02

03

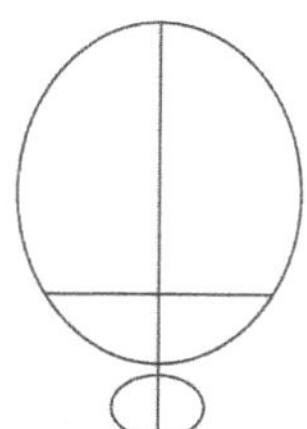

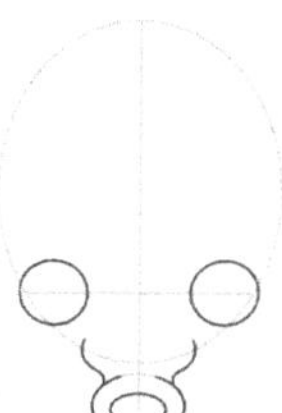

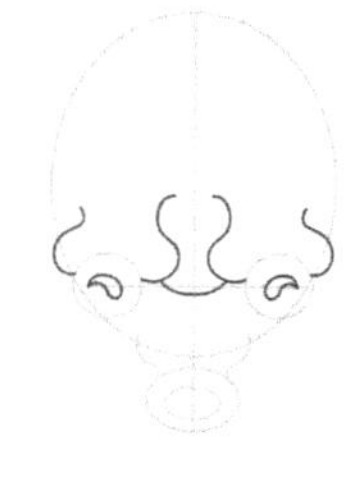

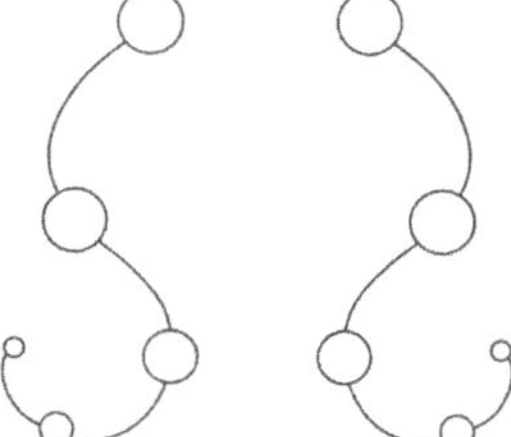

04

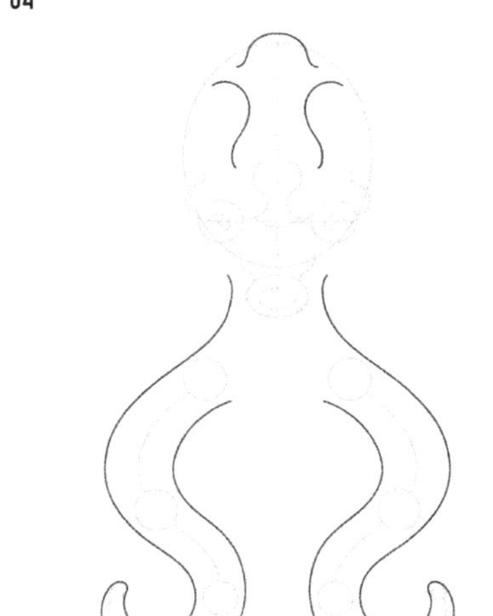

05

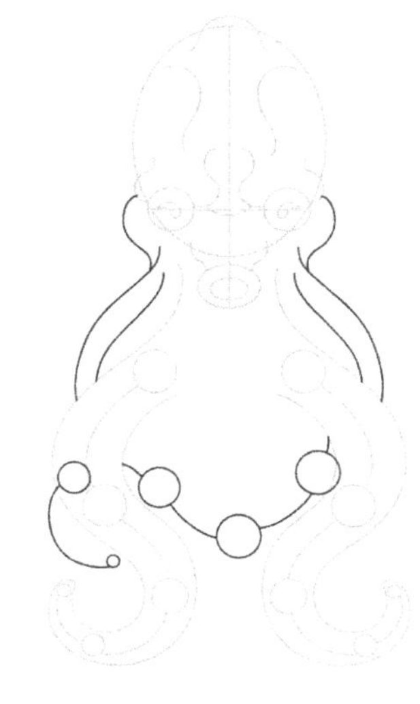

06

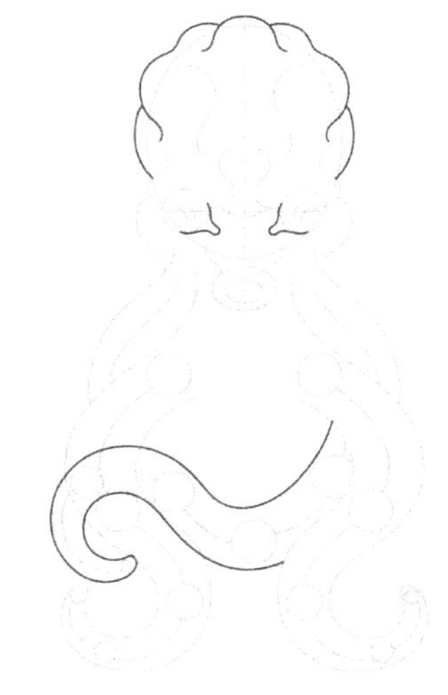

07

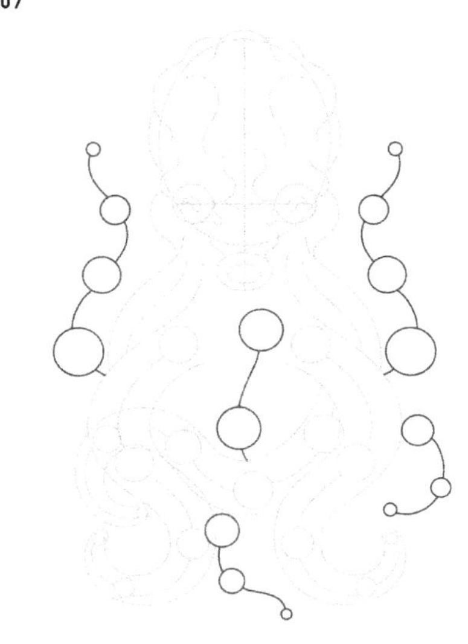

08

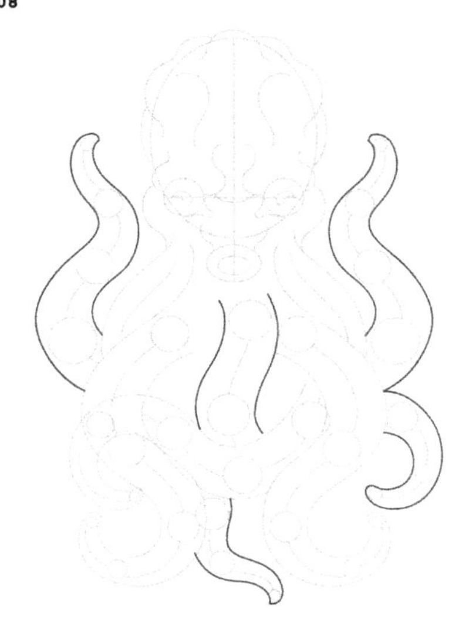

09

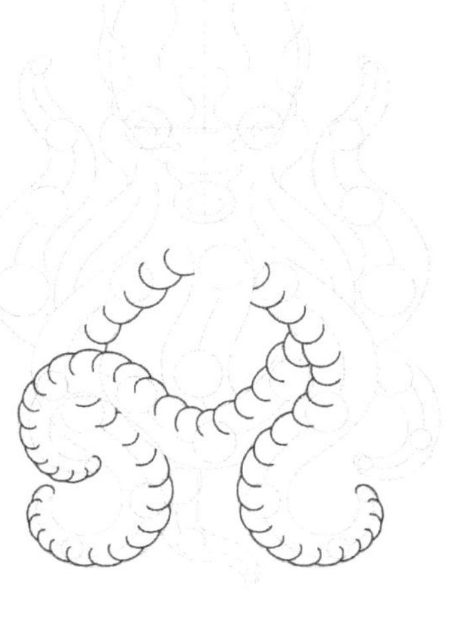

10

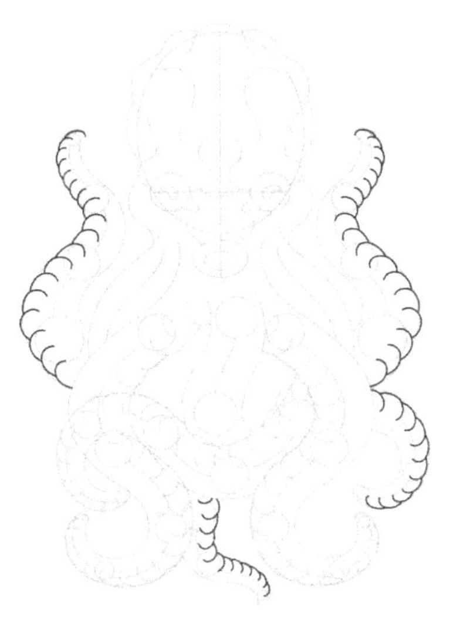

11

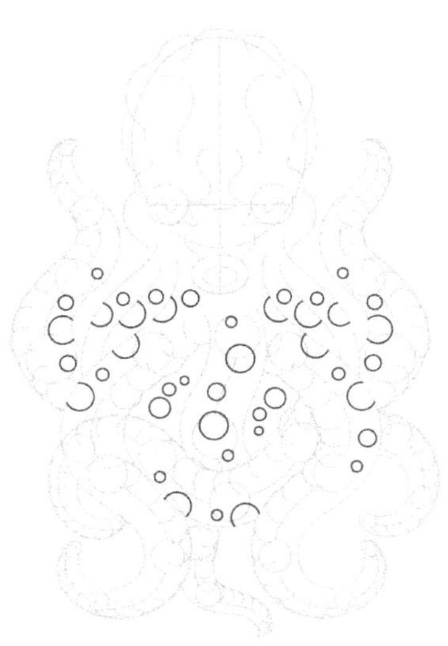

12

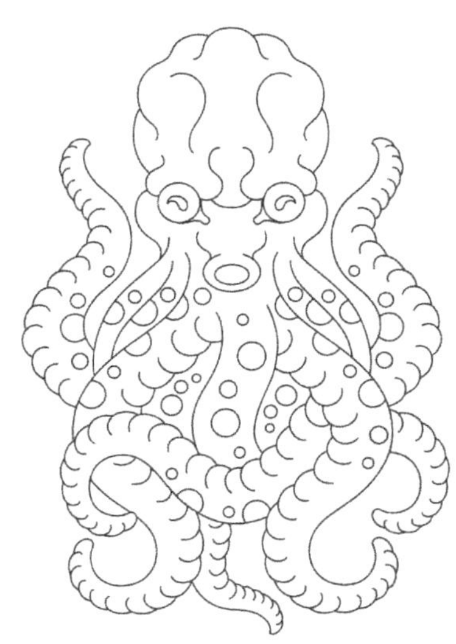

KAPPA

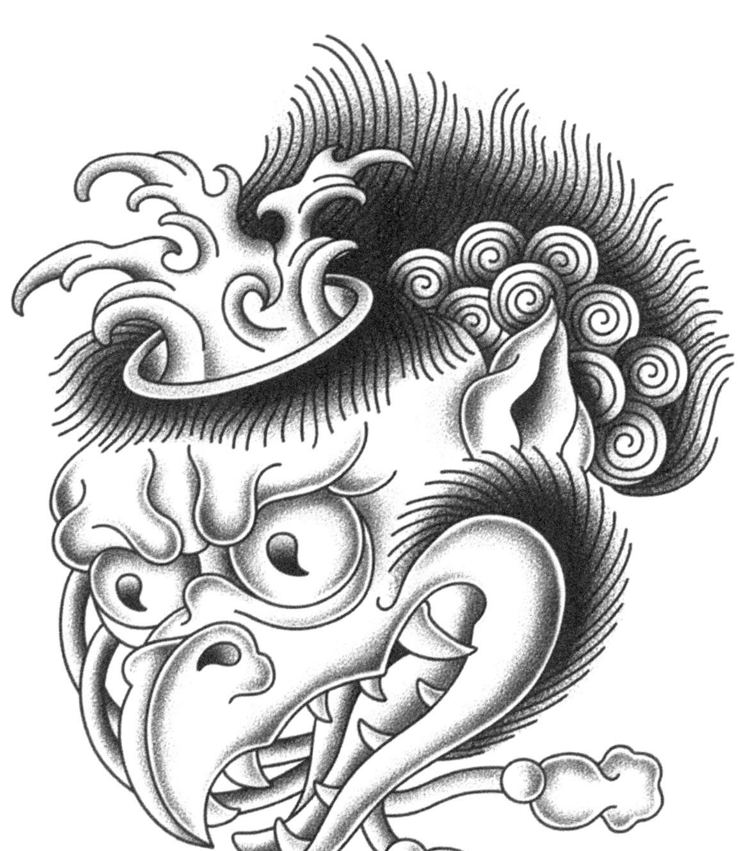

Kappa are mischievous water spirits with turtle-like bodies and a water-filled head dish. They love cucumbers and are known to be tricksters, but they can also be dangerous.

01

02

03

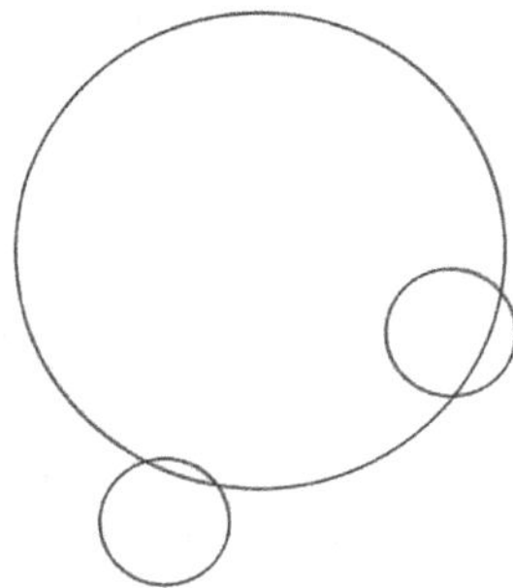

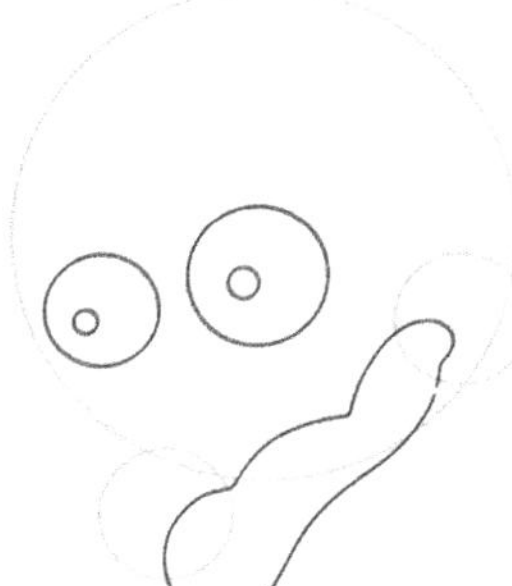

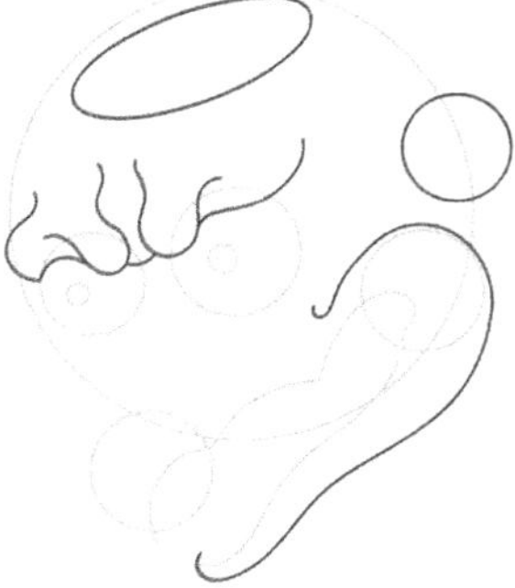

04

05

06

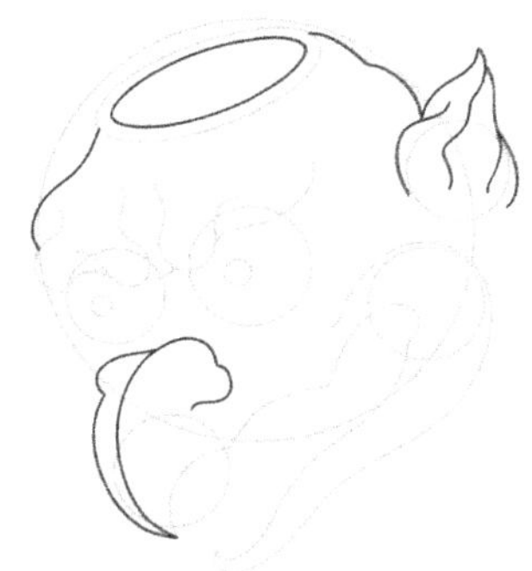

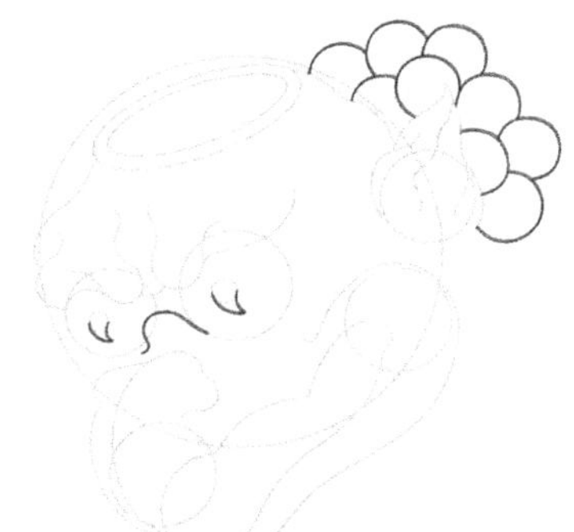

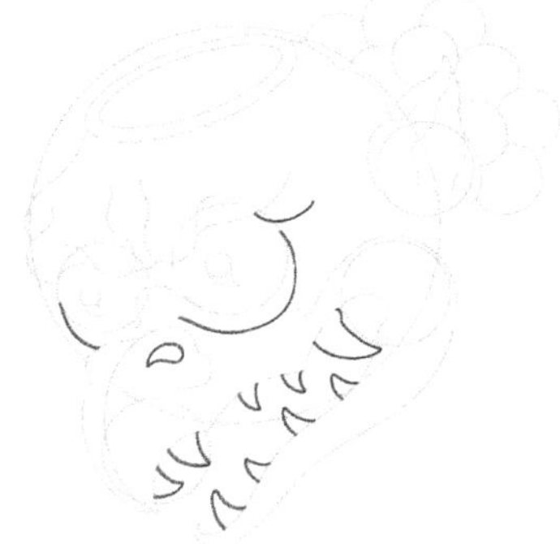

07

08

09

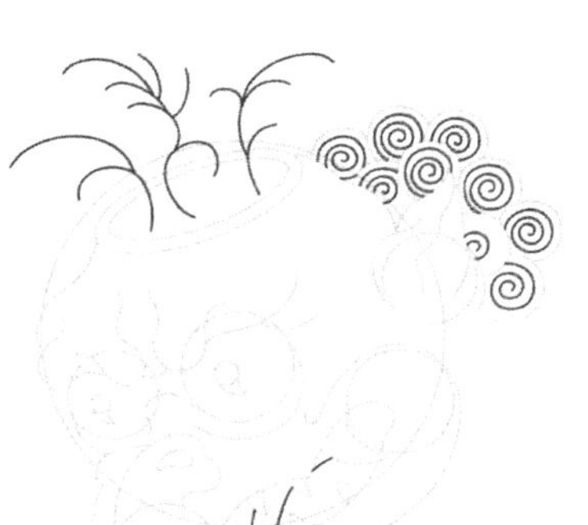

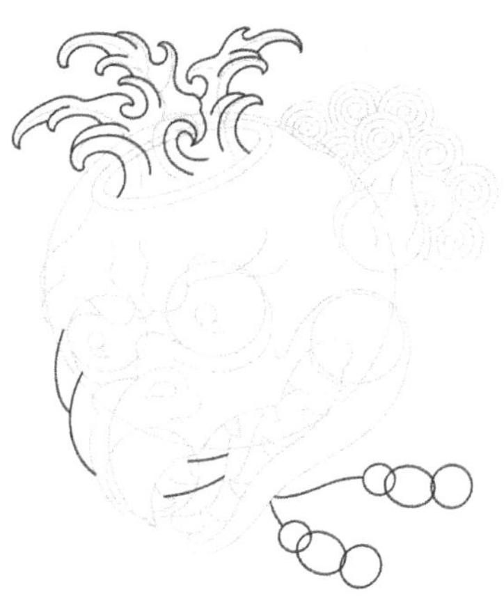

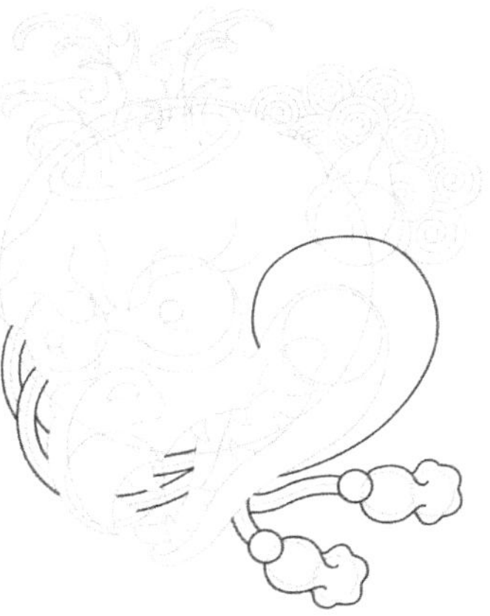

10

11

12

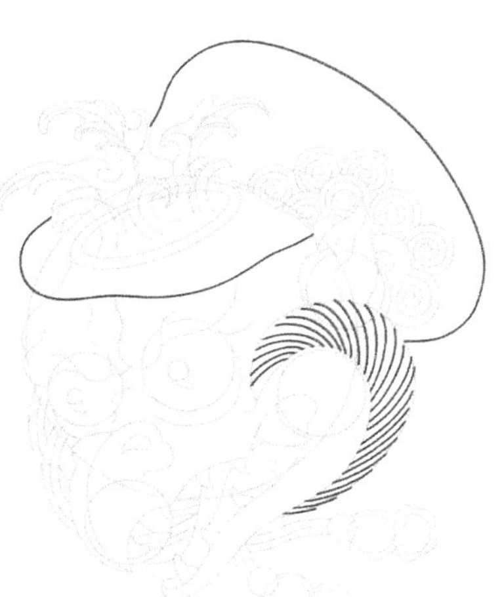

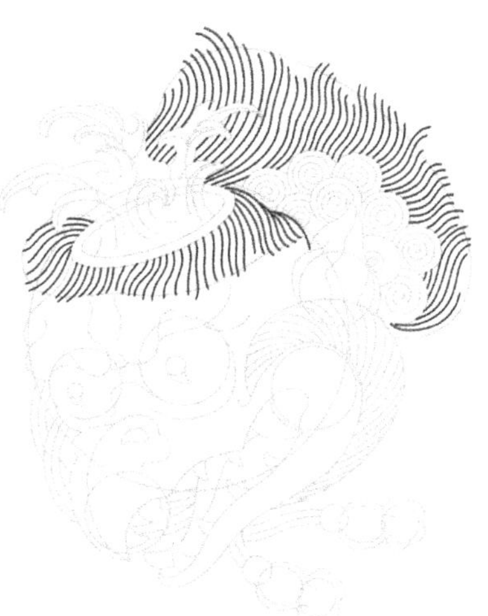

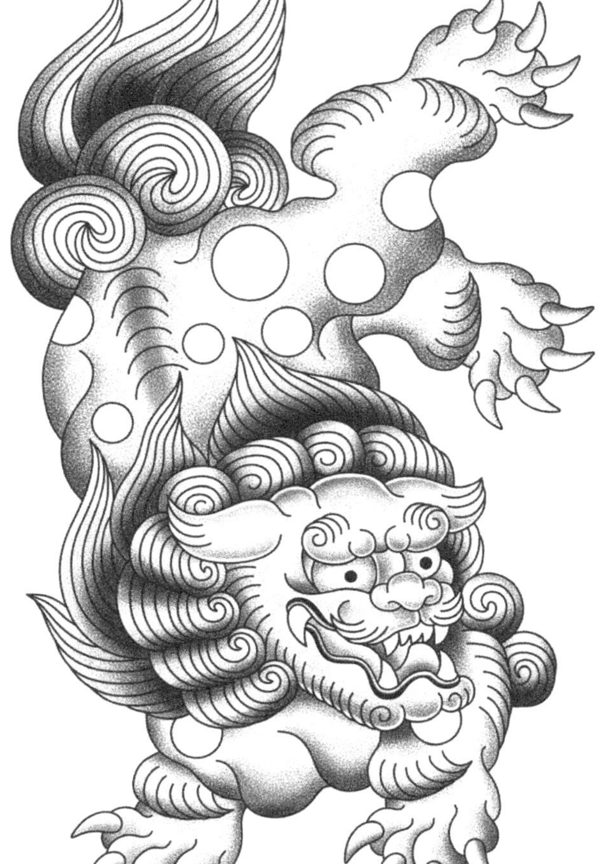

SHISA

Shisa are lion-dog guardians. People place pairs of Shisa statues on rooftops or beside their gates. One opens its mouth to ward off evil, and the other closes it to keep good fortune in.

JAPANESE TATTOOS

01

02

03

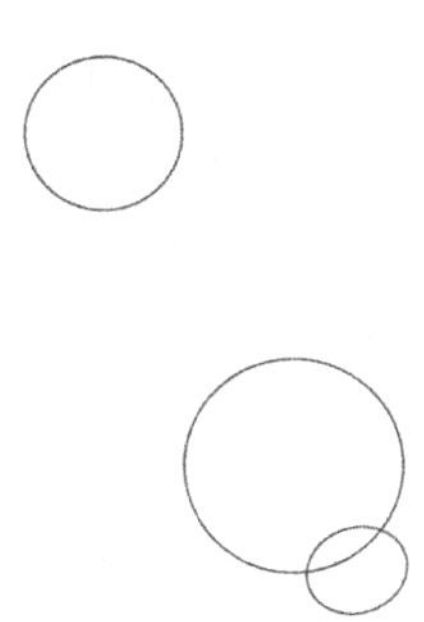

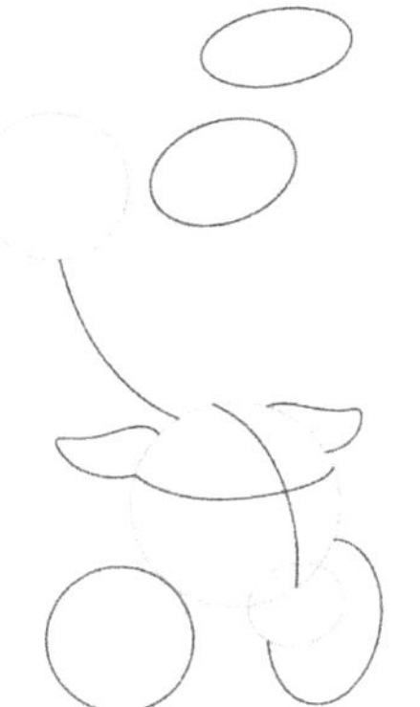

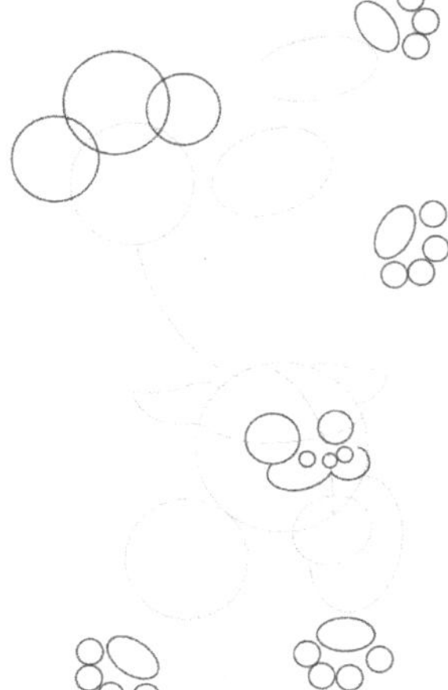

04

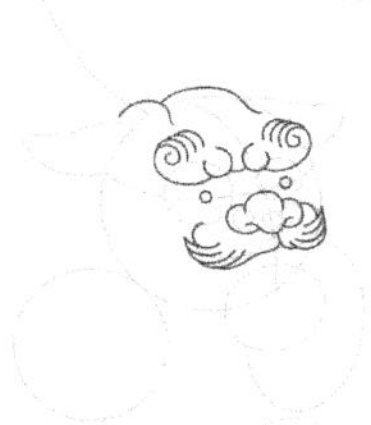

05

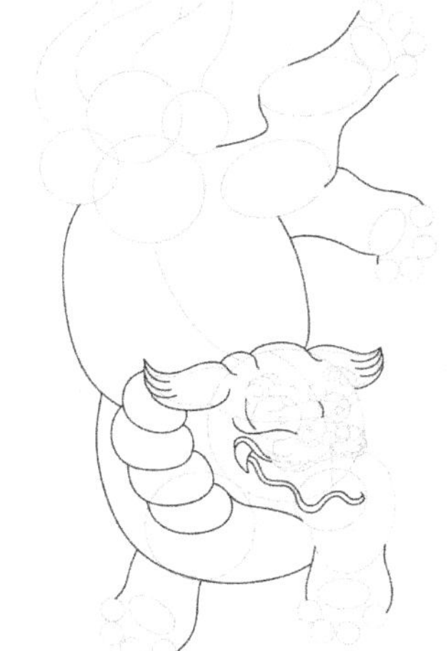

06

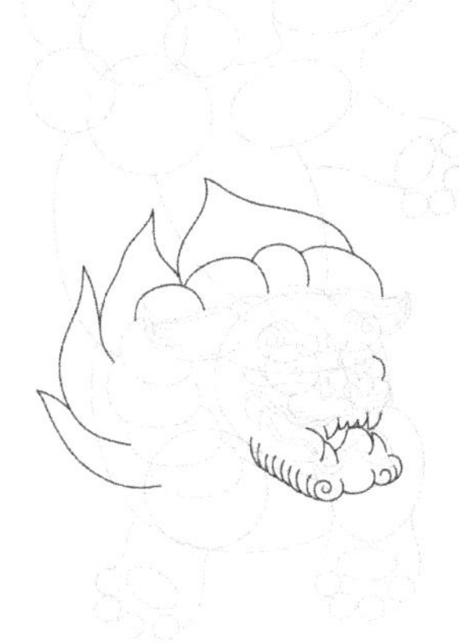

07

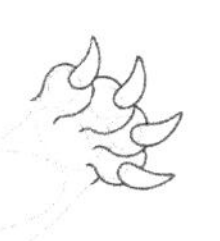

08

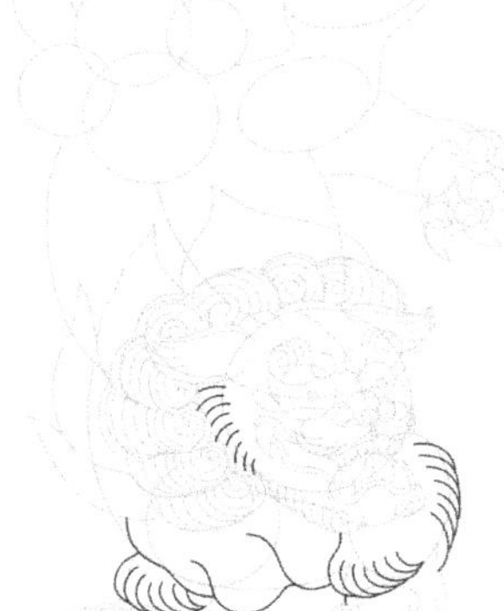

09

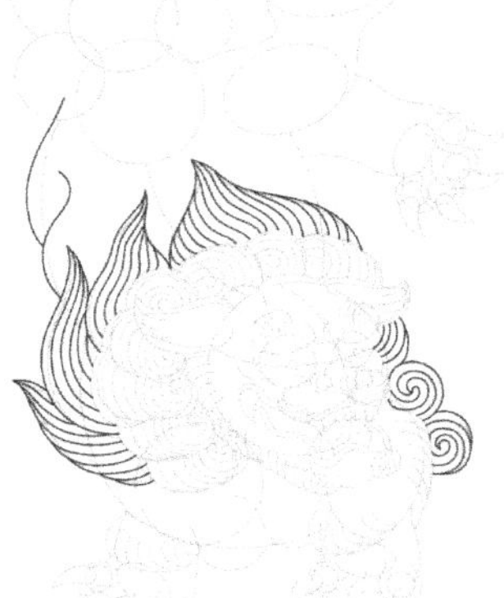

10

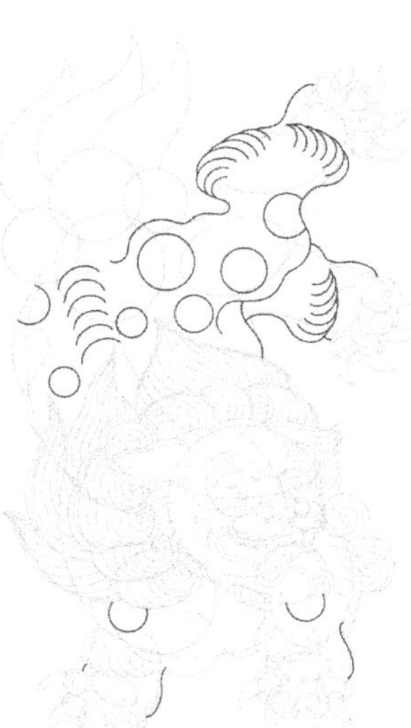

11

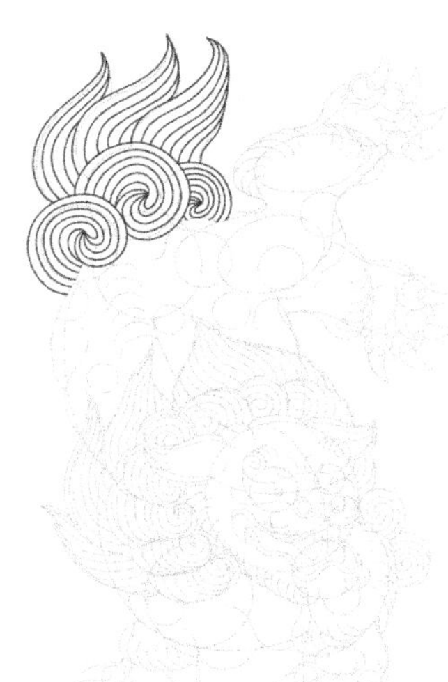

12

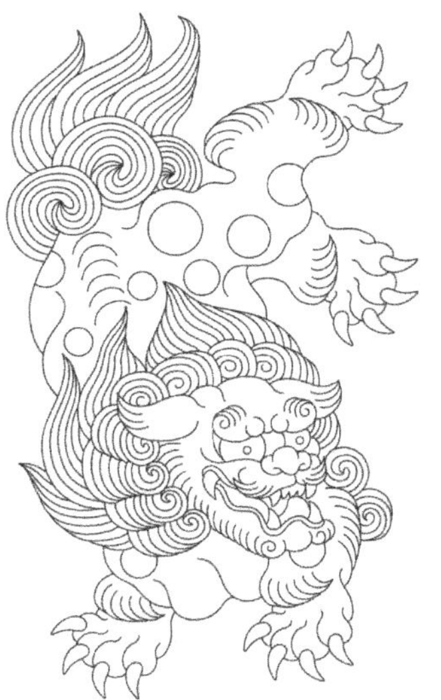

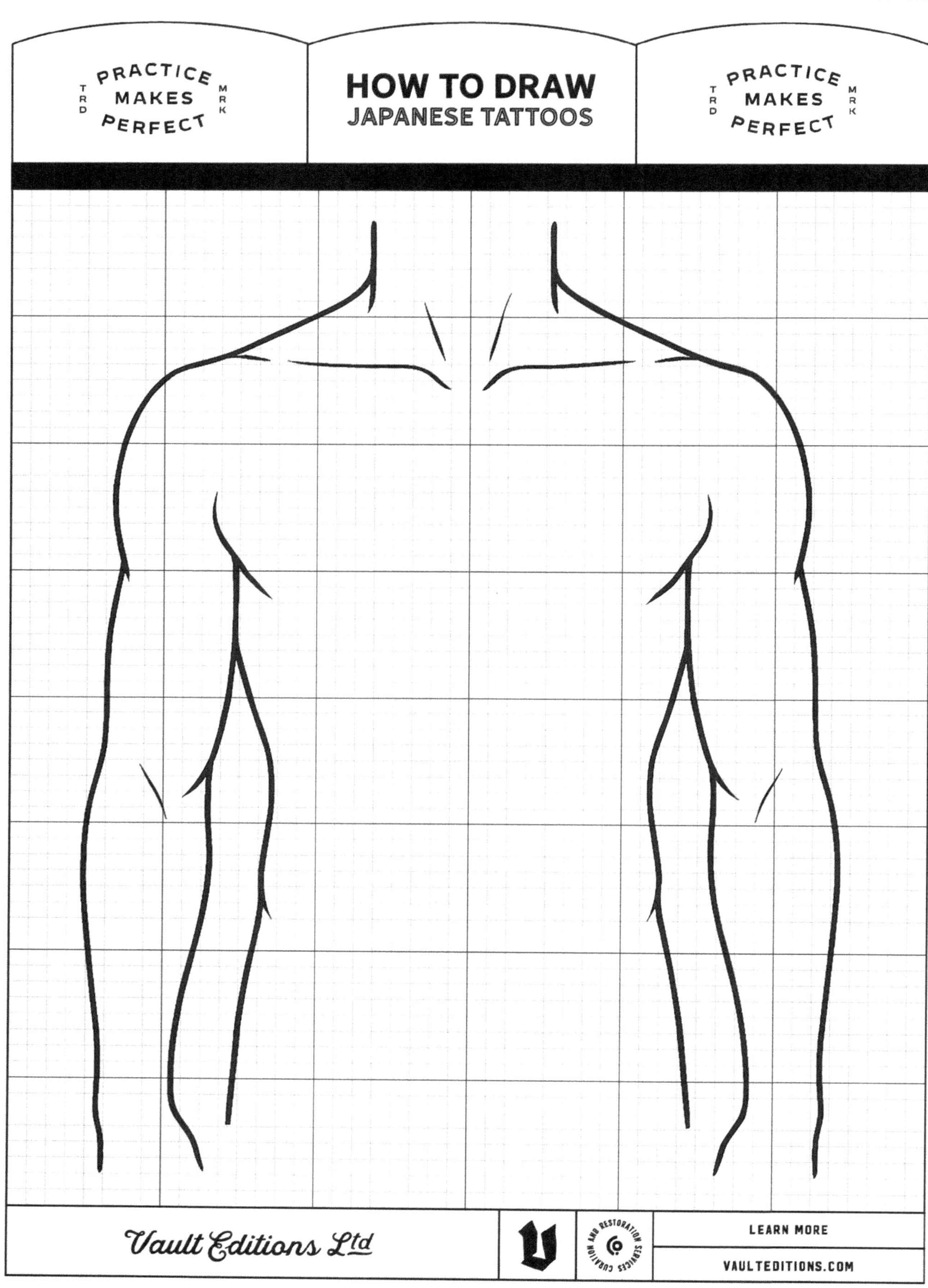
PRACTICE
MAKES
PERFECT
T R D
M R K
HOW TO DRAW
JAPANESE TATTOOS
PRACTICE
MAKES
PERFECT
T R D
M R K
Vault Editions Ltd
CURATION AND RESTORATION SERVICES
LEARN MORE
VAULTEDITIONS.COM

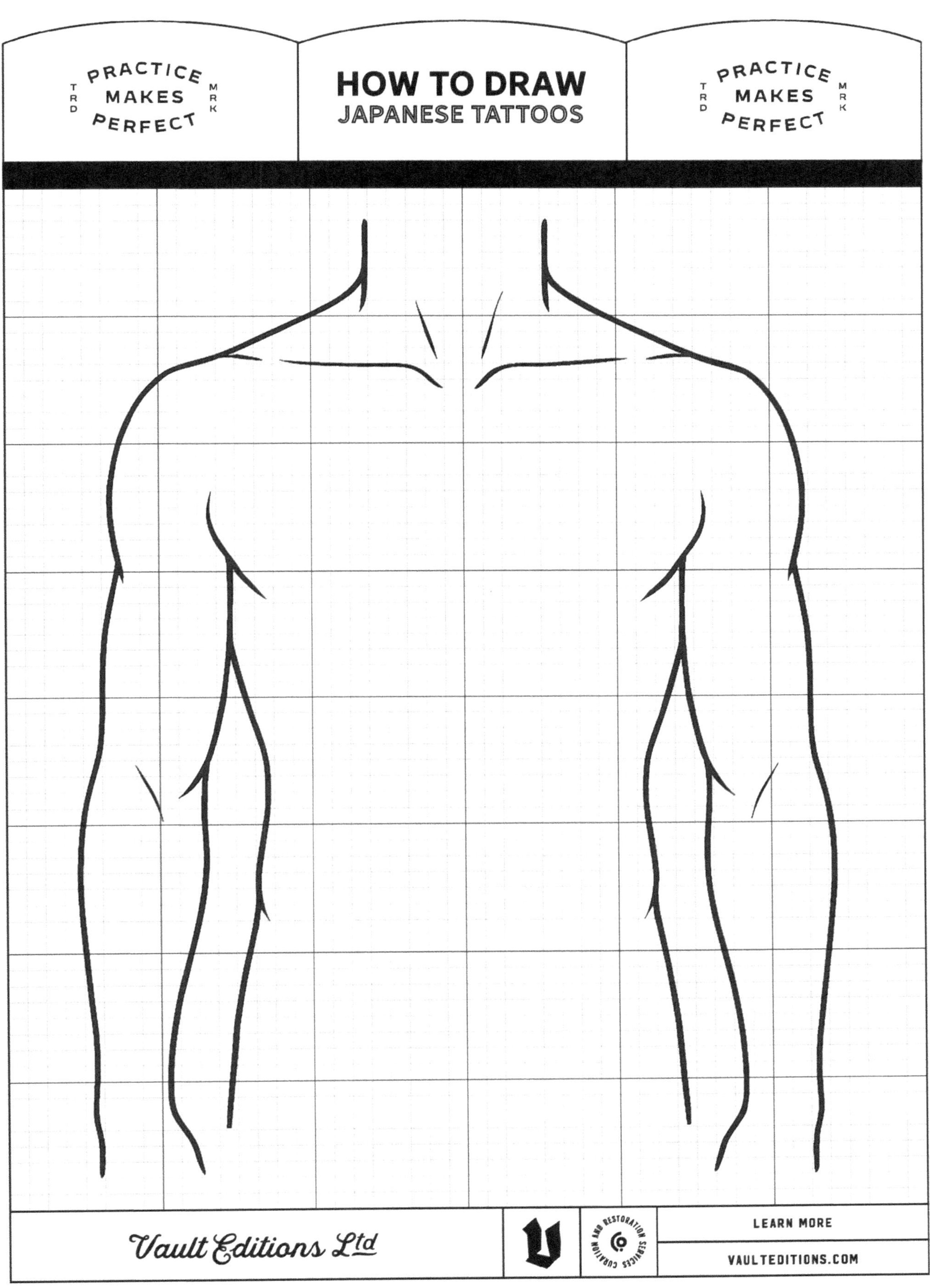
PRACTICE
T R D
MAKES
M R K
PERFECT

HOW TO DRAW
JAPANESE TATTOOS

PRACTICE
T R D
MAKES
M R K
PERFECT

JAPANESE TATTOOS

Vault Editions Ltd

LEARN MORE
VAULTEDITIONS.COM

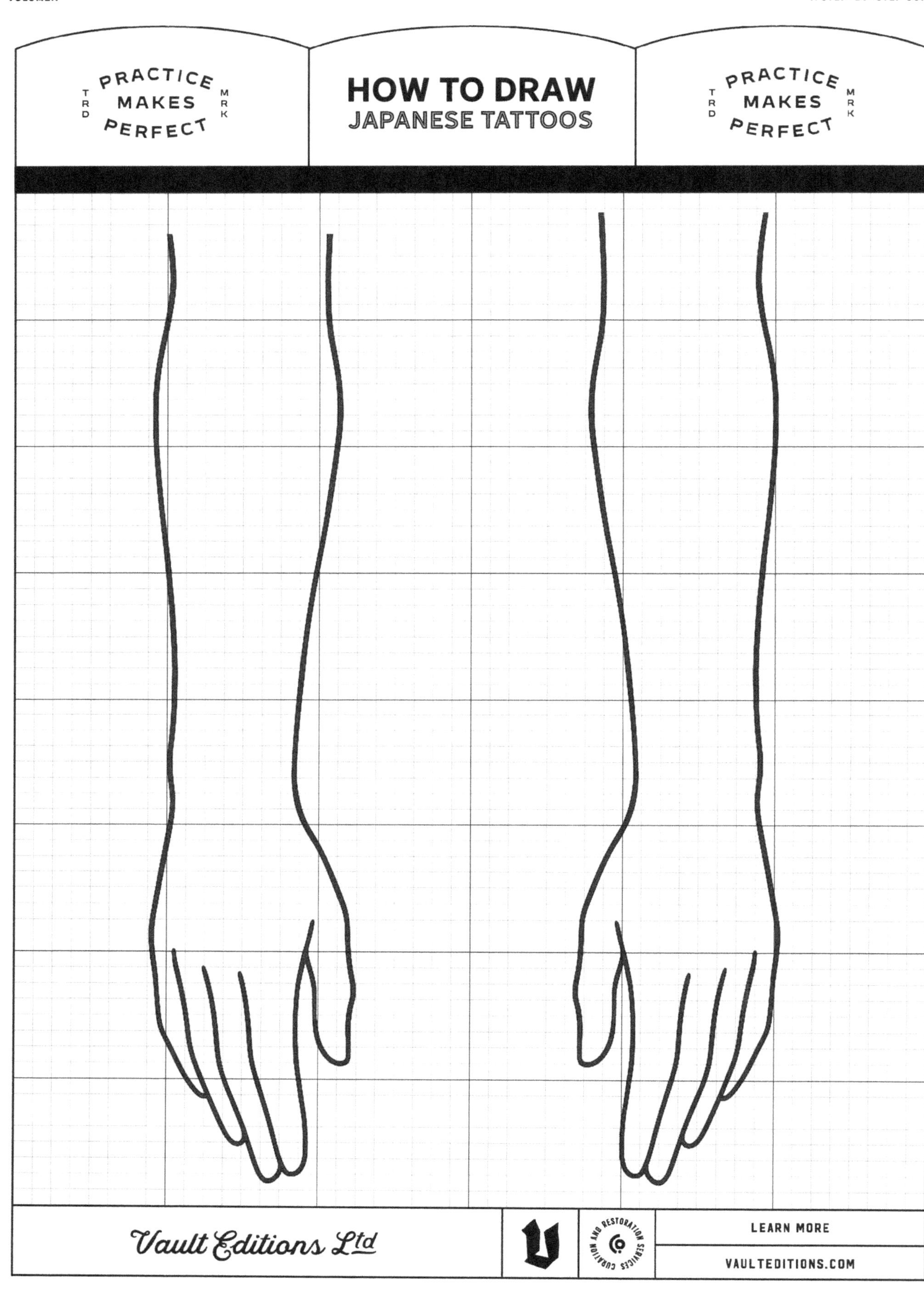
PRACTICE
MAKES
PERFECT
T R D
M R K

HOW TO DRAW
JAPANESE TATTOOS

PRACTICE
MAKES
PERFECT
T R D
M R K

JAPANESE TATTOOS

Vault Editions Ltd

CURATION AND RESTORATION SERVICES

LEARN MORE

VAULTEDITIONS.COM

PRACTICE
T R D   MAKES   M R K
PERFECT

HOW TO DRAW
JAPANESE TATTOOS

PRACTICE
T R D   MAKES   M R K
PERFECT

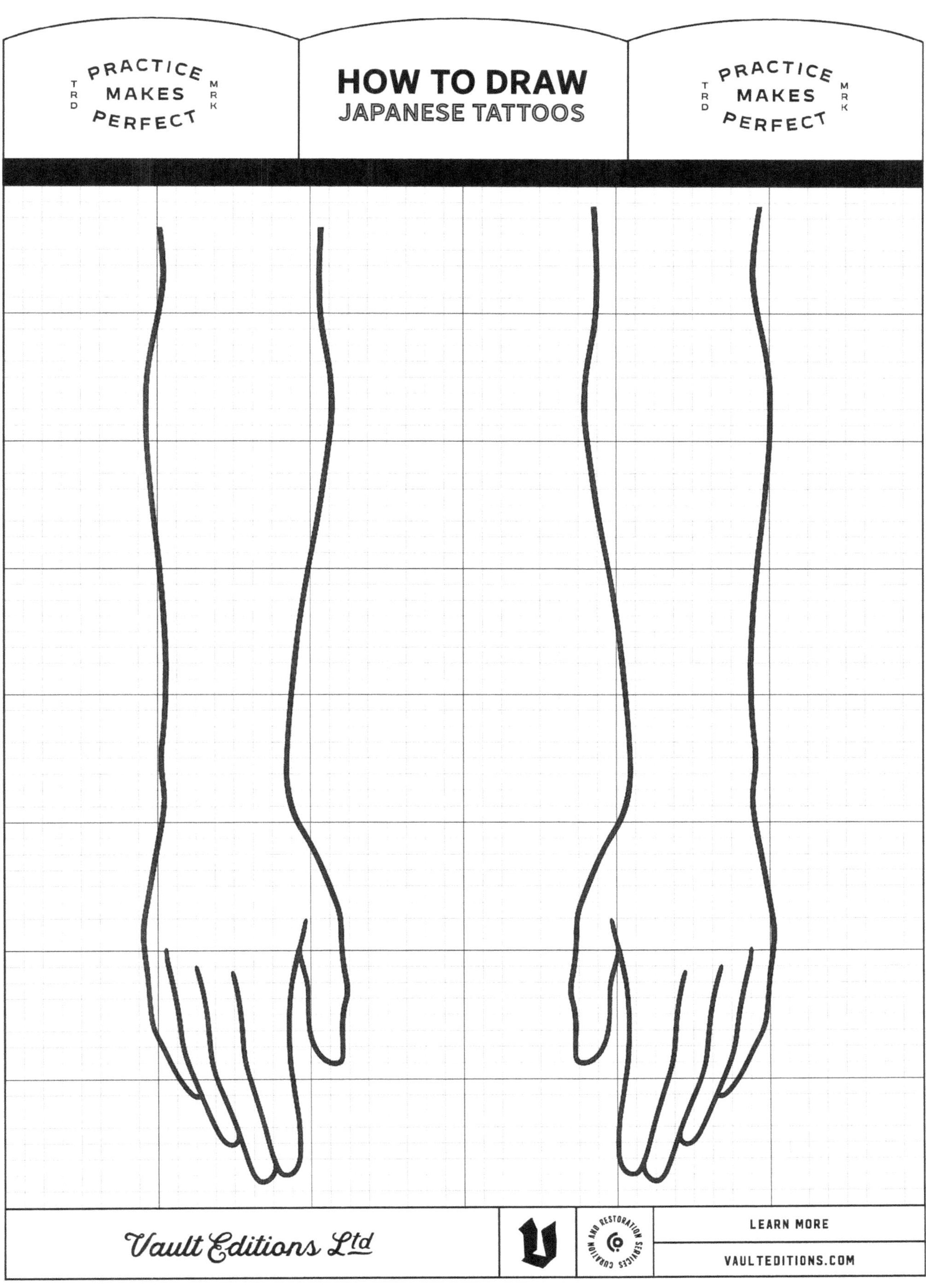

Vault Editions Ltd

LEARN MORE

VAULTEDITIONS.COM

CURATION AND RESTORATION SERVICES

JAPANESE TATTOOS

HOW TO DRAW
JAPANESE TATTOOS

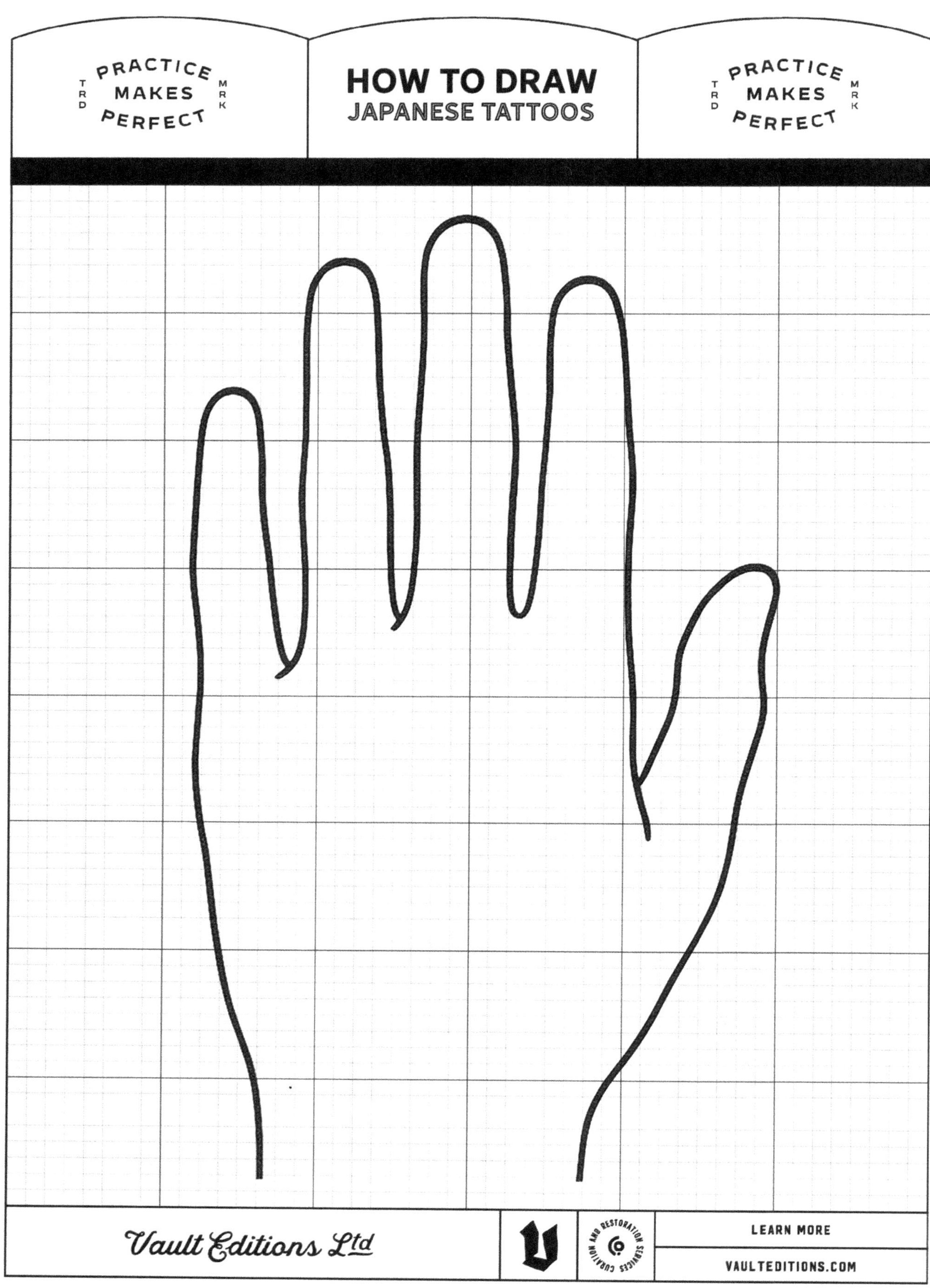

JAPANESE TATTOOS

Vault Editions Ltd

LEARN MORE

VAULTEDITIONS.COM

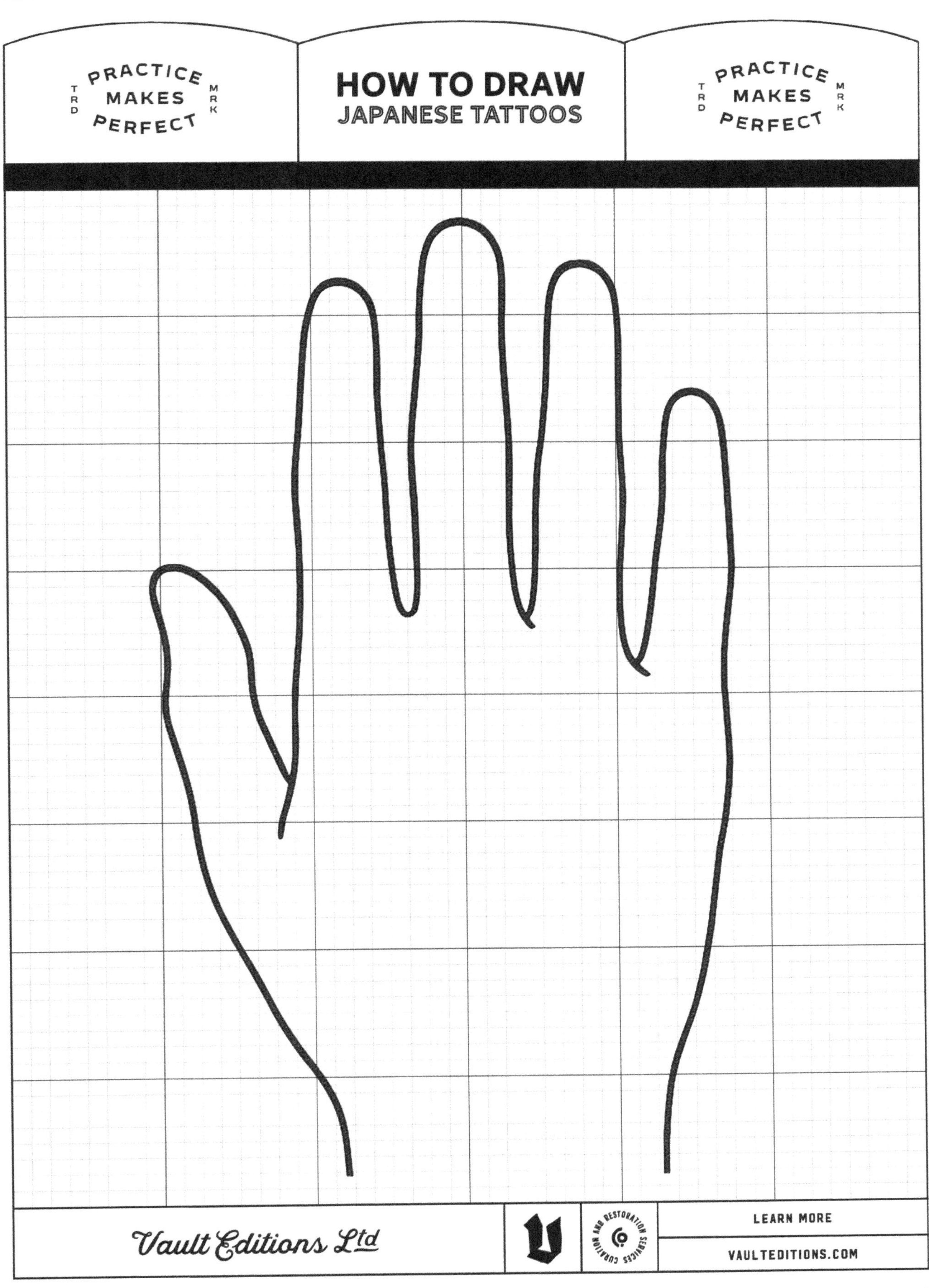

PRACTICE MAKES PERFECT
T R D
M R K
HOW TO DRAW
JAPANESE TATTOOS
PRACTICE MAKES PERFECT
T R D
M R K
JAPANESE TATTOOS
Vault Editions Ltd
LEARN MORE
VAULTEDITIONS.COM
CURATION AND RESTORATION SERVICES

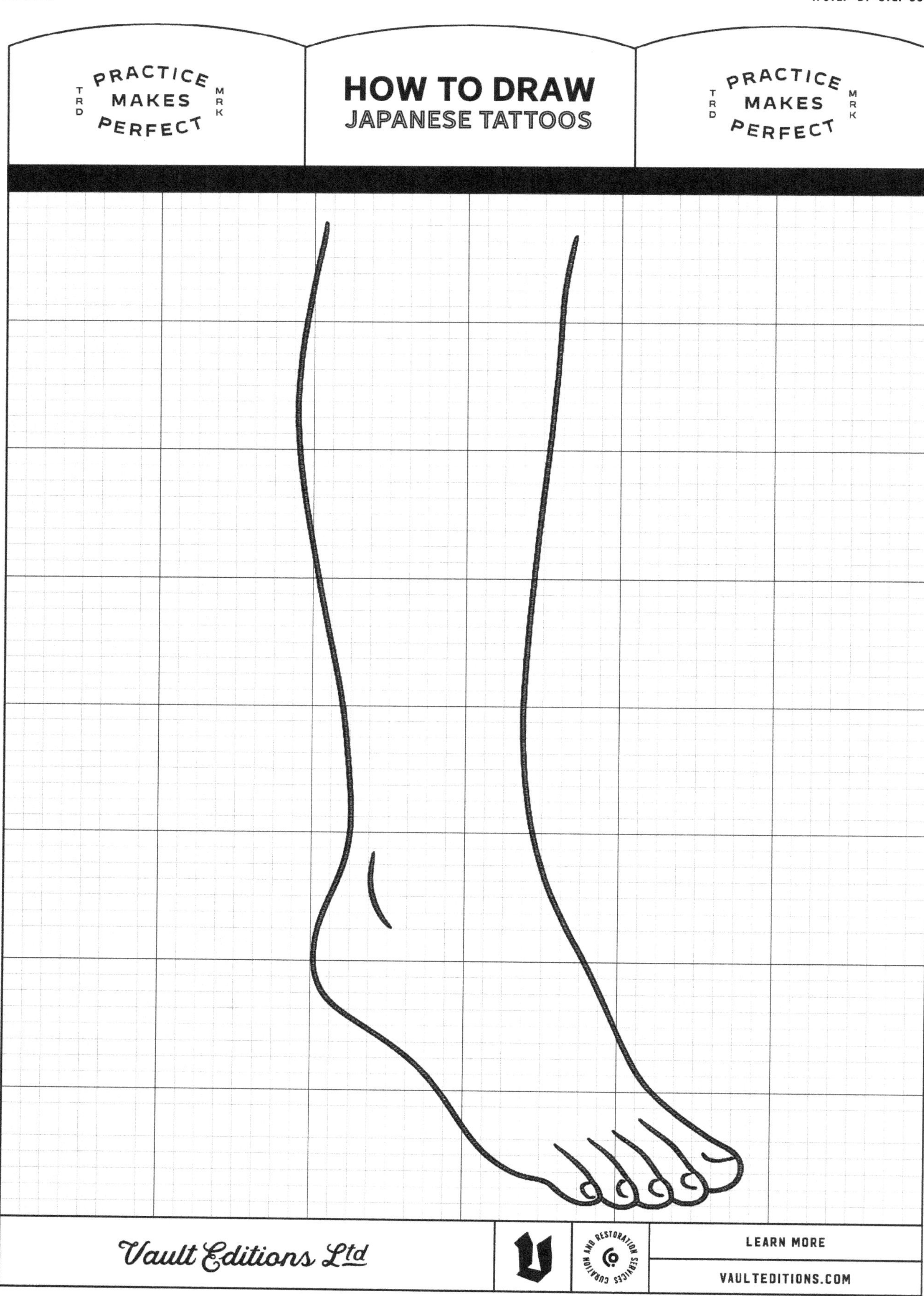
PRACTICE
MAKES
PERFECT
T R D
M R K

HOW TO DRAW
JAPANESE TATTOOS

PRACTICE
MAKES
PERFECT
T R D
M R K

Vault Editions Ltd

CURATION AND RESTORATION SERVICES

LEARN MORE
VAULTEDITIONS.COM

PRACTICE
MAKES
PERFECT
T R D
M R K

HOW TO DRAW
JAPANESE TATTOOS

PRACTICE
MAKES
PERFECT
T R D
M R K

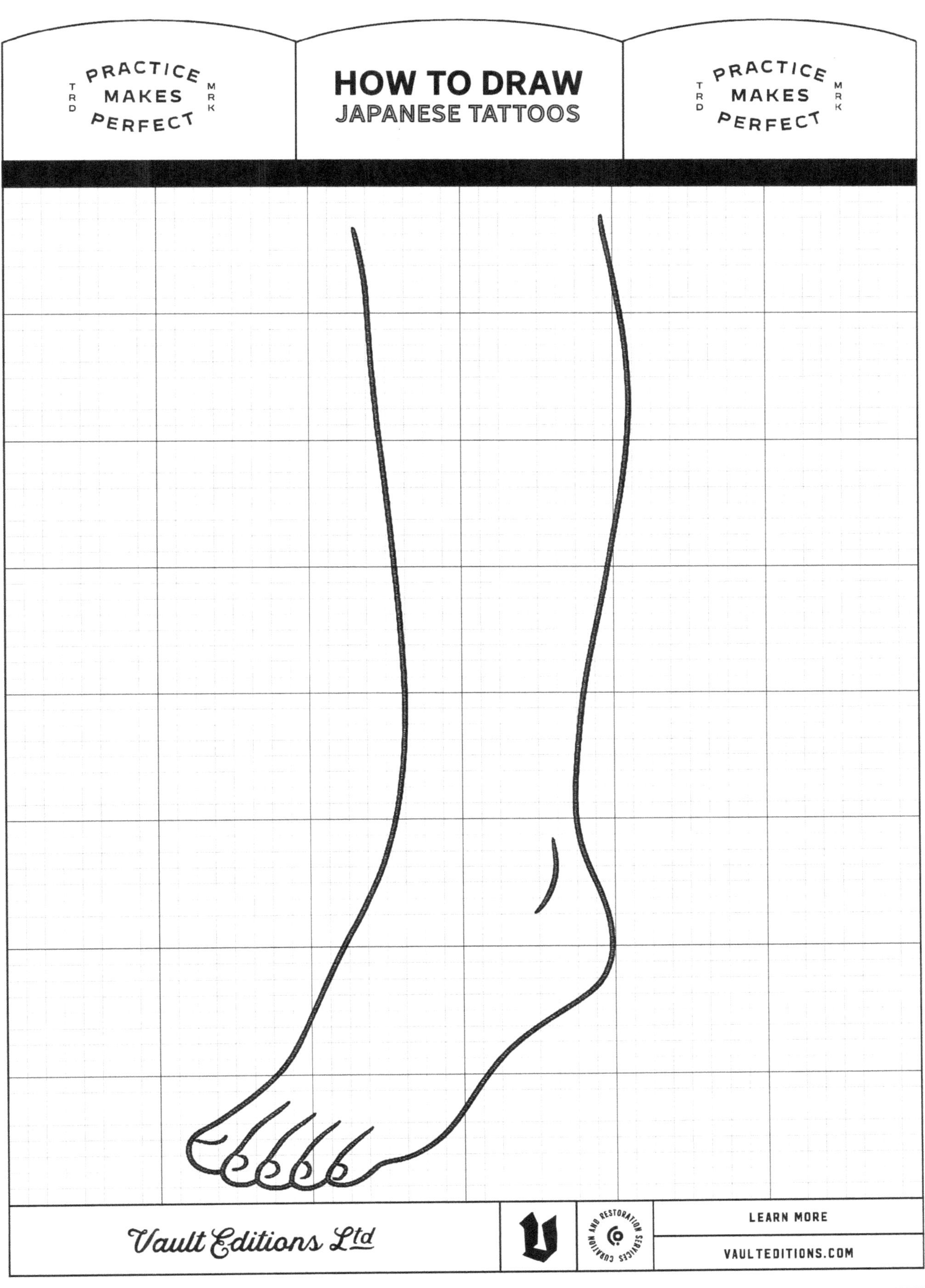

JAPANESE TATTOOS

Vault Editions Ltd

CURATION AND RESTORATION SERVICES

LEARN MORE
VAULTEDITIONS.COM

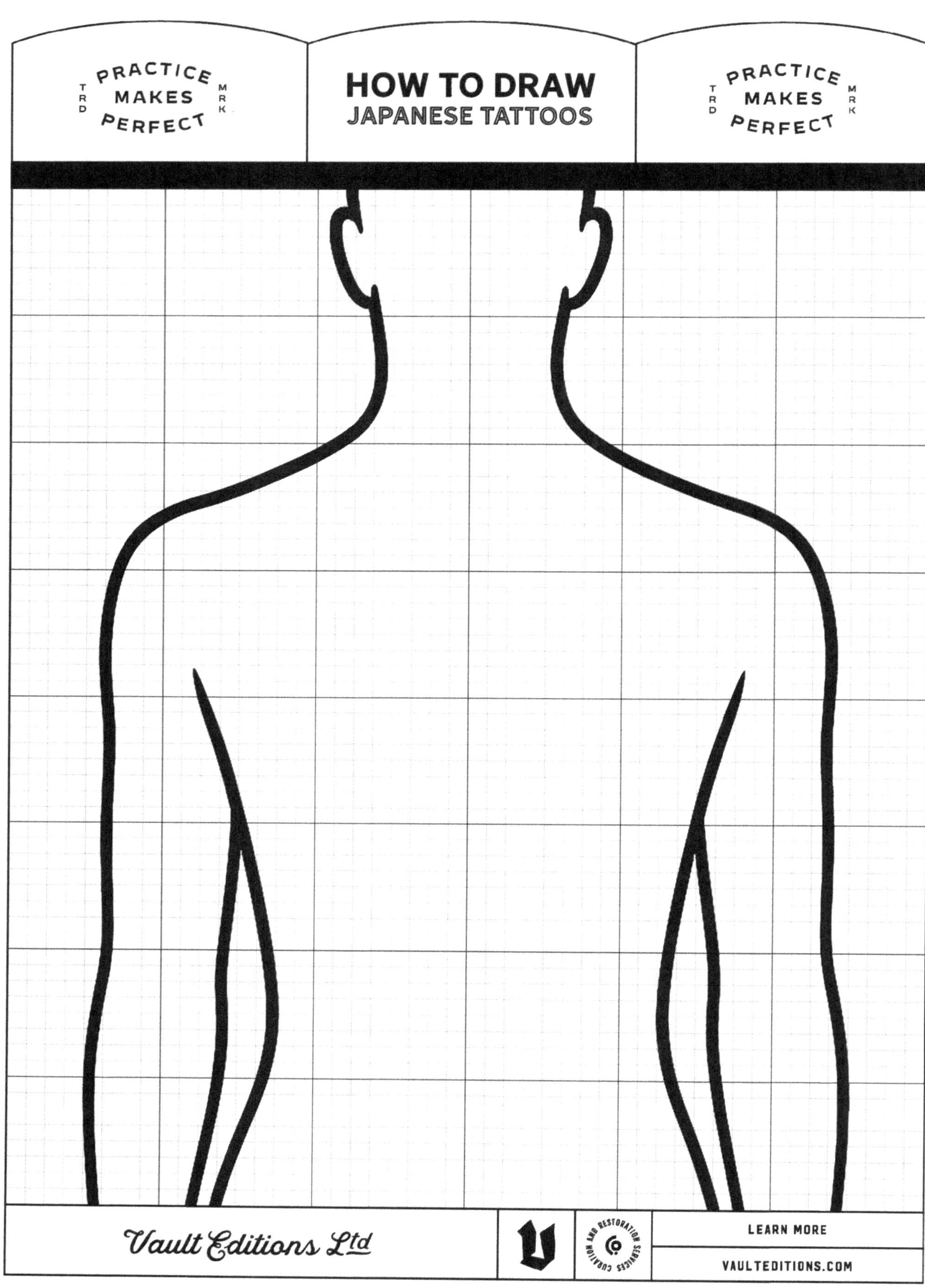
PRACTICE
MAKES
PERFECT
T R D
M R K

HOW TO DRAW
JAPANESE TATTOOS

PRACTICE
MAKES
PERFECT
T R D
M R K

JAPANESE TATTOOS

Vault Editions Ltd

CURATION AND RESTORATION SERVICES

LEARN MORE
VAULTEDITIONS.COM

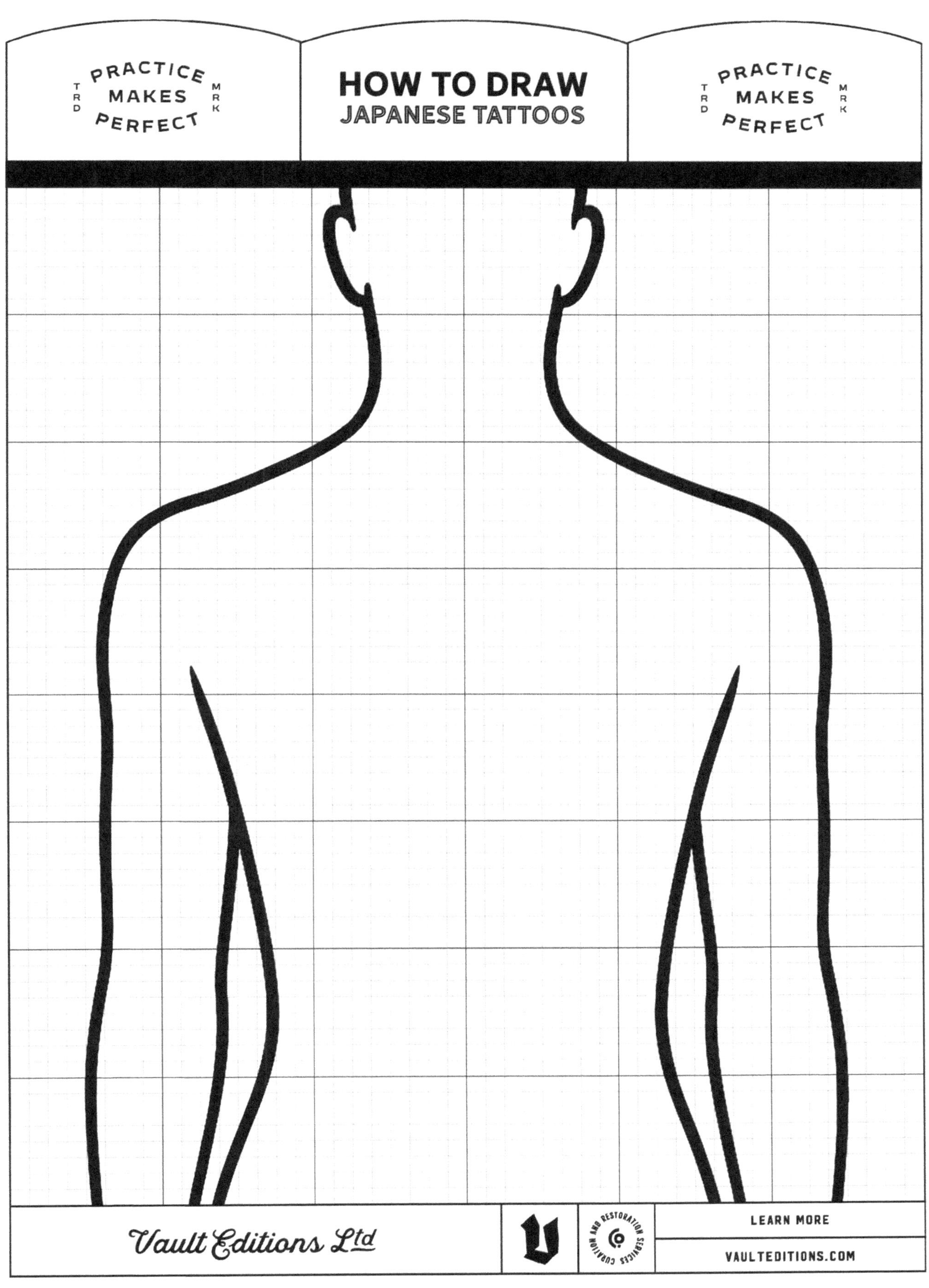

PRACTICE MAKES PERFECT
T R D
M R K
HOW TO DRAW
JAPANESE TATTOOS
PRACTICE MAKES PERFECT
T R D
M R K
JAPANESE TATTOOS
Vault Editions Ltd
CURATION AND RESTORATION SERVICES
LEARN MORE
VAULTEDITIONS.COM

PRACTICE MAKES PERFECT
TRD MRK

HOW TO DRAW
JAPANESE TATTOOS

PRACTICE MAKES PERFECT
TRD MRK

JAPANESE TATTOOS

Vault Editions Ltd

CURATION AND RESTORATION SERVICES

LEARN MORE

VAULTEDITIONS.COM

HOW TO DRAW
JAPANESE TATTOOS

Vault Editions Ltd

CURATION AND RESTORATION SERVICES

LEARN MORE

VAULTEDITIONS.COM

PRACTICE
MAKES
PERFECT
TRD MRK

HOW TO DRAW
JAPANESE TATTOOS

PRACTICE
MAKES
PERFECT
TRD MRK

JAPANESE TATTOOS

Vault Editions Ltd

LEARN MORE

VAULTEDITIONS.COM

PRACTICE
MAKES
PERFECT
T R D
M R K

HOW TO DRAW
JAPANESE TATTOOS

PRACTICE
MAKES
PERFECT
T R D
M R K

JAPANESE TATTOOS

Vault Editions Ltd

CURATION AND RESTORATION SERVICES

LEARN MORE

VAULTEDITIONS.COM

CONCLUSION

As you reach the end of *How to Draw Japanese Tattoos*, you've not only developed your drawing skills but also taken the first steps into a rich visual tradition shaped by centuries of cultural meaning and artistic expression. Through each motif, you've explored a world where line, form, and symbolism come together to tell powerful stories of strength, transformation and protection.

Japanese tattoo design is a compelling visual style, and a symbolic language passed down through generations. Whether you continue refining these designs, begin creating your own compositions, or simply carry forward a greater appreciation for the art form, the skills you've built here are a foundation for lifelong growth.

Thank you for joining us on this creative journey. May your exploration of Japanese tattoo art deepen with skill, curiosity, and a true appreciation for the tradition.

ABOUT THE ARTIST

Abrom Rose, an accomplished artist with a remarkable talent for visual communication and instructional illustration, created the designs in this book. With a background in illustration and design, Abrom brings clarity, precision, and artistic sensitivity to every drawing he produces. His work is defined by confident linework, strong composition, and a deep understanding of form, qualities that make his illustrations both engaging and accessible to learners at all levels.

Abrom's approach to drawing is rooted in careful observation and a passion for traditional tattoo art, which he interprets with originality and technical skill. Whether guiding beginners or inspiring experienced artists, his ability to break down complex motifs into clear, teachable steps sets his work apart.

LEARN MORE

At Vault Editions, our mission is to provide the highest-quality reference materials for artists and designers, offering meticulously curated resources that inspire and empower creativity. If you've found value in this book, we invite you to explore more of our expertly crafted titles at vaulteditions.com, where you'll discover a world of visual inspiration and practical tools designed to elevate your creative work.

REVIEW THIS BOOK

As a family-owned and operated independent publisher, reviews are essential to the success of our business. Please leave an honest review of this book wherever you purchased it.

JOIN OUR COMMUNITY

Are you the creative and curious type? If so, you will love our community on Instagram. Every day, we share bizarre and beautiful artwork ranging from 17th and 18th-century natural history and scientific illustrations to mythical beasts, ornamental designs, anatomical drawings and more; join our community of 300K+ people today by searching @vault_editions on Instagram.

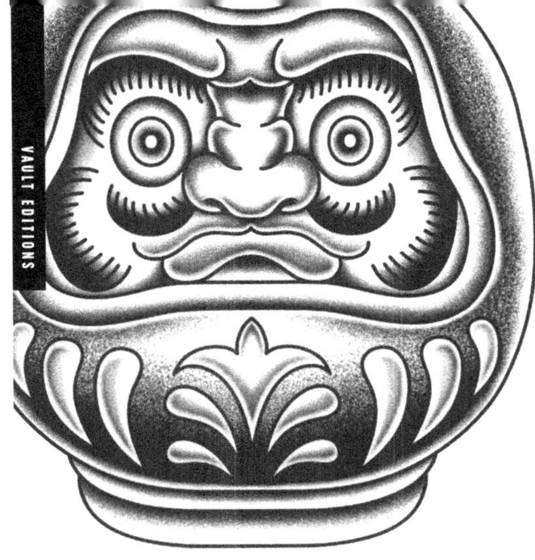

DOWNLOAD YOUR FILES

To enhance your creative journey, How to Draw Tattoo Flash comes with a digital PDF version of the book and a specially designed set of Procreate brushes. These resources are tailored to help you refine your skills and streamline your workflow, whether you're working traditionally or digitally.

The digital PDF provides easy access to the book's contents on any device, so you can reference the designs anytime, anywhere. It's perfect for artists on the go, allowing you to study and practice whenever inspiration strikes.

The custom Procreate brushes are designed to replicate the look and feel of traditional tattoo flash designs, from bold outlining to shading techniques. These brushes make it easier for digital artists to create authentic-looking designs in a digital medium, offering precision and flexibility as you sketch, refine, and finalise your artwork. Whether you're experimenting with new ideas or perfecting your final designs, these brushes allow you to bring your creations to life with the same iconic style that defines classic tattoo flash.

Download yours now and get creating!

STEP ONE

Enter the following web address on a desktop or laptop computer in your web browser.

vaulteditions.com/pages/htj

STEP TWO

Enter the following password to access the download page:

htj2346sxda

STEP THREE

Follow the prompts to access your high-resolution files.

CONTACT

For technical support, please email:
info@vaulteditions.com

Copyright © 2025
Vault Editions Ltd

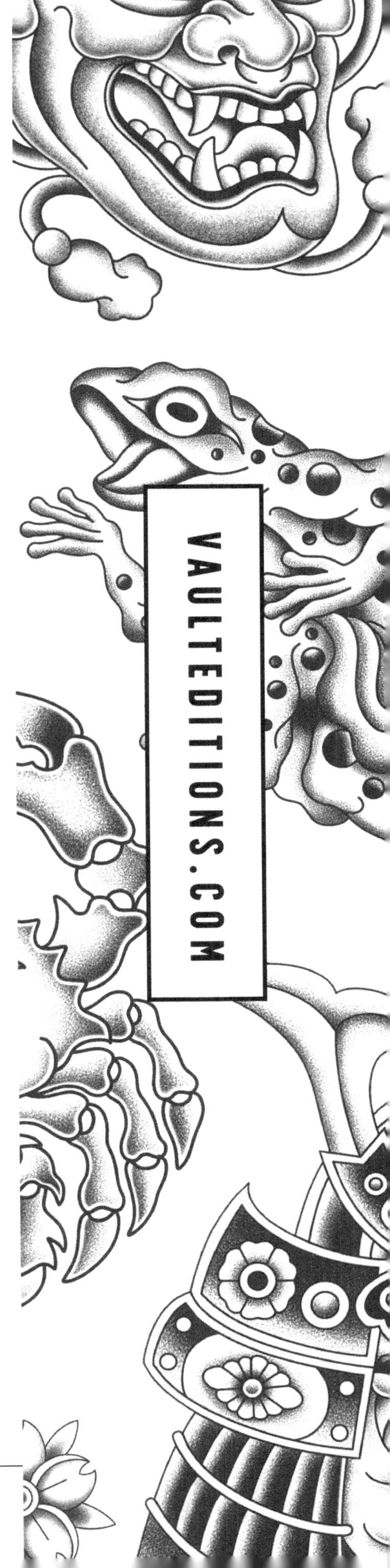

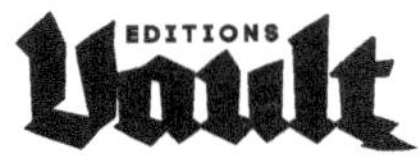

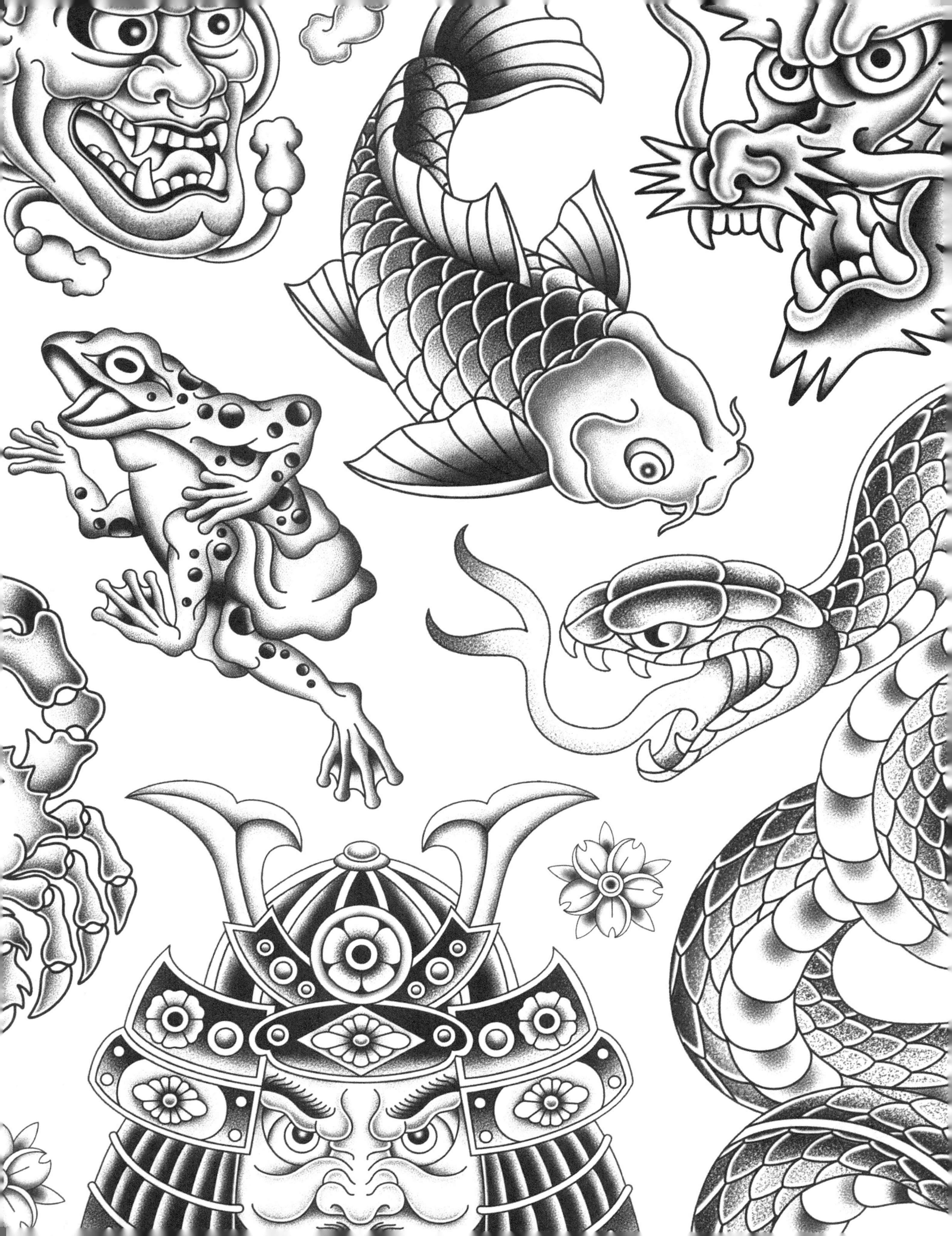